FOR WHOM THE BELL TOLLS

AMERICA OR THE JIHADISTS?

GAUTAM MAITRA

2009

Order this book online at www.trafford.com
or email orders@trafford.com

Most Trafford titles are also available at major online book retailers.

Note for Librarians: A cataloguing record for this book is available from Library
and Archives Canada at www.collectionscanada.ca/amicus/index-e.html

Printed in Victoria, BC, Canada.

ISBN: 978-1-4269-0615-2 (soft)
ISBN: 978-1-4269-1008-1 (ebook)

*Our mission is to efficiently provide the world's finest, most comprehensive
book publishing service, enabling every author to experience success.
To find out how to publish your book, your way, and have it available
worldwide, visit us online at www.trafford.com*

Trafford rev. 8/10/2009

North America & international
toll-free: 1 888 232 4444 (USA & Canada)
phone: 250 383 6864 ♦ fax: 812 355 4082

PREFACE

The roots of modern terrorism can roughly be traced back to 2000 years. As it evolved over the millennia, it managed to retain some of its historical characteristics, such as, 'religious convictions', that motivated its earliest predecessors.[1] It happens to be a fluid concept and assumes specific forms, depending on time, circumstance, and subject. It is a constantly evolving concept and has a 'survival' factor, in that it can be reduced for the time being but not rooted out. That is why, Paul R Pillar in *Terrorism and U.S. Foreign Policy*, looked upon terrorism as 'a challenge to be managed and not solved'[2]. Terrorist tactics, in general, are the most potent and accepted means to vent anger, vengeance, and retribution for any cause, right or wrong, and by any individual, group, or state.

Its objectives may range from secular political, religious, or even environmental and animal rights demands. The 'heart' of any terrorist group throbs as long as there is a smooth and abundant supply of arms and finance. Without these two, terrorism might either degenerate to the level of individual murders or would simply be a hollow concept.

The recent 26/11 Mumbai carnage by the Pakistani based Lashkar-e-Toiba (LeT) group has amply shown that these are mindless killers for whom life has little value. This book considers the most prevalent type of terrorism that is perpetrated in the name of religion— Islamist terrorism. However, the ideology of the terrorist masterminds does not always conform to the original tenets of Islam. Since the immediate goal or objective of fundamentalist terrorist groups, like the al Qaeda, LeT, the Jaish-e-Mohammad (JeM), or any other Mujahideen group happens to be a political one and since for Islam, state and religion are inseparable, it is difficult to comprehend how any such movement could be defined in purely religious terms. The problem has its roots in the initial rift between the two sects, the

Shia and the Sunni, over the devolvement of political and religious authority to the same person.

Many confusions and debates rage around the interpretation of the Sharia. The Sharia covers all the aspects of social, political, and religious lives— including worship, law, human rights, gender equality— of the Muslims and apart from the few original verses, the part of revelation and the Divine Law, the Koran also incorporates the Sunna or the Hadith by the Prophet. The Sharia, in its more specific formulation, is referred to as Islamic law and hence applying it means adopting Islamic law. Yet the all important issue is— how should it be applied? According to H.A.R. Gibb, "The Koran and Tradition, having thus been accepted as infallible sources, how are their rules to be applied? Neither offered a systematic body of legal provisions, but only supplied the materials out of which a system could be constructed. The actual construction of this system thus involved the creation of a new and elaborate science of interpretation or 'roots of jurisprudence'".[3] Mohammad Asad writes about the Sharia, "Being a Divine Ordinance, it duly anticipates the fact of historical evolution, and confronts the believer with no more than a very limited number of broad political principals; beyond that, it leaves a vast field of constitution-making activity, of governmental methods, and of day-to-day legislation to the ijtihad of the time concerned."[4] It is the ijtihad that is being used by fundamentalists to advance and impose their views on Islam on others.

The problem with radical Islamic groups is that they have to interact with a large body of Muslims belonging to different ethnicities and languages, spread across the world, besides the vast non-Muslim populations in other countries. It is the difference in perceptions between the fundamentalists, adhering strictly to religious diktats, and the moderates among the Muslim community, who have little prejudice against western values and ways, that could prove decisive in determining the fate of Islamist terrorism. The moderate or the average Muslims fail to properly comprehend why a political issue should be religion-ised. On the other hand, the jihadists find it hard to understand why Muslims in many parts of the world, remain apathetic to 'aggressive' foreign policies by the United States in the heart of the Muslim holy lands. For example, while moderate Muslims tend to view various state issues through the prism of secular political goals, radical Islamist groups invariably lump religion and politics.

For the Muslims living outside the Middle East, the acceptance level of western values is greater (it must be remembered that the Koranic laws also contain traces of other civilisations, for example, Roman law. In this connection, an important observation from H.A.R. Gibb is worth mentioning. In his article on Sharia, he had written, "As for Roman law, though some of its formulae and contents percolated into Islamic Law, the principles upon which the latter was constructed (one may even say) the whole spirit of its application were entirely unrelated to those of the Roman jurists.)[5] Even, in the Middle East, countries like Saudi Arabia, UAE, and Kuwait have shown permissiveness towards western cultures. This alone raises doubts in the minds of their opponents, that the Mujahideen (one who carries jihad or struggle) have other agenda— the establishment of an Islamic state and empire and then, the Ummah, on a global scale. Yet, the issues behind their jihad happen to be political rather than religious. It has to be so in, at least the short term. Unless they have a political goal, for instance, driving away western powers from the holy lands of the Middle East, they cannot install an Islamic state. In a heterogeneous world, such conflicts may either be solved by force or through negotiation. More importantly, since power centres alternate, there is nothing final, contrary to what the Islamic radicals would have us believe (for the jihadists and the Islamists there is no such concept as relative).

With all these contradictions, the War on Terror, or the jihad, whichever one may call it, goes on. This book thus focuses attention on two key players in this war— radical Islamist terrorists and the United States— and tries to establish that even radical Islamists have a political agenda beneath their religious rhetoric and hence, they too, are amenable to treaties and negotiations, such as the 1993 Oslo Accord. One of the basic premises of this book is that American bullying in the Middle East happens to be the chief cause for the rise and proliferation of Islamist terrorism and that the United States ought to make amendments in its foreign policies by gelding its aggressiveness. Moreover, the book concludes that even a relatively insignificant force, like radical Islamist outfits, can spring a surprise on the American colossus, if the United States continues, heedlessly, its present foreign 'aggressive' policies in the Middle East. The US rulers, on their part, want to isolate the radicals, that is, the jihadists, from moderate Muslims through it's the war on terrorism

The recent Mumbai terror episode forms the bedrock of various analyses contained in this book. 26/11 has served as a big eye opener to the fact that these ruthless terrorists have no respect for humanity. Moreover, they have left no message, religious or political, during that entire operation. Thus they acted in a cowardly fashion to indulge in a blood bath that can only recoil on them. How far can they go on alienating the international community through their radical ideology and still create the Ummah? This book also makes a very up-to-date and in-depth analysis of two of the life support systems— arms and funds— of these terrorist groups and of how the international community, led by the United States, carries on their counter terrorism policies in this regard. Two countries, the United States and Pakistan, occupy a central place in this book.

Finally, I have preferred to use "Islamist' terrorists instead of radical Islamic terrorists, since Islamist terrorism covers both the two components of this book— violent armed jihad and the political agenda and ambition behind such activities. Because of the extreme mobility (reminiscent of the days of Great Crusade when European Christians marched towards the Holy land) of quite a number of young Muslim youths from various parts of the world towards Iraq and Afghanistan, modern Islamist terrorism has indeed taken a turn towards global jihad. This point is also discussed in detail in the second chapter.

References

[1] A Brief History of Terrorism, Mark Burgess, CDI research Analyst, 2 July, 2003, http://www.cdi.org/program/issue/document.cfm?DocumentID=1381&IssueID=138&StartRow=1&ListRows=10&appendURL=&Orderby=DateLastUpdated&ProgramID=39&issueID=138
[2] ibid, Mark Burgess
[3] The Sharia, Mohammedanism, An Historical Survey H.A.R. Gibb, London: Oxford University Press, [1950] (pages 72-84). bestall2u.info/islam/gibb-har-the-sharia.html
[4] Mohammad Asad, The Principles of State and Government In Islam, Islamic Book Trust,Kuala Lumpur, Paperback edition, 1999, p.23
[5] Ibid., H.A.R. Gibb

FOREWARD

The advent of modern, international terrorism is dated to July 22, 1968, when the Popular Front for the Liberation of Palestine (PFLP) hijacked an Israeli El Al commercial flight en route from Rome to Tel Aviv. Since the beginning of the contemporary wave of terrorism, the world has witnessed violence conducted by five categories of non-state threat groups. They are left and right wing (ideological terrorism), ethno-political, politico-religious, state-sponsored, and single issue groups. Ideological, ethno-political, and state-sponsored terrorism were the most dominant forms of violence during the Cold War. With the collapse of the Soviet Union, the ideology of communism lost its appeal and support, and left wing groups diminished. With the end of the Cold War, the Soviet bloc of countries terminated support for socialist governments and left wing groups, and the Western bloc of countries terminated support for right wing governments and right wing groups. While the threat posed by ethno-political groups continued, a new form of terrorism emerged and grew steadfastly into the 21st century. While the end of the Cold War marked the decline of traditional or old terrorism, the post Cold War witnessed the emergence of a new form of terrorism.

Skeptics of new terrorism argument debated until al Qaeda attacked America's most iconic targets on September 11, 2001. With continuity of attacks, the world realized that 9/11 as not an anomaly but a trend. Since 9/11, the global threat of terrorism has grown, and not plateaued. Al-Qaeda and its operationally linked associates in the Muslim world as well as its ideologically affiliated cells in the West are the exemplars of this new terrorism. In addition to mobilizing 30-40 groups in Asia, Africa and the Middle East, al Qaeda has successfully inspired segments of Muslims in both the territorial communities of the Middle East, Asia and Africa as well as the Diaspora and migrant communities of the West. Despite being the world's most hunted class of terrorist groups, al Qaeda, its associated groups and affiliated cells, pose a global and an unprecedented threat. In the early 21st century, preventing and suppressing new terrorism has become priority of most governments.

In his book, "For Whom the Bell Tolls: America or the Jihadists" by Gautam Maitra makes an appreciable contribution to both understanding and responding to the contemporary threat. Unlike most non-Muslim writers, he understands that the threat stems from the misinterpretation and misrepresentation of Islam rather than from Islam, a great faith. He maps the evolution of the political ideology, and its ideological and operational manifestations. Furthermore, he surveys the terrorist and extremist literature and provides insightful comments for decision and policy makers.

Today, India suffers both from domestic and international terrorism. India, hosting the second largest Muslim population in the world, has constantly underestimated the threat from terrorism. Together with Pakistan, Afghanistan, and Iraq, India is one of the four countries in the world suffering from a very high level of terrorism. A vicious by product of ideological extremism, terrorism is spreading both in urban and rural India. Not all of terrorism in India is international, but domestic. A community centric approach is needed to counter the wave of radicalization affecting Indian society. As the devastating Mumbai attacks demonstrated in November 2008, India has failed to develop a comprehensive, national and a strategic approach to fight either operational terrorism or ideological extremism. Gautam Maitra's book will be a useful guide to the Indian policy and academic community in crafting an appropriate response. Gautam Maitra is one of the few Indian scholars with the knowledge and understanding to play a frontline role in formally and informally educating the Indian public, elite and its leaders of the contemporary threat.

Rohan Gunaratna is Head, International Centre for Political Violence and Terrorism Research and Professor of Security Studies at the S. Rajaratnam School of International Studies at the Nanyang Technological University in Singapore. He is the author of "Inside Al Qaeda: Global Network of Terror," published by Columbia University Press, an international bestseller.

TABLE OF CONTENTS

CHAPTER I

YES, THEY TOO CAN DO IT IF...

Introduction

Victor Hugo once said, "Nothing in this world is so powerful as an idea whose time has come". This rings particularly true in the sphere of politics. Major historical or political happenings, right from the American Revolution to 20th century Fascism, Socialism, and Communism, sprung from ideas whose 'time' had come. Yet, those ideas never fructified in a day. They were the products of several decades of probing, investigation, application, and, importantly, consummation of successive 'experiments' in that direction.

Every new idea in history had been viewed with pessimism and suspicion. Many fell aside, but some seemingly impossible, odd, and unconventional ideas saw the light of the day. Few did expect Karl Marx's ideas to hold sway over a large part of the world with such a 'religious' fervour and to surface so pervasively in undeveloped regions like Russia and China, least envisioned by Marx himself. Neither had anyone expected that the ideas of Fascism and Nazism would rise out of the massive destruction brought by the First World War, and that too with such lightning rapidity, in a land burdened with the yoke of the Versailles compensations. In all these cases, unfortunately, it was the brazen display of highhandedness on the part of the ruling elites in these countries or of the victorious adversaries that hastened the realisation of these ideas.

Since the closing decades of the last century, we have been experiencing another type of movement, a more bizarre and a terrific one—radical/ fundamentalist/ *jihad*-ist Islamist terrorism. Its ideas were rooted in a doctrine that hardly enjoyed universal acceptability amongst the vast section of moderate Muslims. This doctrine is now being resurrected out of near oblivion with greater vengeance and vigour, thanks, partly, to bin laden, and partly, to some irresponsible and indiscreet policies pursued by successive American administrations in the past few decades, culminating in the American declaration of 'War on Terrorism' (WOT).

The straw that broke the camel's back was the 11 September 2001 (9/11) attack on the World Trade Center (WTC) twin towers and the Pentagon—symbols of American pride. This most recent form of Islamist terrorism, espoused by bin Laden and the al Qaeda, owes its rise and force to a series of wilful American foreign policy blunders in the last few decades in various parts of the world, especially, the Middle East. As a result, the al Qaeda, as an organisation, movement, and activity, has virtually become the pivot of the global anti-American *Jihad*.

Needless to mention, since 1945, few countries—except those loyal to the United States—have escaped wanton destruction of land and resources, massive civilian casualties, fall of established governments, and unwarranted psychological and physical maiming, because the United States deemed that they ought to follow 'American' ways. In a letter addressed to the then Iraqi President Saddam Hussein, just prior to the 1991 US led UN invasion of Iraq, the then American President George Bush Sr warned that the US military action would not only destroy the industrial-military infrastructure of Iraq, but would also raze Iraq back to the stone age. Incidentally, the then Iraqi Foreign Minister Tariq Aziz, refused to deliver that letter to Saddam Hussein because he found the tone and language of that letter unacceptable. Successive American administrations rarely mend their ways. Nothing has changed since the first Gulf War. Iraq happens to be still on the US radar despite changes in the US administration. The International Red Cross, in a recent report, mentioned that many Iraqi children have to pass dead bodies on the street as they walk to school in the morning.[1]

The intention of this book is not to justify terrorism but to make an objective assessment of contemporary Islamist terrorism in order to see if it really has a religious agenda or a genuine political grievance. The US bullying, especially, in the Middle East, had rather driven an otherwise secular political terrorism into the strait jacket of religion resulting in the emergence of the al Qaeda with anti-American jihad as its chief goal.

The fact is that the rise of Islamist terrorism, which is just a phenomenon in the long chain of international political history, has coincided with the inexorable and inevitable decline in American great power potential. The rise and appearance of bin Laden or the al Qaeda is simply a historical reality resulting from a series of recent American highhandedness in the relentless pursuit of its 'great power' strategic interests in the Middle East (or bankruptcy of the US foreign policy perceptions in the post-Soviet vacuum?). The very foundation of the American 'empire', based on some key assumptions, notably, the supremacy of the western civilisation, now stands somewhat shaken. In this connection, the 9/11 Commission Report deemed that a change in the US policies towards the Middle East was warranted. Indeed, the American misadventures in various parts of the world are but symptoms of its great power decline syndrome. What is ominous for the US is that the phenomenon or the movement of terrorism might pave the way for the rise of another great power or a combination of great powers, taking charge of the world affairs, at America's expense. This is what I had predicted in my earlier book, *Tracing the Eagle's Orbit*.

There are concerns even in the American intellectual and political circles because that country is losing a war that it hoped to bring to an end in the shortest possible time. Many US foreign policy and terrorism experts hold the Bush administration's unwarranted and wilful policies responsible for imparting an 'anti-Islam' slant to the US conduct of foreign affairs. Two undercurrents have chiefly guided American foreign policies in the post Cold War decades: the ghost of the Cold War and the 'subconscious awareness' of an impending clash of civilisations in the backdrop of suspicion generated by an uncertain international political order undergoing American experimentation in the post-Soviet and post-colonial vacuum. America has failed to come to terms with new international political realities.

The crux is that, unlike in earlier reverses—for example, Vietnam— the United States has little 'exit' option this time. Donald Rumsfeld, in a telephonic interview with the New York Sun, remarked, "The idea that you can ignore these enemies or live or let live, or find some accommodation of peaceful existence or détente is just erroneous, it can't be done".[2] In this backdrop, president Obama's policies towards reducing terrorism would be extremely crucial in deciding whether civilisations will head towards a second Great Crusade, this time on a truly global scale.

Because of the anti-American perception amongst a large section of the Muslim community, generated by some ill-conceived American policies in the Middle East, America has already become, to some extent, a 'target' nation—a condition that every country, strong or weak, would try to avoid at all costs. Nothing is more dangerous for any country than to become a 'target'. By target I don't simply mean the wrath of the terrorists, but a general loss of confidence and respect in the eyes of the rest of the world. The US has already lost some credibility and is being viewed by many as a bull in a china shop, thanks to its 'bullying' in various parts of the world.

The word 'target' has great implications in the context of this book. The United States has got to explain to the rest of the world why it is being targeted by the jihadists. Some scholars believe that the 'aggressiveness' inherent in Islam serves as the driving force for jihadists to assert the supremacy of Islam. However, this viewpoint simply fails to account for the decades-long wilful American intervention in the Middle East.

True, the Islamist terrorists don't speak for the entire Islamic community and happen to be a minority compared to their moderate Islamic counterparts, regionally and globally. Yet these jihadists, for example, the al Qaeda, have assumed global influence in a remarkably short time. Does this not prove that the jihadists have got a definite political agenda—ejecting America out of the Middle East—in the guise of religion? The simple logic is that, if the jihadists are in a minority, which is indeed the case, we have to look elsewhere to account for the al Qaeda's rapid proliferation on a global scale—American intrusive policies in the Middle East. Unless these terrorists have some support base in other countries, their 'movement' would have vanished like many other religious-political terrorist movements.

It is this global dimension of jihad which is at the root of the al Qaeda's success in keeping up a prolonged anti-American struggle. For example, it is easy to suppress local insurrections of any type because the insurgents often lack the necessary resources to carry on a protracted engagement with the concerned state power. One of the chief reasons for their premature demise—here an analogy can be drawn from the history of civilizations—is their inability to migrate and expand. Now, the ability to spread and migrate depends on the willingness of a group faced with an issue of survival. This willingness, in turn, is rooted in a conviction in ones purpose and reasoning. No terrorist group or organisation would dare to carry its tirade against a great power, especially, in alien territories, unless it has belief in its objective, anti-Americanism, and unless it feels that the clamour for anti-Americanism resonates on a global scale. There are many Muslim countries that have experienced the baneful effects of aggressive American foreign policies. It is another thing whether the jihadists would be able to translate their anti-American jihad into a mother of battles, in the foreseeable future. The bottom line is that they have a chance if American policies continue to generate hatred amongst people in other countries—an extremely embarrassing position for a superpower.

Worse still, a perception among other countries that the American foreign policies are being used to enhance its geo-political interests, *at any cost*, requires the United States to convince others that it really cares for other countries and their people, in order to avoid a possible isolation in international affairs. The danger for the United States is that if al Qaeda's vilifying tactic continues, the latter might actually succeed in securing legitimacy for itself. This point is extremely crucial. Unlike conventional wars between states, the battle with the jihadists has to be ideological. Force or real political considerations may not hold for long and would do little to offset a possible loss of credibility, especially, in matters of international politics. All said and done, the allegations regarding Islam's forcible expansion may come under any serious consideration only after the jihadists attain their chief objective—driving away the American forces from the Arab lands. The centrepiece of the above arguments is that American foreign policies stand on trial.

People everywhere fail to comprehend why the mighty United States is so 'over reactive' to the activities of the 'trifle' al Qaeda, when that group has to stay on the ground and when that ground belongs not to the al Qaeda but to other states, and when many of these states, including the European allies, have joined the War on Terror, at America's behest! Nevertheless, a section of the US ruling and intellectual circle still believes that the war with the al Qaeda could last for another hundred years, reminiscent of former

Pakistani leader Z. A. Bhutto's famous statement that Pakistan would carry on a thousand year jihad against India!

There are books, like, Mark Steyn's *America Alone*, Craig Winn's *Prophet of Doom*, and Tony Blankley's *The West's Last Chance: Will We Win the Clash of Civilizations*, that have become quite popular in the United States. These and many other books exaggerate the possibility of a clash of civilisations by pointing to the declining trends in the western civilisation, the 'aggressiveness' of Islam, and the relative advantages that Muslims enjoy in respect of demography and able bodied youth vis-à-vis their Western counterparts. These are simply aimed at upping the ante and the hype. I don't think such mindsets would facilitate communication between the Muslims and the United States, which is the need of the hour.

On the other hand, some experts like Alan Chouet, a former senior officer of France's Director-General for External Security, DGSE, feel that WOT was already a doomed war since the US invasion of Afghanistan in 2001. He says, "...it's as ridiculous as a 'war on anger'. You do not wage a war on terror you wage a war against people".[3] Michael Scheur, the Head of the Osama Bin Laden Unit from 1996 to 1999, observed, "We're clearly losing. Today, Bin Laden, the al Qaeda and their allies have only one indispensable ally: the 'US' foreign policy towards the Islamic world."[4]

What Laden wants

A close look at the principal grievances of the al Qaeda under bin Laden's leadership simply confirms the veracity of the above arguments. The al Qaeda wants: (1) a total withdrawal of American forces from the Middle East; (2) overthrow of all pro-American government in the Middle East since they have become corrupt, insincere, and 'infidel' by being subservient to America; and (3) establishment of rule of Islam in other parts of the world by defeating the infidels in order to do 'God's justice'.

Both the fatwas issued by bin Laden and his associates — the 1996 Declaration of War Against the Americans Occupying the Land of the Two Holy Places and the Declaration of the World Islamic Front for Jihad against the Jews and the Crusaders of 1998— cover all these three requirements. Bin Laden, in his 1996 fatwa, was extremely critical of the Saudi rulers for their highly repressive acts on the Ulema (scholars) and the Da'ees (callers), at the instigation of the 'Crusaders' and the 'Zionists'. Besides declaring jihad against America and Israel for defiling Islam and the Holy land, the 1996 fatwa contained a litany of political-economic-religious deprivations. Laden's emphasis on ensuring and spreading drinking water facilities for everyone reminds one of the social welfare activities of the Hamas and the Hezbollah. That fatwa also contains a definite hint towards a counter sanction on the US trading interests. Laden deemed it extremely necessary to cut the taproots of the US trading interests in Muslim countries, as the revenues accrued therefrom were bound to enhance the repressive capacity of the American rulers. Two important components of the 1996 fatwa were the call for the mobilisation of the Islamic world in order to thwart the US design to undo the establishment of a global Ummah and avert split and internecine feuds between various groups and factions of Islam.

The 1998 fatwa ruled that killing Americans and their allies, civil and military, was an individual duty for every Muslim in every country, in order to liberate the Al-Aqsa mosque and the holy mosque of Mecca from their grip, and to compel the US armies to move out of the Islamic lands, "defeated and unable to threaten any Muslim". Why was this fatwa issued? According to Laden, "this is in accordance with the words of Almighty Allah', to fight off the pagans 'until there is no more tumult or oppression, and there prevail justice and faith in Allah.'[5] One noticeable difference this time was the absence of the call for mobilisation of Islam on a global scale and Laden's silence on the Saudi role. The ideological foundations of these fatwas got more focused and were made more concrete when Al Zawahiri, in his *Knights under the Prophet's Banner*, gave a call for the creation of an operational base within the Arab heartland to convert terrorism into a real movement for the liberation of the Muslim homelands.

The reasons behind the promulgation of 1998 fatwa were the following: American occupation of the Arabian peninsula for the last seven years (it should now be read as, last eighteen years since more than a decade has elapsed after that fatwa was issued) that resulted in plundering its riches, dictating its rulers, humiliating its people, terrorising its neighbours, and turning its bases in the peninsula into spearheads to fight the neighbouring peoples with, and above all, the American support for Israel.[6] According to Laden, America wanted to demolish Iraq, "the strongest neighbouring

Arab state, and their endeavour to fragment all the states of the region such as Saudi Arabia, Egypt, and Sudan into paper statelets and through their disunion and weakness to guarantee Israel's survival…"[7]

This book does not support the mindless killing and violence perpetrated by Islamist terrorists. Rather, it seeks to emphasise that today's jihadist's owe their rise and justification to some tacit American 'approvals' during the days of the Soviet-Afghan war. Indeed, the US had provided all sorts of help to fundamentalist Mujahideen to undo Soviet occupation of Afghanistan, stoking the 'pet' idea of Islamic jihad as a counterweight to communism. Past sins are now revisiting America with greater vengeance. The US is now in hot pursuit in the Gulf and adjoining regions to chase out and chastise the very Mujahideens that it had nourished during the Soviet-Afghan war. Little wonder that American cities have now become targets of the jihadists.

What is more puzzling is that while America has waged the War on Terror, it continues its arms supplies to various groups and states that support terrorism, discussed in some detail in the next chapter. It must be remembered that uninterrupted supply of funds and arms happen to be the two principal arteries of jihadist activities. All these leave enough doubt about the American sincerity in carrying out the War on Terror. Does America have a hidden agenda? Would not the American half-hearted approach aid the jihadists? Islamist terrorist groups like the al Qaeda, thus would be too keen to convert their 'beliefs' and 'ideas' into an international ideological and political movement, and in the process, may inflict an upset defeat on their near 'invincible' adversary!

Can anybody deny that theirs' (the Islamist terrorists) happens to be an idea or a belief system born out of a reaction against the 'unlawful' US 'occupation' of Arabia and American bullying in that region for the past few decades? This idea or belief system of jihadists has its roots nearly a century ago, in a similar reaction to the colonial and imperialist domination of the erstwhile European colonial powers, like the Muslim Brotherhood established by Al Banna in 1928. Now, it is the al Qaeda that has taken upon itself the responsibility of carrying on jihad against American neo-colonialism. It is not difficult to see that in the absence of at least three developments in world politics—unchallenged American supremacy in the post-Cold War era, the US propensity to rely on the use of force to chastise the 'devils', and the American support for the Mujahideen during Soviet-Afghan war—the world today may not have known an entity called the al Qaeda.

Almost one and a half decades ago, Laden himself, in a private conversation with Abdel Bari Atwan at Tora Bora, admitted that the US had used the Mujahideen for their own ends, exploiting their "Islamic fervour to rid a Muslim land of infidel occupiers".[8] Abdullah Azzam, Laden's mentor and founder of the Makhtab al-Khadamat (MAK), was so fired up by the successful outcome of the Soviet-Afghan War that he wrote a book, *Defending the Land of the Muslims is Each Man's Most Important Duty*, in which he stressed that the fight would continue and jihad would remain an individual obligation until all other Muslim dominated lands were freed. While, in 1989, Azzam had given a call for global jihad, Al Zawahiri in his book, written a decade later, felt that reforms and free elections could take place only when these lands are liberated. All these clearly emphasise *political* agendas of the jihadists.

Laden and his followers had long known how the American bullying and intransigence, especially, during the 1980s turned Lebanon and other parts of the Middle East into a tinderbox region. The endless bloodletting unleashed by CIA-backed covert operations, aimed at setting one religious group against the other, along with other intrusive US policies in that region, bear ample testimony to American callousness towards the suffering and plights of common civilians. Laden also saw how helpless had been Iraq before the might of this formidable adversary in the 1991 and the 2003 Gulf Wars. Growing American intervention in the Middle East in the post-Cold War era rather hardened the resolve and resistance of hardliners in these countries. They viewed these American overtures as ploys to ensure Israel's security on a permanent basis. With too many odds to overcome, the Islamist terror groups had only one course left, targeting the US soft spots.

After all, both Laden and the Mujahideen fighters had some idea as to where the vulnerability of the Americans lay, thanks to their interaction with the CIA during the Soviet-Afghan war. Laden was smart enough to realise that the same tactics that had created so many problems for the Soviet forces could very well be used against the Americans, especially in the rugged terrains of Afghanistan. He went a step further and reasoned that "surprise and clandestine" attacks on the lone superpower's soft targets, especially on American soil, could have great repercussions on a global scale. It is doubtful if 9/11 attacks would have taken place had the world order remained bi-polar or multi-polar. This is the strategic reality of post-Cold War international politics, which has so much to do with the rise of the jihadists.

War on Terrorism

Former US President George W. Bush, in his 20 September 2001 speech to the Joint Congress, vowed that his country would direct every resource at its command, "every means of diplomacy, every tool of intelligence, every instrument of law enforcement, every financial influence, every necessary weapon of war -- to the destruction and to the defeat of the global terror network."[9] He, elaborated on the kind of war that his country would wage, said, "Our response involves far more than instant retaliation and isolated strikes. Americans should not expect one battle but a lengthy campaign unlike any other we have ever seen... we will starve terrorists of funding, turn them one against another, drive them from place to place until there is no refuge or rest. And we will pursue nations that provide aid or safe haven to terrorism. Every nation in every region now has a decision to make: Either you are with us or you are with the terrorists".[10] The American President did not miss the opportunity to declare that it was not just America's war but that of the entire international community.

It is now widely acknowledged in the American academic and political circles that despite its formidable military might, the US now happens to be at the receiving end of the ongoing War on Terror. As early as 2006, The Center for American Progress and Foreign Policy magazine carried out a survey, The Terrorism Index, amongst 100 top foreign policy experts. Most of them believed that the US was not winning the War on Terror. Nearly 86 per cent of the experts felt that the world had since become more dangerous for the Americans to live in.

A few years back, an anonymous CIA officer had claimed in his book, *Imperial Hubris* that America was losing the War on Terror. He held that the US invasion of Iraq in 2003 was responsible for shifting America's main focus on War on Terror, away from Afghanistan. He rather felt that the 2003 campaign in Iraq was like a "Christmas gift" for the al Qaeda and vindicated

Laden's oft-repeated claim that the US design in the Middle East was to attack and soil the holy places in the heartland of Islam. In an interview given to the NBC's Chief foreign affairs correspondent, Andrea Mitchell on 24 June, 2004, this anonymous CIA officer further observed that Laden had succeeded in bringing various ethnic and linguist Muslim groups all over the world to carry on jihad against the United States. Incidentally, Bruce Hoffman, another terrorism expert, feels that such a conglomeration of the various heterogeneous elements in a common body, the al Qaeda, would rather work to the disadvantage of the jihadists and enable the United States to create divisions within their ranks. The above CIA officer believed that the US had underestimated the size of the al Qaeda and its various networks and that American aggression had actually inflated its membership and its inflow of funds several fold! The above views are now shared by many foreign policy experts in the US.

Jon Basil Utley, a Robert Taft fellow at the Ludwig Von Mosses Institute, had listed thirty six ways that the US was losing the WOT. At least a few of his contentions are worth mentioning, such as, Laden's success in creating a support base among Muslims in Asia, Africa, and Europe, on the basis of anti-American feeling, the 'meta-sizing' of the al Qaeda into smaller and independent local cells working as 'new semi autonomous groups' in various parts of the world, and the withdrawal of vast Arab funds from America for fear of getting confiscated due to various US counterterrorism financial measures, thereby, causing a serious drain on the US economy.[11] According to the July 2007 National Intelligence Estimate, the al Qaeda had not only regrouped in Pakistan's northern border region but there has also been a significant rise in the number of new and independent, smaller terror groups sympathetic to the al Qaeda, in various parts of the world.

On the other end of the spectrum, we have the viewpoint of the US administration. The then US president in his address to the nation on the fifth anniversary of 9/11 said, "Five years after 9/11, our enemies have not succeeded in launching another attack on our soil, but they have not been idle. The al Qaeda and those inspired by its hateful ideology have carried out terrorist attacks in more than two dozen nations. And just last month, they were foiled in a plot to blow up passenger planes headed for the United

States. They remain determined to attack America and kill our citizens-and we are determined to stop them."[12]

The most ominous part of his speech related to the Iraqi situation. He said, "We are training Iraqi troops so they can defend their nation. We are helping Iraq's Unity Government grow in strength and serve its people. We will not leave until the work is done. Whatever mistakes have been made in Iraq, the worst mistake would be to think that if we pulled out, the terrorists would leave us alone. They will not leave us alone. The safety of America depends on the outcome of the battle in the streets of Baghdad."[13] Elsewhere in his speech he said that America was in the early hours of this struggle between tyranny and freedom. These are the views of the head of the mightiest state on earth five years after waging the War on Terror, not against a formidable state power, but against a few mobile, non-state, and clandestine groups!

Another important issue is how to determine win or loss in a kind of war lacking any known official instruments to do so. It may be that the vanquished terrorists would temporarily move into oblivion, as they have done many times in the past, only to resurface with greater vengeance,later. Conversely, it may also be that the US may prefer a temporary retreat from active involvement in world affairs, and some of its European allies may step into its shoes. However, none of the indicators like the retreat of the enemy or reduction in striking capacity of the terrorists, temporary feeling of safety on the part of the state powers consequent on such reduction, or even temporary success in thwarting and forestalling the plots of terrorist groups guarantee a definite outcome in such kinds of warfare. That is why, the former US President, George W. Bush said that this war was not merely a military battle but a decisive ideological battle of the twenty first century. On the other hand, since one of the key demands of Islamist terrorists is the US withdrawal from the Muslim lands, they would definitely feel triumphant if they succeed in this respect

On 20 September 2001, the former President George W. Bush, described the al Qaeda as a "collection of loosely affiliated terrorist organizations", "a fringe movement that perverts the peaceful teachings of Islam", whose goal is not to make money, but "remaking the world and imposing radical beliefs on people everywhere".[14] It is, however, incomprehensible how a fringe ideological movement can create a 'radical Islamic empire' on a global scale when democracy and rule of law happen to be long standing and internationally accepted political practices. Did President Bush have any hidden agenda behind this War on Terror or did the American administration underestimate its adversaries?

The answer to this question can be found in a recent statement by Dr. Anthony H Cordesman, Arleih A. Burke Chair in Strategy, Center for Strategic and International Studies, made before the House Committee on Foreign Affairs, Sub-committee on the Middle East and South Asia.[15] Dr. Cordesman said that the new US President, Mr Obama's shift in strategy was still not really a strategy but a change in tactics of 'hold and build', underlining the stark fact that such a type of insurgency can never be won by military means but would have to be won at the local level.[16] The reader may be surprised to note that this happens to be the real situation in Afghanistan, after almost eight years of the War on Terror that had taken a toll of nearly 650 Americans! In what respect does this war still lack a strategy and continues to be so?

While he was dwelling on the 'to-do' list of present US administrations' policies, he didn't fail to mention that the American failures in setting 'clear benchmarks for action, progress, or to measure success' goes back to the previous administration that had started the war. He said, "we do not yet have a clear plan for using the US troops, improving the role of our allies, and solving NATO's command and caveat problems".[17] More appalling is his admission that "our top intelligence and policy officials admit that we do not yet have the range of metrics to fully understand what is happening and measure success or failure."[18] Cordesman felt that for all these years, American policy makers have rather 'over promised and under performed'.

At the very beginning, Dr Cordesman mentioned that America was not winning the war and that tactical victories would be meaningless if the insurgents continued to find 'sanctuaries' in Pakistan and continued to expand their areas of operation. How could Dr Cordesman say that the US was at the receiving end of the war? He took some crude trends, like rise in violence, rise in the numbers of IED explosions, of insurgency attacks in peak months, and in allied casualties. For example, in respect of IEDs and roadside bombs, the number rose from 22 in 2002 to 83 in 2003, 325 in 2004, 782 in 2005, 1931 in 2006, and 2,615 in 2007, while the number of major incidents rose from 50 in 2002 to 160 in 2007, and 120 in the first half of 2008. According to his estimate, the number of IED attacks alone in 2008 rose by 27 per cent while the number of attacks on Afghan personnel registered a rise of 119 per cent. The number of NATO/ISAF deaths rose by 355, while suicide attacks showed just a 5 per cent decline. The overall situation continued to worsen through 2008 till the first quarter of 2009. He further reported that the size of high risk areas in Afghanistan and that of the 'Green Zone' kept steadily increasing over the years.[19] Cordesman's statement clearly shows how misplaced was the American perception of its much vaunted War on Terror waged in 2001. Was America serious about the dangers from the jihadists or did it have a hidden agenda?

Advantages for the Islamist Terrorists

Indeed, the jihadists stand a good chance of success in this war against America. Common people can only choose between alternatives. People feel that their chances of bargaining vis-à-vis the establishment might increase several-fold if an *alternative* exists. It is this human tendency that terrorists try to exploit. Note the difference here, between terrorists and the drug mafia or smugglers. By its very nature, a terrorist group, political or religious, cannot do without influencing the masses, whereas, smugglers and drug peddlers must work stealthily and out of public notice. That is why the conventional state powers strive desperately to club terrorists, smugglers, and drug traffickers in the same bracket in a bid to deglamorise terrorists.

If the War on Terrorism lingers on for forty years, as President Bush, said in an interview last year to Richard Engel, NBC News Correspondent and author of *War Journal: My Five Years in Iraq*, then the war might work to the great advantage of the terrorists. Mr. Bush said, "...in forty years the world would know if the War on Terrorism and conflicts in Iraq and Afghanistan, had reduced extremism, helped moderates, and promoted democracy."[20] Why did the former US president feel that it won't be less than forty years? Was he hitting on an arithmetic calculation based on a natural law, that in forty years bin Laden, his associates, and the first and second generation of the jihadists would die or be too incapacitated to carry on the war? My

to recreate their feats! [24] Consequently, it is easy for the jihadist groups to produce an unlimited number of fresh recruits in contrast to others.

Generally speaking, Islamic countries are not averse to accepting modernization, but they are loath to relinquish their traditional beliefs and practices. This has been highlighted by Huntington in his book on the *Clash of Civilizations* with reference to Malaysia, Indonesia, Saudi Arabia, etc. Even some top intellectuals within the Muslim community are rarely free from such feelings. The Indian police investigating last year's serial blast cases in various Indian cities have found one computer programmer working as a software engineer at Yahoo in Pune. He was believed to be at the head of a "media terror cell" comprising some "highly qualified, computer savvy people belonging to good and educated families". Mohammad Mansoor Peerbhoy, the alleged IT personnel, was believed to have drafted the emails on behalf of a jihadist group, the Indian Mujahideen, just before or immediately after the blasts in Delhi, Ahmedabad, and Jaipur. The Joint Commissioner of Mumbai police, Mr Rakesh Maria told reporters that the "The Indian Mujahideen started a media wing with software engineers."[25] Even though the charges are yet to be proved, one thing is certain— the use of emails for sending prior warnings from hacked wireless Internet sites that is beyond the knowledge of the average terrorist activists. Even the Pakistani Interior Minister, Rehman Malik, admitted before the media that the terrorists used sophisticated techniques in conducting the 26/11 operation in Mumbai.

Terror experts and common people, alike, are puzzled regarding the involvement of Muslim doctors implicated in the London and Glasgow airport terror conspiracy on 29 and 30 June 2007. Stephen Schwartz mentioned a few Islamic groups, like Al-Muhajiroun and Tablighi Jamaat in UK which recruit medical students. He wrote, "Many Muslim doctors have adopted the extremist doctrines espoused by the Muslim Brotherhood, Saudi Wahhabists, and Pakistani jihadists."[26] This presence of 'elite intelligentsia' is bound to shape and swing the opinion and leaning of average Muslims in the jihadist direction. Although not much data is available on this extremely sensitive issue, it is up to the state authorities to tackle it, even if these may be stray cases. Incidentally, the Government of India had the past record of successfully dealing with cases of bright intellectuals and students involved in the Naxal movement in the 1970s and permitted most of them to return

16

to mainstream of society. Many of those bright students later went on to fill top bureaucratic and administrative posts in the government.

Given the 'forty years' earmarked for them by Mr Bush, terrorists shouldn't have much trouble in climbing up the ladder of 'legitimacy'! The borderline between terrorism and rule of law has every reason to get thinner over time. After all, enemies often trade their attributes through prolonged interactions. This is evident from an unintended remark by Dr Condoleezza Rice on 3 December 2008 at a Press Conference in New Delhi that since 2001, the US has learnt a lot about the modus operandi of the terrorists. To repeat, protracted engagement with terrorists may well mean the legitimisation of Islamist terrorism. That way, it may be said that terrorists can be successful in their objectives if the US allows them the space of manoeuvre.

Another important advantage that Islamist terrorists have is that many lower class Muslim youth in various parts of the world, fortunately or unfortunately, flock to retail businesses associated with mobile phones and computer, the two livewires of modern communication. Many among these youths have a practical knowledge (though not much theoretical knowledge) in repairing and even in altering the settings. What is more, familiarity with computers and the Internet at such lower levels carries the terrorist battleground into cyber world. The enormous proliferation of jihadist web sites in recent years simply acts as magnets for terrorist groups and their sympathisers. Every detail from bomb making to training facilities can be found in many of these web sites. Such a trend helps the sprouting of home grown cells enormously, rendering it extremely difficult to track them.

Terrorist groups often exploit the weaknesses of state authorities by testing the latter's willingness in going all out for the terrorist hunt. Generally, the state machineries are slow to act, as in the recent Pakistani deliberation to eject Taliban from the Swat valley. Even the United States had been slow to react to intelligence warnings prior to 9/11. One reason may be the cost-effectiveness of a particular counter terrorist measure. It is here that terrorists like to enhance the odds against state entities. For example, constant recourse to new tactics by the terrorists may render even extremely ambitious and prohibitively costly counterterrorist measures redundant after a certain point. Consequently, the number of costly campaigns tends to mount. So do financial expenditures. It is the state machinery that finds the cost of countering terrorism too prohibitive while the terrorists often successfully get away with low budget campaigns. After the release of the 9/11 Commission Report, it is now well known how the terrorists manage to carry out big operations with low budgets. For example, the 9/11 campaign had cost the terrorists just $ 4, 00, 000 to $ 5, 00, 000 excluding the $ 2, 70, 000 that they spent in America for flight training, travel, housing, and vehicles.

The al Qaeda deputy, Ayman Al Zawahiri, draws from Paul Kennedy's views that the overstretch factor and the subsequent rise in costs of maintaining the American bases and forces would prove too much for the US to bear in future.[27] For example, the first five years of the Iraqi war, according to various sources, had cost the United States anything between $500 billion to $700 billion, including future costs. According to Joseph Stiglitz, a Nobel Prize winner in economics, the Iraqi war expenses, so far, might have cost anything between $1 and $2 trillion, including future costs.[28] Bin Laden, in an address to American people, said that the jihadists had forced the US President to resort to emergency budget to cover the cost of continuing the Afghan and Iraq wars and that this alone proves "the success of the plan of bleeding [America] to the point of bankruptcy, Allah willing".[29]

I have discussed in a later chapter, how a radical Islamist group like the al Qaeda procures money and arms through the creation and use of front organisations. Any American counter measure to block such a flow of finances might evoke strong reactions from the concerned diaspora and from local politicians who feel that such action might jeopardise the voting patterns in their respective constituencies. The jihadists are always on the lookout for exploiting the openness of the western societies. This alone accounts for the spread of the Wahaabi influence to various parts of the world and the takeover of Middle Eastern studies programs at various US universities, mainly through Saudi funding.[30] We shall discuss some more advantages that terrorist have, a little later in this chapter.

The US Advantages

Despite the above advantages to the Islamist terrorists, one must not lose sight of visible rifts and conflicts between various groups, sects, and even states within Islam. This gives an advantage to the opponents of

Islam and to countries engaged in fighting Islamist terrorism. Bin Laden, in a 1996 fatwa, had specifically appealed to Muslims all over the world to avoid all such factionalism. The US cleverly exploited such differences and successfully marginalised Saddam in the 1991 Gulf War. That is why bin Laden accuses the US of being a divisive force, particularly for the Islamic world. Conversely, there is a difference in perception between the US on the one hand and its European allies and the rest of the world on the other, which may work to the advantage of the terrorists.

America happens to be the largest and the mightiest international power for quite some time. It has a grand record of defeating enemies, for example, the erstwhile European colonial powers and the erstwhile Soviet Union. It has vast experience in fighting conventional wars. It has a robust intelligence network that is simply unmatched and an armoury that shapes military tactics of other nations. It sells arms to almost every nation on the globe and to many other non-state entities. The US has readymade, comprehensive, and detailed lists of members of every terrorist organisation, which is upgraded from time to time.

The US has the unique advantage being in a position to summon the community of nations, that is, the United Nations and other international bodies, in the shortest possible time, to meet any emergency situation. The US has surveillance networks on land, sea, and air that are difficult to bypass. The US is the repository of a vast array of counter-insurgency intelligence covering every part of the world, thanks to its Cold War experience. The US, through its intelligence agencies, has carried out coups and even individual killings—both as a state terrorist and as a state sponsor of terrorism, as we shall discuss in greater detail in a later chapter. It is equally adept and vastly resourceful in carrying non-conventional forms of warfare. Depending on its national interest, it had supported and continues to patronise select terrorist and insurgent groups as well as rogue states. It has established a global financial empire surpassing that of its precursor, imperial Britain. It can turn a foe into an ally with the twinkle of an eye, by flexing its financial and 'physical' muscles. It has an enviable record of getting intractable and rival neighbours to the negotiating table against the normal run of events, for example, the 1978 Israeli-Egyptian peace agreement at Camp David. Now the Obama administration is on the job of getting the 'Two State Solution' in

Palestine accepted by Israel. In short, the US happens to be God and the devil at the same time. It is a great benefactor to some and Satan to others. It has thus all the attributes to sustain its super power status and to lead the world, unless it ruins its chances through monumental blunders or intransigence.

It is easily imaginable how helpless can the non-state entities like the al Qaeda be before the might of such a military colossus. Thus, it sounds ridiculous on the part of the head of such a formidable state power to declare 'War on Terrorism' which some expert call 'war on anger'. America's only problem is its titanic ambition to undo the 'overstretch' liabilities, to maintain status quo as a super power, and more importantly, to perform the impossible job of transforming rest of the world into its ways and image. All these above considerations leave sufficient ground to doubt the sincerity of the US in waging the War on Terror. Isn't America using this war to buy precious time with a view to completing the above mentioned 'unfinished' jobs? It is difficult to believe how America missed several occasions to capture bin Laden when it could pluck out Saddam Hussein from a dark cave and when it could easily secure the extradition of dreaded terrorists like Abu Nidal and even Laden, from more than one country. Equally incomprehensible is the US diversion of war from Afghanistan to Iraq, when it ought to have directed its hunt on Pakistan to totally stamp out the al Qaeda and the Taliban from the face of the eqarth. What is more, the Mumbai massacre has simply served to expose the misplaced American trust on Pakistan.

Despite the advantages and the disadvantages of both the contending parties, that is, the jihadists led by the al Qaeda and the international community led by the United States, a speedy resolution of the War on Terrorism (if it qualifies the definition of war) may range from an unilateral US retreat, albeit, temporary, from the Middle East to the US efforts in isolating terrorists from the general Muslim population through an array of initiatives like the successful resolution of the Arab-Palestine-Israeli standoff, and most importantly, on America's ability to counter the jihadist ideals and propaganda with the injection of a broad package of secular values and ideals. In my earlier book, I had predicted that the US may have to curb its penchant for resorting to unbridled unilateralism in contemporary world affairs. Incidentally, quite a number of American politicians and counter terrorist experts have changed their earlier jingoistic rhetoric and now profess a softer approach to tackle Islamist terrorism.

Finally, the US has another important advantage in discharging its foreign policy obligations. Being a bi-partisan polity, in which the administration changes hand every 4 to 8 years, it is easy for new American leaders to put the blame of foreign policy failures on their immediate predecessors, yet carry on with new 'experiments' on the same issues. Vietnam offers one such glaring example. The United States often links its foreign policies with its geo-political interests and it resorts to special 'catch words' or pleas towards that end, for example, 'WMD' during the 2003 US invasion of Iraq, and now 'Central Front' in the ongoing War on Terror.

Now, a new administration has assumed office in Washington. Predictably, the new president had little problem in laying the blames on the Bush administration's policy failures in Iraq and then coming up with a new 'Obama' package. This time the focus is on Afghanistan and Pakistan and, as just mentioned, the new catchword is 'Central Front', with reference to the Afghanistan-Pakistan border regions, and the objective: destruction of the al Qaeda and Taliban once and for all. The new American President, while announcing his plan to shift the focus of the War on Terror back to Afghanistan and Pakistan, did not fail to remind the world that the 2001 US invasion of Afghanistan was in retaliation to 9/11 terror attacks on America that had left 3000 Americans dead. The basic objective of the new policies spelt out by President Obama in respect of the War on Terror remains unchanged: the safety of America and its people and preventing any possible repetition of a 9/11 type of attack on American soil. American policy makers believe that this can only be done by pegging and totally annihilating the al Qaeda at the Afghanistan-Pakistan border, far away from the United States. Strangely, American leaders have suddenly woken up to the reality that the masterminds of 9/11 happen to be in Pakistan and Afghanistan! The main objective of the War on Terror will now be to "disrupt, dismantle, and defeat The al Qaeda in Pakistan and Afghanistan, and to prevent their return to either country in future."[31]

Understanding Islamist Terrorism

Ethnic, political, and religious issues have always appealed to tribes, groups, and individuals. Every student of history must know how an impassioned speech by Pope Urban II triggered off the Great Crusade. In his November 1095 speech at a gathering of nobilities and common people, Pope Urban II gave a clarion call to wrest the Holy Land from the Seljuk Turks due to the latter's alleged acts and inhuman atrocities on Christianity and its followers. Yet, if we go by the account of Robert Monk, the chronicler of the First Crusade, the Pope's speech was clothed in politico-economic incentives: "This land which you inhabit, shut in on all sides by the seas and surrounded by the mountain peaks, is too narrow for your large population; nor does it abound in wealth; and it furnishes scarcely food enough for its cultivators. Hence it is that you murder one another , that you wage war, and that frequently you perish by mutual wounds.... wrest that land from the wicked race, and subject it to yourselves..... God has conferred upon you above all nations great glory in arms. Accordingly undertake this journey for the remission of sins, with the assurance of the imperishable glory of the kingdom of Heaven"[32] Modern Islamist terrorism too has the same politico-religious slant. This is discussed in detail in the next chapter.

Radical Islamist terrorism, the spearhead of modern terrorism, happens to be uncompromising and, as its name suggests, it is motivated by religious objectives. It resorts to the scriptures of the Holy Book to justify its actions. It is rooted in a reinterpretation of Islam wherein the state, politics, and every social custom must adhere to the Sharia and the original verses of Koran. Radicals or the fundamentalists work on a narrow and conservative theory based on *their* interpretations of an enlightened religion, Islam. According to reputed Islamic author and journalist Muhammad Asad, while the Prophet bade that Islamic practice, law, and the state must always conform to the original Koranic verses, there are numerous instructions in the Hadith that required successive generations to be imaginative and adaptable to the needs of the time and common people. Asad writes, "And this is where ijtihadi legislation rightly comes in."[33] This difference in perception over the correct interpretation of Islamic teachings between moderates and radicals within the Muslim community works greatly to the advantage of the US.

One inevitable fallout of such differences is definitely the rise of Islamist terrorism of the contemporary era.[34]

On the other end of the spectrum, Islam as a religion has always commanded a large body of 'voluntary' converts that keep on increasing over time because they find Islam an enlightened and tolerant religion. There are still many Islamic countries that have not declared Sharia as the law of the land and have kept their windows open to new ideas coming from the West. Even conservative Islamic countries like Saudi Arabia, Sudan, and Iran have demonstrated their willingness to interact with the US in various fields. Even the Gulf States like the UAE, Oman, Kuwait, etc., that abide by the Sharia have little compunction in demonstrating some sort of tolerance in certain areas, like, permitting limited a number of bars (intake of alcohol is barred in Islam) and clubs for the sake of tourism, an important source of revenue for these countries. More interestingly, quite a few leaders of Islamist terrorist movements, as we shall discuss later, are not disinclined to accept Western ideas on science and technology. This works greatly to the American interest.

Middle-East, the birthplace of Islam, have produced quite a number of fundamentalist leaders and theoreticians and it is this region that still acts as a focal point for the spread of Islamic ideas, activities, and movements to other parts of the world. One can, of course, include a few other Islamic states in South Asia where the *mullahs* and clergies exert considerable influence in important political and social issues. Former President of Bangladesh, Hussain Mohammed Ershad, amended the secular constitution in favour of Islam because of the pressure from the conservative lobbies. The assassination of Benazir Bhutto or the recent BDR revolt in Bangladesh were believed to be carried out at the behest of fundamentalist Islamic groups who would hardly allow any space for liberal Western political values to operate in their lands. However, this is not the case with Muslims in other parts of the world. Once again, it is these differences in the perception and the gravitational pull of tradition and history that create uncertainty and tension within the Islamic world.

Evolution and Definition of Terrorism

Modern terrorism has come a long way from the early days of the first millennium when the Zealots or *Sicarii* (dagger men) used to carry out secret missions against the Roman occupying forces in the small Jewish province of Judea, to liberate their territory.[35] Doesn't the al Qaeda follow the same tradition when it seeks to liberate Arab lands from the neo-colonial fold of the US? The Zealots, however, met their doom at Masada. Another terrorist entity, the Assassins, sprung up in the early centuries of the second millennium. Assassins were a breakaway Shia faction, under the leadership of Hassan-i-Sabbah, based in Northern Iran. They indulged in suicide killings of enemy leaders like the modern day 'Fidayeen'. Between the Zealots and the Assassins, human civilisation had enough of the ravages wreaked by the terrifying Goths and Huns in Europe.

It is obvious that both the above forms of terrorism were motivated and sustained through religion. The same tradition of individual killings and suicide missions continues—to a lesser extent, in contemporary secular political terrorist movements, and to a greater extent, in contemporary religious terrorist movements. It must be mentioned here that terrorists, irrespective of any brand, tend to adopt tactics employed by other terrorist groups, now and then. The suicide missions carried out by the Viet Cong forces during the Vietnam War consisted of detonating the explosives strapped around their bodies by ramming motor cycles or stolen jeeps straight into their intended targets. They also employed suicide female bombers.[36] Many later terrorist organisations, like those in Lebanon in the 1980s, took a leaf out of the Viet Cong book and made frequent use of suicide bombs. The LTTE also made use of female suicide bombers, for example, in the horrific assassination of the Indian Prime Minister Rajiv Gandhi. Surprisingly, even the al Qaeda has made use of female suicide bombers in recent times, contrary to their principled stand. Perhaps, necessity knows no law.

In the days of kingdoms and principalities, the warring kings used to hire militia and warlords. With the Westphalia agreement in the mid seventeenth century, rulers of the newly formed nation-states developed effective administrative tools to quell domestic unrest and insurrections. However, this was short lived. Terrorism assumed a far more organised form under the Jacobins during the Reign of Terror, 1793-94, culminating in the spread of state terrorism and state supported terrorism.

The French revolution fired the imagination of many revolutionary groups in other parts of Europe— from Greece to Serbia, for example, the Narodnaya Volia and the Black Hand— till the Bolsheviks took up the terror baton after Bolshevik revolution in the guise of 'red terror'. Simultaneously, the First World War gave tremendous boost to political, ethnic and religious movements in the 1920s, thanks to the spread of the right to self-determination nations. Many of the national liberation movements during this period made increasing use of terror tactics, for instance, India and Ireland. Likewise, some radical Muslim groups, like the Muslim Brotherhood, sprung up in the Middle East in reaction to the European cultural intrusion in their lands. The end of the Second World War resulted in the liberation of a large number of erstwhile colonies However, the euphoria of the nationalist-patriotic fervour of the initial days gradually waned over time, as ethno-religious tensions and irredentism began to unravel across the world.

Nationhood came to be increasingly defined by race, ethnicity, and religion. However, there was a reverse trend, too. The simultaneous spread of the Soviet and Chinese style communism in various part of the Third World, gave further fillip to centralised state powers and acted as a deterrent to separatist movements based on ethnic, racial, and religious lines. With the liquidation of communism, these suppressed ethno-religious movements found an outlet out of this gorge and spread to various parts of the world, setting the stage for one of the most sanguine and terrifying conflicts of the Century. All these provided ideal breeding grounds for the emergence of a peculiar blend of terrorism based on religion and politics—Islamist terrorism or jihad. Worst of all, a lop-sided international political ambience or uni-polarity also acted as a catalyst for the spread of Islamist terrorism.

Definition of Terrorism

According to Professor Chomsky, the US Army Manual clearly defines terrorism as "the calculated use of violence or threat of violence to attain goals that are political, religious, or ideological in nature. This is done through intimidation, coercion, or instilling fear."[37] Extending that definition to cover low intensity conflicts in various parts of the world at

American instigation, he blamed the US foreign policies serving as a vehicle for the spread of the US state terrorism. Consequently, he sees in the killings of innocent civilians in Afghanistan not a War on Terrorism but a glaring example of state terrorism on the part of the US.[38] This definition of terrorism helps to identify one type of terrorism, that is, state terrorism, conducted by the state machinery, for instance the army, police, or the administration.

State sponsored terrorism, on the other hand, refers to the help provided to terrorist organisations or rebel separatist groups by 'interested' states, in terms of funding, arms, training, and logistical information, with a view to attain important political objectives. In recent decades, Pakistan has become the number one state sponsor of terrorism, even though the US prefers to turn a blind eye to it. Interestingly, Pakistan, the United States, the erstwhile USSR, and Communist China (in the past), satisfy criteria of both state terrorism and state sponsored terrorism.

Another form of terrorism, widespread on a global scale, is sub-state terrorism or that which is carried out by clandestine and sub-national groups. These groups have existed since historical times, in one form or another, discussed above. This type of terrorism may assume many forms— from left wing to right wing nationalist groups and activities. The Soviet Union, during the Cold War, was responsible, directly or indirectly, for fostering many such terrorist groups, for example, the PLO and its associates. The Red Brigades in Italy and the Red Army Faction in Germany typically led the left wing terrorist movements in Europe, seeking to overthrow capitalistic economic and social orders. The right wing type, on the other hand, has been concerned with recreating past national glories, for example, the neo-Nazis and radical Islamic terrorist groups. There is another type of terrorist movement that has ethnic-nationalist-separatist objectives, for example, the insurgency movements in various parts of North-Eastern states of India and the LTTE in Sri Lanka, and in other parts of the world. However, this book deals chiefly with Islamist terrorism that has wreaked havoc in recent years on a global scale.

Nevertheless, identifying the various forms of terrorist movements (done in the latter chapters) helps us gain better insight into the nature of specific terrorist groups and their range of activities, their aims (religious or secular political) and capabilities, and their staying power and resilience.

This last component is especially important since many a religious terrorist movement, for example, the Khalistan movement in Punjab, vanished into the blue after a few years. My definition of terrorism emerges from the following considerations. Needless to say, such considerations are but exercises that would help readers to tread the broad landscape covering the scope of terrorism.

Terrorism is, in the first place, an offensive (first strike) tactic or a combination of such tactics, capable of generating an equivalent or even greater amount of fear. It is the element of shock, fear, and surprise that forms an indispensable part of the activities of the terrorist and his group. The terrorist becomes the embodiment of terror and fear, at least he likes to be projected so. The bottom line is that terror tactics would cease to exist without this element of shock, surprise, and murder. Professor Yonah Alexander highlighted this psychological aspect of fear in framing a definition of terrorism when he said, "this element of fear through propaganda, psychological warfare and physical force, certainly poses a serious threat to humanity throughout history and particularly in contemporary times."[39]

Yet, one can terrify only in proportion to one's capacity to inflict real harm. Therefore, one extremely important component of terror tactics is the weapon with which the terrorist terrorises others. Nobody would feel terrified if lightning had no death dealing power. Likewise, it is the *weapons* at the disposal of the terrorist that embolden him to resort to indiscriminate, violent, and cruellest of acts. Just as opportunity makes a thief, so also the weapons at the disposal of even an ordinary fellow, let alone a terrorist, might lead him to indulge in violent acts at the slightest provocation. An individual may behave meekly even when he is tortured, provided he has no weapons and if he lacks support. Interestingly, the same fellow may react aggressively at the slightest sign of torture if he has weapons and support of other groups, for example, the tribals in Lalgarh in the West Midnapore District in West Bengal.

A murderer may create panic and fear through a surprise attack on his target but the victim in most cases is either known or related to him. The arms of terrorists, however, may stretch to totally unrelated and unknown persons (for example, the Mumbai massacre) who may not have harmed him in any way. On the other hand, war, insurgency, or even revolution may cause panic in the minds of common people but these don't come as surprises. These are predictable phenomena having defined ends even if the means they make use of may contain elements of shock, surprise, and violence. Prior awareness of war, insurgency, or revolution, neutralises some of the 'surprise' factor that accompanies them. Terrorists, however, prefer to project themselves as embodiments of shock, hatred, surprise, and cruelty, and they can only kill and get killed, *provided they have arms.* The terrorist or his group can have arms and requisite training provided the organization he belongs to has the necessary funds or he *has* a patron. *Thus for a terrorist, fear, shock, surprise, violence, arms, funds, and patrons are prerequisites.*

Title 22 of the United States Code 2656 f(d) defines terrorism as "premeditated, politically motivated violence, perpetrated against non-combatant targets by subliminal groups or clandestine agents, usually intended to influence an audience." Notably, there is no mention of religious motivations in this definition that gives an impression that either religiously motivated terrorism is not significant or that they too have a common 'political' objective.

The US Department of Defence, on the other hand, views terrorism as, "calculated use of unlawful violence or threat of unlawful violence to inculcate fear; intended to coerce or to intimidate governments or societies in the pursuit of goals that are generally political, religious, or ideological." This definition is, at best, a partial one, which everyone may not agree to. There is a shrewd attempt here to differentiate between lawful and unlawful violence. While the police and the army reserve the exclusive right to perpetrate fear in the minds of others on the pretext of maintaining the rule of law, the same is denied to extra governmental or sub-state actors. The fallacy with this kind of definition lies in its inability to explain nationalist and anti-colonial movements. How can the US justify its own revolutionary war of independence in that case?

The same flaw marks the definition given by the FBI, "Terrorism is the unlawful use of force and violence against persons or property to intimidate or coerce a government, the civilian population, or any segment thereof in furtherance of political or social objectives." It is not clear if social objectives include 'religious' motives. The US State Department has a more restricted and narrow definition, "premeditated, politically-motivated violence, perpetrated against non-combatant targets by sub-national groups or clandestine agents, usually intended to influence an audience." Here, the use of the words dealing with fear and intimidation of the 'government and civil bodies' have been done away with. However, modern terrorists are not afraid of targeting military and hence combative forces and it is not clear from the above definition whether casualties inflicted on members of an armed force by a terror group does actually terrify the former or not!

The United Nations removed the word "unlawful" from its 1992 definition of terrorism and defines it as "An anxiety-inspiring method of repeated violent action, employed by (semi)-clandestine individuals, groups or state actors, for idiosyncratic, criminal, or political reasons, whereby—in contrast to assassination—the direct targets of violence are not the main targets." This definition is largely satisfactory but the fact is that direct targets are very much their (terrorist's) main targets. Terrorists aim for soft targets only when hard targets are hard to come by.

Thus it is necessary to arrive at an appropriate definition of terrorism in an unbiased way. This definition must also take into account the motives of terrorists. Parents and teachers, sometimes, 'terrify' children to bring them back to their senses. Lightning may be terrifying or terrific but they lack subjectivity. Secondly, as discussed above, murder and other criminal activities differ in nature and degree from those perpetrated by 'indoctrinated' and 'framed' terrorists. Besides, there may be other types of localised terrorist activities that are concerned purely with individual or monetary gains. Anti-socials and criminals, too, use terror tactics, but they are rarely branded as terrorists. There are specific laws to penalise such transgressors. Moreover, criminals, dacoits, thieves, or smugglers prefer to stay out of public focus or exposure. Terrorists, on the other hand, prefer media exposure and for that reason they must carry out their surprise attacks in public places and on public targets.

A more correct definition of modern terrorism can be formulated on the basis of the above discussion: *terrorism is the deliberate, step-by-step, and organised use of violence and fear tactics by an armed group, carried with fanatic zeal and commitment, to shockingly impact the government or people of a society, to convert a chance, possibility, or a thought or idea— idiosyncratic or circumstantial, secular, political, or religious, rational or irrational, temporary or of prolonged duration, into reality.* Such an all inclusive definition of terrorism helps in gradually bringing terrorist activities into the legal net. Widespread legal networks, based on an international consensus, might go a long way towards in reducing terrorism and in negating the oft repeated notion that one man's terrorist happens to be another man's ally. Moreover, the above definition, takes into account the 'idea' and the 'thought' behind the whole issue of terrorism since 'ideas', 'thoughts', or 'perceptions' provide the last line of defence in a battle between the conventional state and the non-conventional, non-state actors.

The above definition happens to be an open one in that it includes words like 'circumstance', 'rational', 'deliberate', and 'temporary', which were lacking in the earlier definitions. For example, there may be circumstances when a particular rebel or insurgent group may feel that the powers that be have become too intransigent and repressive and that resort to force and violence is the only recourse left. For example, in the introduction to the *Declaration of Independence—A History,*[40] we find:

"Nations come into being in many ways. Military rebellion, civil strife, acts of terrorism, acts of treachery, a thousand greater and lesser clashes between defenders of the old order and supporters of the new. All these occurrences and more have marked the emergence of new nations, large and small. The birth of our nation included them all. The birth was unique, not only in the immensity of the later impact on the course of world history and the growth of democracy...

Nor have we been wanting in attentions to our British brethren. We have warned them from time to time of the attempts by their Legislature to extend an unwarrantable jurisdiction over us. We have reminded them of the circumstances of our immigration and settlement here. We have appealed to their native justice and magnanimity, and we have conjured them by the ties of our kindred to disavow these usurpations, which would inevitably interrupt our Connections and Correspondence. They too have been deaf to the voice of justice and of consanguinity."

Contemporary religious terrorism enjoys another key advantage over other forms of terrorism. While every other form has a particular theatre of operation because it is limited by its specific goal and strength, Islamist terrorism has a trans-national goal that makes it look more formidable, omnipresent, and hence more awe-inspiring. Terrorists may know the time and place in advance but not necessarily the victim and hence the victim has no idea where, when, and who would decide his next moment. Because of 'awe and surprise' elements, the scope of religious terrorism may thus range from infinity to infinitesimal, depending on information and intelligence. The only thing that a terrorist genuinely fears is the forestalling of his plot by intelligence agencies. It is quite likely that future terrorist movements may be more violent because of the terrorists' desperation to overcome that risk posed by 'intelligence' agencies.

For terrorists, especially, the jihadists, death is not much compared to the satisfaction of seeing his campaign succeed. Atwan, however, observed that many suicide attackers blew themselves up even before hitting the intended targets, which meant that terrorists preferred self-sacrifice over everything else. But this may not always be the case. These failures may be due to technical snags beyond the attacker's control, for example, the December 2001 abortive attack on Indian Parliament. Islamist terrorists, indeed, have a special feeling for suicide missions, and they can lay down their lives in battalions backed by a promise from their leaders that they would enter their promised land, the *Jannat*, only if they can make supreme sacrifices for the cause. But the very fact that they do so for a 'cause' renders that 'cause' or 'ideal' more important.

Among the other advantages that the Islamist terrorists enjoy are, dedication of their fellows or comrades, easy immigration facilities, free access to various centres of learning in developed countries, latest technological know-how,[41] shelter offered by supporters and sympathisers, a 'tailor-made' detailed map of a particular area, target, or locality, and advanced communications networks. All these plus points 'conspire' to tempt terrorists or terrorist organisations, particularly, those which have a global reach, to have a go at soft targets, even those of a great or super power. Without these advantages, terrorism would never have assumed its deadliest form in the contemporary era.

All said and done, it must be noted that terrorism tends to be 'time and situation' specific. For example, specific decades have specific forms of terrorist activities— the 1960s and 1970s saw aviation terrorism preponderate while the 1980s saw suicide and truck bombings and the 1990s rife with indiscriminate attacks on soft targets on a large scale, urban guerrilla attacks, etc. Yet the above two indices of fear and surprise remain in every form of terrorism, irrespective of era and situation.

There is no dearth of instances when a particular movement and its leader might have been branded as terrorists, but later on, the same leader returned to the mainstream political processes once the purpose or the objective was achieved. Both Menachem Begin and Nelson Mandela, once dubbed as terrorists, were awarded Nobel Prize for their role in international peace initiatives! There are many instances when some rebel groups or even states, for example communist China and the erstwhile USSR, were long unrecognised for their 'undemocratic, totalitarian, and 'anti human rights activities'. Yet both these countries went on to become indispensable members of the Security Council! The US keeps its options open even in respect of rogue states which sponsor terrorist activities or insurgent groups indulging in terrorist acts, for example, Sudan, Libya, and North Korea, or the PLA. Since there is no permanent friend or foe in politics (because time, interests, views, circumstances, actors, policies, and priorities change), it becomes all the more difficult to frame a single or a unified definition of terrorism. This necessitates the framing of a time and situation specific definition.

Once we determine an appropriate or even a workable definition of terrorism, it is necessary to probe the modus operandi of some major terrorist groups of the recent decades, like the al Qaeda— how its networks and surrogates work in various parts of the world, its principal sources of sustenance, that is, finance and arms, whether its networks have combined with other criminal networks, like drug traffickers etc., whether, and if so, how far the al Qaeda influences and shapes the legal and conventional areas, like, the economy, army, and the general public, how they are different from extremist groups engaged in insurrections and ethnic conflicts, and a host of other questions. It is also necessary to probe how Islamist terrorist groups interact with other secular forms, and how it uses modern communications facilities to plan and carry out its attacks, how the jihadists recruit and motivate their members and, of course, and who happen to be their leaders. That would give us an idea of the thoughts and direction of Islamist terrorism.

More importantly, it will enable us to pinpoint counter terrorism measures. All these are discussed in the subsequent chapters of this book.

American problems

My claim, laid out at the beginning of this chapter, is that the Islamist terrorist groups like the al Qaeda may succeed in their missions if conventional powers like the US commit blunders. The main focus of this book happens to be the US and the Islamist/ jihadists, since the War on Terrorism is being fought, primarily, between these two entities. It is thus necessary to look at the reasons behind the American commitment to fight the War on Terrorism and the problems it faces in this regard.

The US determination to fight terrorism to its finish was made amply clear by the then US President Bush in his 20 September 2001 speech, just nine days after 9/11. The stated objectives of this War on Terrorism were: identify, locate, and destroy terrorist networks along with those of their associates, not to make any difference between the terrorists and their sponsors, states or any other agencies, strengthen the international effort to fight terrorism and to enable even the weak and the failed states for this purpose, persisting with reluctant states and compelling the unwilling states to help America in its War on Terrorism, deny sanctuaries, safe haven, finance and arms supplies to the terrorists, interdict and disrupt material support for the terrorists, ensure protection of US citizens and US interests at home and abroad, getting world bodies like the UN to take prompt and effective measures while ensuring unity among its members to combat terrorism. But all these measures are predicated upon the premise of maintaining human rights standards and, more importantly, the limits set by the US Constitution.

The al Qaeda members on their part take full advantage of the last two limitations to keep the US constantly guessing. They are extremely mobile, skilful in adapting to changes, and are known to be good learners. This was highlighted by Donald Rumsfeld who, in a keynote address to the Annual Claremont Institute Dinner in honour of Winston Churchill, said, "Their decentralised networks have been able to effectively employ the tools of the Information Age, while the U.S. government remains ponderous, muscle bound, and unable to respond in real time to the deceits of these enemies."[42]

Indeed the al Qaeda has supporters and sympathisers in every part of the world, with numerous home grown cells that can independently take charge of any terrorist operation, as in the case of the London bombings in July 2005. All these create policy problems for the US in taking strict counter measures because of unanticipated backlash effects.

The USA PATRIOT Act, so far the most comprehensive package of counter terrorism, has already given rise to many grievances in the US. Innocent Muslims complain that they are being penalised for no fault of theirs. The US is handicapped by both these types of terrorist operatives— the organised as well as the home grown sectors. America is thus faced with a difficult job of separating the radicals from the common Muslims, besides the responsibility of upholding the sanctity of Islam. The Islamist terror groups thus try everything to provoke an American response that may alienate the Muslim community living within and outside of America. That is why, former President Bush, in the same 20 September 2001, speech stressed that America's enemy happens to be a radical terrorist network and not the Muslims or the Arabs. "The terrorists practice a fringe form of Islamic extremism that has been rejected by Muslim scholars and the vast majority of Muslim clerics, a fringe movement that perverts the peaceful teachings of Islam", he told the Joint Congress.

The US is hampered by another key consideration: how to formulate and implement the above policies while making due allowance for its great power 'interests' in international politics. The American geo-political and trade interests happen to be its chief concerns in world politics, and it is precisely these concerns that require America to stay at the centre of global activities for quite some time, if not forever. In fact, the US won't be the same again if its trade and 'base' empires shrink. This, in turn, means that it must have stakes in every region and in various conflict situations. For example, any tension in South Asia between two sub-continental nuclear neighbours, India and Pakistan, becomes more of an American headache. Incidentally, these are areas that are specifically targeted by the al Qaeda.

Besides its European allies, the US also has problems with other Islamic countries in the Middle East. For example, Saudi Arabia is home to limitless future recruits who are being trained in various *Madrassas* of the country, as well as in many other countries receiving Saudi aid, that serve as conduits for the spread of Wahhabism. Jordan is not too keen to follow counter terrorist measures proposed by the UN and the US. Neither are Kuwait and the UAE. If the international consensus on War on Terror is lacking, it would again prove to a major hindrance for America in tackling terrorism.

Pakistani Perfidy and Designs

Pakistan happens to be another problem area for the US, although the latter has so far acted like an affectionate guardian of a 'rogue' child. More specifically, between an American victory and unbridled anarchy let loose by the jihadists stand two countries, the US (through its impetuosity, intransigence, and lack of direction) and the Pakistan (through its insincerity and perfidy), the latter acting as a quicksand drawing the US to abysmal depths. Both the US and Pakistan seem to be locked in a vicious spiral that can spell doom for both these countries. For example, Pakistan can't survive without the US financial aid. On the other hand, all talk of War on Terror would fizzle out if Pakistan throws down the towel and declines to do the fighting on America's behalf. Most importantly, Pakistan offers the US a firm foothold in this part of the globe that the latter so desperately needs. The US would also need Pakistani help in any of its future campaigns against Iran. The bottom line is that none of them can escape midway as their fates are tied. Yet, Pakistan happens to be the crucible for the jihadists.

Such a condition provides an ideal setting for Pakistan to extract as much concession as possible from the US, even by 'fooling' that super power. One such occasion that instantly comes to mind is when it managed to prevail on the US regarding signing peace treaties in 2005 and 2006 with South and North Waziristan, respectively, pretending that such treaties may assuage the grievances of the tribal militants and create divisions between the moderates and the hard liners within the Taliban ranks. But the real Pakistani design was to provide a safe haven for the Taliban and the al Qaeda fellows who had flocked to the Pakistan-Afghan border regions, driven out from Afghanistan in the aftermath of the American War on Terror in 2001. The inevitable followed as the tribal regions in and around the Pakistan-Afghan border become fertile breeding grounds for the al Qaeda, Taliban, and their new recruits.

Another instance relates to February 2009 treaty at the Swat valley. Pakistan agreed to reinstate 'Sharia' in the Swat valley in lieu of a 'no aggression pact' with the local insurgents (predominantly under the influence of the Taliban). On both the occasions mentioned above, Pakistan, in fact, was playing a double game with the US by touching a raw nerve in the U.S foreign policy perceptions— creating rifts between moderate and extremist elements within the Taliban. Earlier, such divisions might have yielded spectacular results elsewhere, for example, in Lebanon, but this is unlikely to be the case in Swat, particularly, at a time when America has declared war on the al Qaeda and the Taliban, and more importantly, when Pakistan considers Taliban as a strategic ally vis-à-vis India. On the other hand, Pakistan needs American dollars and sophisticated conventional weapons and last but not the least, an American presence in the sub-continent as a protective cover against 'unfriendly' India and Russia, waiting close by.

American campaign in Afghanistan has failed to eradicate the al Qaeda hide outs and has simply resulted in the proliferation of that group to other regions, like Central Asia, Chechnya, Georgia, and most notably, Pakistan, not to speak of Iraq. This failure can be attributed partly to American foreign policy blunders and partly to Pakistan's insincerity and 'betrayal'. Pakistan, like bugs, simply keeps sucking American blood by deliberately prolonging the War on Terror. The US harbours a misplaced hope that it can attain eventual victory over the jihadists and that too with the help of another Muslim country! What an illusion!

Madeline Albright, the former US Secretary of State has categorically expressed her displeasure when she called Pakistan a 'migraine' for the international community. As mentioned above, the new US President Barrack Obama, has charged Pakistan with hoodwinking the US and diverting most of the American funds and arms (meant for use against the al Qaeda forces in the Pakistan-Afghan front) towards increasing and modernising its conventional arsenal in preparation for a possible showdown with India. President Obama in his first ever Press Conference as the 44th US president said in Washington on 10 February 2009, that like the US, Pakistan is equally endangered by the al Qaeda.

Former CIA analyst Bruce Riedel had recently accused Pakistan of "extracting billions of dollars from Washington even while it allowed the al Qaeda to regroup in its tribal lands."[43] He even mentioned the possible link between the ISI and the Islamic militants on the Pakistan-Afghan border. Riedel also asked the US administration not to sell 'big ticket weapons' to Pakistan. The new US Secretary of State, Hillary Clinton, said on 7 March 2009, following the terror attacks in Lahore on Sri Lankan cricketers, that most of the world's terrorist activities are being designed on the soils of Pakistan and Afghanistan. The Chairman of the Senate Foreign Relations Committee, John Kerry, in a recent report, admitted that a nuclear Pakistan with a population of 17 crores had become a sanctuary and a fast breeding ground of spiralling radicalism. Many American officials are convinced that top the al Qaeda members, including bin Laden, enjoy a safe haven in Pakistan.

How sincere is America in waging and continuing the War on Terrorism

After nearly eight years into the War on Terror, more and more people are getting used to the fact that the US is losing that war, entailing colossal waste of dollars. According to Ken Dilanian, the total figure for the two wars—Iraq and Afghanistan— could be around $2.4 trillion through the next decade while Thomas Kahn, staff director of Spratt, thought that the Iraq war expenses alone, could cost around $1.9 trillion, including $564 billion in interest (since a large part of war expenses is funded through borrowed money).[44] According to a CRS report, updated on 15 October 2008, the Congress had approved a total of about $864 billion from military operations, base security, and reconstruction to foreign aid, embassy costs, and veterans' health care. This total amount covers all war related appropriations from the financial year of 2001 through part of 2009, in supplementals, regular appropriations, and continuing resolutions.

The Afghan campaign, after its initial success, has long turned into a wild goose chase for America. As early as the early 2002, barely a few months into the American War on Terror, many foreign policy experts in the US doubted the rational of wasting billions of dollars in 'grinding rocks' in the inaccessible terrains of Afghanistan. The Taliban has subsequently regrouped on the outskirts of Afghanistan and now even in its interiors (Taliban and the al Qaeda, these days, frequently attack foreign targets in the main Afghan cities), and, ominously, in the tribal border regions in Pakistan. The Taliban has virtually laid siege on the Afghan capital, with checkpoints in at least three out of the four roads that run out of Kabul. Recent terror strikes in the US, Indian, and German Embassies in Kabul and the daily procession of corpses in the streets of Kabul tell a tale of US failures in its War on Terrorism. As for Iraq, there are conflicting reports because of the administration's recent claims that there has been a significant fall in suicide attacks.

At this writing, a spate of suicide bomb attacks in and around Baghdad killed over 60 and injured more than 150, just a couple of days back. On the very day of his first ever press conference as the US president, Barrack Obama admitted that at least four American servicemen were killed in Iraq, that day alone. The body languages of neither the new US President, nor his subordinate staff appearing in various fora, are anything but encouraging. The simple fact is that the decision to go for the War on Terror was either taken in a fit of frenzy, retaliation, and hubris, or else there might have been some hidden design on the part of the US policy makers with little thought about its consequences.

If the US really meant to extirpate the al Qaeda and the Taliban from Afghanistan, they would have followed things through once they succeeded in driving the latter from the main cities of Afghanistan. The next step would invariably have required the US to destroy terrorist training camps and networks in Pakistan, especially on the Pakistan-Afghan border and in the Federally Administered Tribal Areas (FATA) where many the al Qaeda fellows took refuge and from where they continued to carry on their activities against the NATO forces in Afghanistan. Worse still, the al Qaeda managed to forge alliances with other jihadist groups in the Pak occupied Kashmir (PoK). The US intelligence knew about this. The US administration even warned that the American forces might strike within Pakistan to flush out and destroy the al Qaeda outfits. However, America has rarely ventured into Pakistani territory. It is hard to believe that the US did so only for the sake of respecting Pakistan's sovereignty, considering the fact that the former had declared a *War* on Terrorism. The all important question still remains—

why, instead of capturing them, the American and the Northern Alliance forces halted and allowed The Taliban forces to take refuge in the fringes of Kandahar? It is only recently that the US President Barack Obama has termed the 2001 US campaign in Afghanistan as a 'drift'! Is this what the US means by the War on Terror?

The same issue of respecting sovereignty of other nations was brushed aside in the case of Iraq when the US invaded that country on a false plea of Iraq's possession of WMDs or WMD materials (it is only recently that both the US President and the US Vice President have openly admitted their mistakes before the media). But the US refrains from repeating that feat in Pakistan, despite the fact that India has constantly alerted it of the increasing dangers posed by the Pakistan's (ISI) training of radical Islamic terrorists. India further informed the US administration that jihadist groups like the Jaish-e-Mohammad and Lashkar-e-Toiba had strong links with the al Qaeda. But to no avail. Pakistan was, perhaps, an exception to American strictures to the rest of the world, that the states sponsoring terrorism or providing shelters to any terrorist group in any part of the world would not be treated differently from the actual terrorists. Ironically, it is only recently that American diplomats have admitted that Lashkar-e-Toiba (LeT) could pose a threat to the US mainland.

The US is only interested in fighting terrorism when it hurts US citizens and its interests abroad. That is a contradiction in itself. While America wants to internationalise both the War on Terror and its counter terrorism measures, these are done merely to secure the lives and properties of US citizens, at home and abroad. Such a selfish attitude on the part of the US betrays its real intention to *fight* terrorism, all the way (although, very recently, the US president Obama in his historic speech at the Cairo University had denied that the US happened to be a 'self interested' nation). That means, the US is not concerned about fighting the terrorists so long as it affects other countries and other people. According to a State Department report, in 2007 (and I don't think that the picture has changed in later years when the number of attacks on various Indian cities had risen by leaps and bounds), India topped the list of countries sustaining most terrorist attacks, especially, from groups based in Pakistan. No American official has cared to visit India after any of these attacks, except for the 26/11 Mumbai massacre when six Americans were killed! The American perception (the US believes that the Kashmir dispute is at the root of such attacks) and the muted US response following a series of recent terror attacks in various Indian cities by Islamist terror groups, can only embolden the latter to contemplate a second strike in the American heartland. The US didn't bother to comment on the recent revolt by the Bangladesh Rifles in Dhaka, which was believed to have been masterminded by fundamentalist terrorist groups receiving finance and training from Pakistan. Nor was the US forthcoming in condemning the recent attack on Sri Lankan cricketers in Lahore, except in a very casual and perfunctory manner.

After the 9/11 attacks on American targets, President Bush vowed that he wouldn't have a 'restful sleep' till terrorism was rooted out from every part of the globe. If that means only securing American targets everywhere, then the US has failed in that mission. American personnel and tourists still continue to be the targets of the al Qaeda. The recent Mumbai terror casualty list also bears out the truth of my claim. The US is at pains to pressurise its long-term ally, Pakistan, despite the fact that the US law requires its intelligence agencies to follow any terror probe to its logical end, wherever Americans are targeted.

Pakistan's support for terrorist groups to torment and destabilise India runs counter to the US and the UN anti terrorism laws, which categorically state that any country sponsoring terrorism or giving safe haven to terrorists must be held equally responsible and must face the consequences. Recently, the Indian Prime Minister, Mr. M. M. Singh, speaking at a meeting of the state Chief Ministers in New Delhi, categorically stated that given the sophistication and military precision with which the terrorists carried out the November 2008 Mumbai mayhem, it was obvious that such an attack would not have been possible without the active support from an "official agency" in Pakistan. The US though, continues to overlook Pakistan's designs.

The US knows Pakistan's covert support for various terrorist groups (like in the Kargil episode of 1998) very well, but has either ignored it or deliberately downplayed it. One can't go on defending a wrongdoer for long as that would simply embolden the latter to shift from passive and covert to an overt support for the terrorist groups on a global scale. Such pretence of denial and growing realisation that the United States is apathetic even to genuine claims by India, simply enhances Indian suspicion about America's real intentions in the subcontinent. Facts are stubborn things and truth cannot be hidden. The recent row between the US and Pakistan is not so much about the latter's support for terrorist groups as it is over the 'Drone' attacks in the border regions of Pakistan, which rather proves the latter's complicity with the terrorists. It is only recently that the US, again acting out of self interest (danger posed to the Pak nuclear arsenal by the growing Taliban influence in Pakistan), had prevailed upon Pakistan to wage war on the Taliban firmly entrenched in the Swat valley.

Incidentally, one Pakistani newspaper had recently published an excerpt from a book written by the New York Times White House correspondent David E. Sanger, *Inheritance: the World Obama Confronts and the Challenge to American Power*. The author of that book wrote that the US decision to intensify Drone attacks followed a US National Security Agency (NSA) revelation that the latter had intercepted telephonic messages of high level Pakistan army officials praising the Taliban as "strategic assets for Pakistan". One NYT PTI article of 26 March, 2009 cited top US government officials claiming that the recent widening of Taliban campaigns in Southern Afghanistan was due partly to 'direct support from operatives in the Pakistan's military intelligence agency'[45]. Such 'betrayal' on the part of Pakistan has left the US officials struggling to understand the nature of such allegiances.

One can't go on endlessly fighting a stateless enemy unless one has a 'hidden' agenda. Already, the duration of the US War on Terror has exceeded those of the World Wars in the last century. The American casualties in Afghanistan and Iraq combined are not much compared to those incurred in those wars. Many experts in the US have questioned the legitimacy of carrying on this war for so long against a stateless entity with whom one can't even sign any peace treaty!

The US declared the War on Terror out of its sole concern to defend its citizens and its homeland and, therefore, to quarantine the al Qaeda in an area far off from the American homeland. But why war had been the only option against an adversary bereft of the requisite conventional war materials when the US internal security measures alone would have been sufficient to attain that objective? More importantly, does the US assumption or policy or theory seeking to justify war in a far off land (while keeping US soldiers and bases in these very countries, perhaps on a permanent basis) to keep the enemy at arm's length, hold good against an adversary bent on demanding a complete withdrawal of the American forces from the Middle East?

A far better option would have been to secure the American borders and its interiors through tight counter terrorism measures. America still has relatively permissive borders even as it seeks to avoid a repetition of 9/11 type attacks. It is not prudent on the part of the US to maintain a lenient immigration policy at a time when it resorts to force in other parts of the world. After all, one can't live in a house made of glass and throw stones at others. It would be absurd to think that such American highhandedness in many parts of the world, particularly the Middle East, would go without a response, particularly from the jihadists. A vast country like America could easily become increasingly vulnerable if the prevailing rates of immigration from other parts of the world continue. Already many diaspora groups in various states of America exert considerable economic and political clout, both in the White House and Capitol Hill. There have been many instances when foreign immigrants and nationals, knowingly or unknowingly, set up numerous home grown cells and charity organisations that turned out to work as front organisations for Islamist terrorist groups like the al Qaeda. No wonder, the presence of Muslim diaspora abroad might have simply fanned the desire of these radical Islamic groups in resurrecting the dream of a global Ummah. To make matters worse, these diaspora groups oppose stringent counter financial measures aimed at blocking such 'proxy' funding to the al Qaeda.

Usually, a country goes to war either when it is attacked or when it intends to enhance its geo-political interests. In the First World War, a terror attack might have been the last straw that broke the camel's back, yet, all the warring parties like Russia, Britain, and Germany had their eyes transfixed on their respective geo-political interests. Likewise, in the Second World War, geo-political interests proved crucial, yet again. 9/11 was a terror strike on the American homeland. Terror strikes have also taken place at the heart of Moscow in the closing years of the Cold War, but none could be categorised as acts of war. In that case, it is highly likely that the second option, that is, geo-political interests must have served as that all important 'hidden' agenda behind America's conduct of the War on Terror.

The happenings on that fateful day, and even the developments leading to that 'apocalyptical' terror strike, clearly reveal colossal intelligence failure on the part of the US. One is left wondering how the months long preparations and plots hatched in multiple cities of Europe, prior to the September 11 terror strike, escaped the notice of the various intelligence bodies in the US and Europe? How is one to explain the same intelligence failure on America's part when four hijacked planes roamed over the sky of American cities for hours? And if the lapse was due to intelligence failure, then is it not clear that the solution lies in revamping the intelligence and legal machineries to combat terrorism? After all, many counter terrorism measures of the 1970s and 1980s, went a long way in reducing hijackings and hostage takings.

Former American President George Bush, in a speech in September 2006, claimed that not a single attack took place on the American mainland since 9/11 and that there were at least nineteen occasions when such terrorist plans were forestalled. The President attributed this success both to domestic measures to fortify the country as well as to the war on the al Qaeda. While the various internal security measures that the US had adopted after 9/11 yielded spectacular results, it is hard to give the same credit to the American War on Terrorism abroad.

What is the reality? One outcome of the war is that the al Qaeda and the Mujahideen have rebuilt themselves and even proliferated to different parts of the world—from Bosnia, Chechnya, and Somalia, to Iraq. Incidentally these are also the countries that had become the scene of the American War on Terrorism. As mentioned above, the Taliban has gained an upper hand over the Northern Alliance in Afghanistan—first in the fringes, and thereafter, gradually extending their influences in the interior.

President Bush had commented, "if we leave Iraq now, they will pursue us." This is important. What does this mean? This simply means that the US had only a short term view of the war when it waged the War on Terror. Obviously it had underestimated the strength and tenacity of its adversary. It thought that there won't be any consequence since the opponent, a non-state entity, would hardly withstand the American blitzkrieg. The folly on the part of the lone superpower was that it had failed to understand the 'self procreating' capability of the jihadists, armed as they are with a religious doctrine.

The American prescription, whenever American interests were hurt, has always been the same—use of force irrespective of the nature of the enemy and the situation. Use of force, however, may not achieve the purpose where the opponent is so resolved (thanks to American highhandedness, again) and programmed with a religious doctrine that would hardly tolerate foreign oppression. Further, one can't hope to win against a 'war loving' enemy (recent pictures from the Swat valley by a Geo TV reporter, killed brutally, clearly shows how the Taliban lives and sleeps with assault rifles by their side). To this one may add the constant 'self procreation' and the resultant swelling of the ranks of new recruits. Did the United States, in a fit of impatience and hubris, simply overlook this reality?

The US counter terrorism expert and the counterterrorism coordinator, Ambassador Dell Dailey, conceded that sticking to the policy of destroying terrorist groups won't pay and that the US should think of constructive engagements instead.[46] Doesn't this admission mean that the pragmatic and vastly experienced policy makers in the White House had other things in mind when they launched the War on Terrorism? They knew well that such a policy might be counter-productive and a colossal waste on the tax payers' money. That is why, following some resounding success in Afghanistan in the initial months of the war, the US lost no time in minding its geo-political interests by shifting its focus to another theatre of great strategic importance— Iraq

The US has got to set its house in order by making adjustments both in its domestic and external policies. The two American pillars in respect to international relations in modern times, globalisation and immigration, despite having trans-national dimensions may also work in a reverse way and pave the way for a return to pre- Westphalian days of micro-nationalism, the opposite of what the US policy makers intend. The rise in ethno-religious tensions after the Cold War clearly points to this danger. Ironically, the US is hamstrung by its own Constitution, economic, and geo-political compulsions, and by other traditional political values like democracy, liberalism, and free trade to alter its immigration and foreign policies and bring them in line with its various counter terrorism measures.

Instead, it hopes that other nation states would accept the American ways and views and relinquish their traditional values in favour of a global culture. Even America's western allies have reservations in this regard. They feel that such a policy perception is at odds with a large body of world population and that ethno-religious feelings are as difficult to stamp out as terrorism itself. As a result, the US runs the risk of being the odd man out in the field of international relations. American foreign policies are being viewed with suspicion in many Islamic countries, too. Chomsky rightly felt that the US, as a great power, feels it beneath dignity to seek consensus from others.

But there is a crux. Would American policy makers dance to the tune of a few terrorists and make the US immigration policies stricter? The US has a reputation of being the land of settlers and immigrants. To talk of strengthening its immigration policies is to strike at the very root of some fundamental assumptions on which that country was formed. Thus, the US has to ensure that its counter terrorism policies target 'terrorist' movements only and not the general flow of immigration in a bid not only to frustrate the designs of the jihadists but also to marginalise them. Such conflicting tasks render it too difficult for the US to frame a clear and unified counter terrorism policy.

America has other problems, too. The growing divergence between the US and its western allies on matters relating to trade, environment, international politics, and even terrorism, is another block in America's way for continuing the War on Terror. While its allies did lend their psychological and limited physical help in war against Afghanistan after 9/11, they remained highly critical of the US designs when the latter invaded Iraq in 2003. The US had to ignore the findings of the UN and override the objections of some of its key allies in launching its Iraqi campaign. Such wilful and premeditated acts on the part of the US could simply undermine international support in America's War on Terrorism.

Conclusion

The US has already shown some of its cards in fighting the War on Terrorism. Just as the United States had gained new insights into the workings of the al Qaeda, so also the opposite is true. The al Qaeda has not only grown more flexible but has, so far, successfully evaded many stringent counter measures taken by the US. That means, the US have to depend more on other countries to successfully carry out its anti-terrorist campaigns and treat terrorism on a regional basis. In my previous book, *Tracing the Eagle's Orbit,* I have discussed how such an approach would be more effective in combating terrorism. Now, both the Afghan and the Pakistani authorities, in response to Obama's new policies on War on Terror, have appreciated the US policy of combating terrorism, on a local and regional basis. That way, the terrorists would be deprived of safe havens and would have to be on the move constantly, till they are left with little ground to live on.

Another effect of such localised tackling, instead of relying on a global War on Terror, would be that the burdens, in terms of finance as well as casualties, will be shared between many countries, which would neutralise the accusations of 'bullying' and 'cultural molestations' against a super power. But this is not to say that the US would continue to retain its forces and bases in other parts of the world, especially, in the Middle East. Otherwise, any hope and effort towards a long-term solution in this respect would be extremely farfetched. The issue is simple— since jihad has taken an anti-American turn as a reaction to the frequent US meddling in the Middle East, the bell rings, at least, for a temporary American withdrawal from that region.

But there is snag here. Other countries, Like the US too, are concerned about *their* interests and they would leave no chance to 'exploit' America (like, Pakistan does). That, in turn, means that America may have to rein its impetuosity and resort to more vigorous diplomatic manoeuvring in summoning international support and in maintaining international unity. The more the US over-hypes the War on Terrorism the greater the odds against it, as others will see 'motive' behind this.

To complicate matters further for the US, bin Laden has recently made overtures towards a *quid pro quo* arrangement with the European countries and offered not to strike at the latter's targets provided they disassociated themselves from the American global War on Terrorism (GWOT). The message is clear: if the US fails to decentralise the War on Terror, the jihadists would do so and, worse still, on their own term. This change of attitude on Laden's part followed the Spain's decision to withdraw its troops from Iraq. It may be mentioned that the European countries snubbed a similar offer from Laden in 2004. That could mean a victory for the terrorists and a diplomatic defeat for the US. This is America's Achilles' Heels—to maintain international unity for long when other countries might feel that peace could easily be gained by acceding to the offers of these terrorist groups, to a certain extent, rather than dragging the War, indefinitely.

Prior to 9/11, most of the terrorist attacks took place far off from the American homeland. The US thus had no problem in involving the international community through various Conventions and International Laws. The al Qaeda soon made its intentions clear as it took the fight to the American camp by focusing on American targets, sometimes in the American heartland. Now a day, terrorists have become more selective and they are on the lookout, chiefly, for US nationals, and to a lesser extent of its allies, for example, the Mumbai terror incident. They target other foreign nationals and armed personnel occasionally, but these are done to send a message to the concerned countries not to help the US in the War on Terrorism. This makes the American job that much difficult. The United States finds it hard to convince others that Islamist terrorism happens to be an international problem and that they ought to perceive and treat terrorism the same way that America does. The American teleological attitude and perception that the rest of the world must act and react in the same way on such issues as globalisation, communism, or terrorism simply adds to American problems.

However, forging and maintaining such a kind of unity on an international scale over a long period is extremely difficult even for a mega power like the US. There are bound to be many 'ifs' and 'buts' besides many other considerations. For example, if the US can tame the jihadists, this would, be a bonanza, as this would definitely deter other major powers from challenging the American global supremacy.

Terror tactics have been exercised by rebel bands or groups against great power rules since historical times. The same tradition continues as Islamist terrorists seek to undermine the pride and legitimacy of a super power like the United States in the 21st Century. In a world dominated by print and electronic media, any irresponsible behaviour on the part of the strong, say, the US, may help the terrorists in gaining more political mileage and public sympathy. What is more, use of force by a super power often evokes stronger public reaction and hatred, which may lend further boost to the cause of the terrorists. Success in campaigns and greater media attention is what the terrorists need to keep themselves afloat and gain legitimacy. This is also their only hope for transforming terrorism into a real political movement.

I had written earlier that it would be an utter folly on the part of the US to rely on another Islamic state, say, Pakistan, to fight the jihadists. This is more so when the US is losing the War on Terror. Recent American reverses in Iraq and Afghanistan, and the US problem in carrying out its follow-up policies, that is, nation building through successful installation of new governments with a view of ensuring peace and stability in both these countries, add to that worry. On the other hand, the al Qaeda takes advantage of rise in ethno-religious and political turmoil in these countries by cashing on these American failures. The al Qaeda has been more successful in setting up numerous cells to continue its subversive and terror activities because it knows that America is in trouble now.

With the US now at crossroads in the War on Terror, such tactics would be employed more frequently and would become the paradigm for the jihadists in pushing America against the wall. Henceforth, we might see the jihadists increasing the scale and frequency of their activities in those Muslim states where the US seeks to intervene, overtly or covertly. Take the case of Somalia where we find the same American foreign policy blunders. Alarmed by the developments in Somalia, the US tried to prevent that country from becoming a breeding ground of jihadist groups, like the Al Shaba, seeking to impose Sharia law in Somalia. Al Shaba has claimed to have the al Qaeda connections. The US backed an invasion by Ethiopia in 2006 to oust a group of hard-line Islamic courts from Mogadishu.[47] However, that American policy backfired as diplomats, regional analysts, and US officials admitted that the insurgency in Somalia had become more violent and stronger than ever.

The al Qaeda already has a significant influence in Yemen. So is the case with Algeria. With an increase in the numbers of new, young jihadists in its ranks in Algeria, the al Qaeda in the Islamic Magreb, AQIM, (a merging of the al Qaeda forces and the indigenous group, the Salafist Group for Preaching and Combat, GSPC), in 2006, unleashed numerous suicide attacks against the government and military targets. Here, as in other jihadi hotspots, the US prescription has either been to foster moderates within jihadist groups or to isolate the al Qaeda by supporting tribes and local politicians hostile to the al Qaeda. The rationale behind empowering moderates stems from the need to prevail over the jihadist ideology, the mainstay of the global jihadist movement led by the al Qaeda.[48]

However, sceptics doubt the efficacy of such a change in American policies in Iraq and Afghanistan. Steven A. Cook, Douglas Dillon Fellow at the Council on Foreign Relations and author of *Ruling But not Governing: The Military and Political Development in Egypt, Algeria, and Turkey*, doubts that the American policy of boosting moderate Islam and refining extremists may not work in view of the unsatisfactory track record of the 'moderates turned radicals'. The very popularity and even the survival of the extremists, like the Hamas and Hezbollah and Turkey's Justice and Development Party (AKP), depends on their 'radical' images. Steven Cook feels that any policy based on empowering the moderates would only amount to asking for trouble because of a thin borderline that separates radicals and moderates in Islam.

This is quite understandable. American efforts in this direction may easily be gainsaid unless a primary condition demanded by the jihadists is met—withdrawal of American troops and American influence from the Middle East. For example, the moderates may soon turn extremists if the American policy makers continue to resort to 'misadventures'. Nevertheless, no one can deny that the moderates wield enormous pull on the Muslim community in the Arab world. Carrie Wickham, Associate Professor of Political Science at Emory University has written that the Islamists have "emerged as the Arab world's loudest and most 'authentic' advocates of political accountability, social justice and the defence of Palestine (and Arab and Muslim rights, more generally)…"[49] According to him, Muslim Brotherhood in Egypt, The Islamic Action Front In Jordan, the Nadha party

49

in Tunisia, the Islamic Constitutional Movement in Kuwait, and the Justice and Development Party in Turkey happen to be reformist Islamist groups. They take part in parliamentary elections, and they compete for leadership positions in students unions and professional associations.[50]

Nevertheless, the crux remains. Bernard Lewis thought that all Muslims have the same attitude towards the Koran. Undoubtedly, the fundamentalist/ radical and the reformist Islamic groups, both hope to create a political system based on Sharia. One important distinction between the fundamentalists and the reformers is the former's rejection of and the latter's acceptance of the *ijtihad* (individual reasoning) that allows them to take into account the changes in modern times. Wickham rightly concludes that the followers of moderate Islamic parties far outnumber those of militant groups. Yet, everything depends on one condition: American attitude towards the Middle East. Incidentally, prior to the US invasion of Iraq, he had written, "a massive American military operation in Iraq would be sure to unite the moderate and militant wings of Islamic movement."

Another ramification of this development is that American bullying abroad might alienate other secular and neutral countries. And this may work to the great advantage of terrorists. *The Islamist terrorists have, in this context, a political equivalent of the nuclear bomb to humble the mighty United States.*

The Islamic fundamentalists know that their dreams of creating the Ummah on a global scale are not be far-fetched, if only they can persevere in their goals and terror tactics. The success of the Hamas in the Gaza strip in respect of social welfare services or the relief works by the Lashkar-e-Toiba (LeT) in the 2005 earthquake in Pakistan need to be mentioned. The Hamas has little difficulty in replicating the various activities of conventional states and institutions, such as taking part in elections and getting involved in administrative and social and humanitarian works. Yet both the Hezbollah and the Hamas have never relinquished their violence.

People tend to support groups or political parties which have sound economic and political agendas irrespective of their ideals. For example, the All Hurriyat Party Conference (AHPC) in Kashmir was believed to enjoy support of the Kashmiri people for advocating an independent state of Kashmir. The AHPC gave a call to boycott the 2008 Assembly elections as they felt the elections were a futile exercise and would hardly fulfil the aspirations of the common people.[51] But the subsequent election results showed that their radical views appealed little to the common people, who voted freely for political parties having sound socio-economic agendas. Former US President Bush, while hailing the Hamas electoral victory in the Gaza strip, remarked that the Hamas victory should serve as a reminder to Mehamoud Abbas (PA Chairman) that his government and party failed to serve the people and eradicate poverty and unemployment and that the Hamas win would create a competition between the Hamas and the Fatah. Mr. Bush hoped that Hamas would come to the mainstream of politics.[52]

It must be remembered that a win, here and there, for the terrorists, and any reversal for US, could act like an 'Islamic' torrent on a global scale. This would be possible only if the US loses composure and indulges in acts of indiscretion. The US is still the decisive player in the international sphere. President Obama's new policy orientation on the War on Terror could prove decisive in this respect.

The jihadists have a big problem. What if the common masses get used to their 'shock and surprise' tactics and get used to living with terrorism? When that happens (and this may well happen if the global War on Terror becomes regional), the core component of terrorism, the surprise element, would be substantially regularised and that could be the 'death' bell for the jihadists. That is why Al Zawahiri, in his book *Knights under the Prophets Banner,* had given a definite and concrete direction to jihadist movements in the following words: "jihad must dedicate one of its revolutionary wings to work with masses, preach, and provide services". He advocated a reciprocal love relationship with the general masses. What does it imply, other than highlighting the political objective within jihad?

References

[1]'Trauma severe for Iraqi children', www.usatoday.com, 16 April 2007. *http://www.usatoday. com/news/world/iraq/2007-04-15-cover-war-children_N.htm*
[2] Eli Lake, 'Victory Will Come as in Cold war, Rumsfeld Predicts', 19 November 2007. the Sun. Available at http://www.nysun.com/national/victory-will-come-as-in-cold-war-rumsfeld_ predicts/66643/
[3]'Michael Moulot, 'Washington is Losing War on Terror: Experts', 5 July 2006, Agence France Presse, Common Dreams News Center, *www.commondreams.org/headlines06/0705-03. htm*
[4] ibid,.

[5]'Jihad against Jews and Crusaders', World Islamic Front Statement, 23 February1998.

[6] ibid.

[7] ibid.

[8] Abdel Bari Atwan, The Secret History of Al-Qaeda, 2007, Abacus, p.51

[9]'Justice will be done',Transcript of President Bush's speech To Joint Congress, 20 September 2001.

[10] ibid.

[11]36 Ways the US is Losing the War on Terror', www.AntiWar.com, 3 August 2004.

[12]President Bush on Fifth Anniversary of 9/11, www.About.com: US politics *http://uspolitics. about.com/od/speeches/a/9_11_bush_3.htm*

[13]Ibid.

[14] ibid.,Justice will be done,

[15] *U.S. Strategy For Afghanistan: Achieving Peace And Stability In The ...*Cordesman, CSIS. foreignaffairs.house.gov/111/cor040209.pdf, published on April 2, 2009

[16]*ibid.*

[17]ibid.

[18]ibid.

[19]ibid.

[20] Drudge Retort, Bush: Iraq Will Take 40 years, 4 June, 2008, www.drudge.com/archive/108534/bush-iraq-take-40-years

[21]Barry R. Posen, 'Exit Strategy: How to disengage from Iraq in 18 months' , Boston Review, Jan-Feb, 2006, Available at *www.bostonreview.net.*

[22]Cousin Marriage Conundrum: The ancient practice discourages democratic nation-building', Steve Sailer, The American Conservative, 13January 2003, pp.20-2. Available at http// www.isteve.com/cousin_marriage_conundrum.htm

[23]Veil of Fears, Why the Veil: Why we should leave it alone,' S. Kurtz, 28 January 2002, National Review. Available at http://www.nationalreview.com/28jan02/kurtz012802/shtml

[24] Ibid, Atwan

[25]'Yahoo worker accused of role in India terror', The Guardian, 8 October 2008. Available at http//www.guardian.co.uk/world/2008/oct08/india.terrorism).

[26]'Scientific Training and Radical Islam', Stephen Schwartz, Middle East Quarterly, Spring 2008, pp 3-11, Available at http://www.meforum.org/article/1861.

[27] ibid.,Atwan, p.258.

[28]'Cost of Iraq war could surpass $1 trillion', Martin Wolk, 17 March 2006, www.msnbc.com.

[29] ibid.,Atwan ,p.259

[30]Future Jihadists: Terrorist Strikes Against the West', Walid Phares, Palgrave Macmillan, 2006.

[31]'Obama: Taliban and Al Queda must be stopped', The Associated Press, 28 April 2009,. google.com/hostednews/ap/article/ALeqM5hiC0RYf3aBQerPjTXcfWlnx5Tk4Q...

[32]Pope Urban II, Wikipedia, the free encyclopedia Robert the Monk's account of Urban's speech, Urban II: Speech at Council of Clermont, 1095, Five versions of the Speech (available as part of the Internet Medieval Sourcebook). www.fordham.edu/halsall/source/urban2-5vers.html

[33]Muhammad Asad, The Principles of State and Government in Islam, Islamic Book Trust, 1999, p 15.

[34]9/11 Commission Report. Final Report of the National Commission on Terrorist Attacks Upon the United States, Official Government Edition, http://www.gpoaccess.gov/911/

[35]Early History of Terrorism, Terrorism Research. www.terrorism-research.com

52

[36] ibid.,Atwan, p.88.

[37] Chomsky, US Army Operational Concept for Terrorism Counteraction, TRADOC Pamphlet, no. 525-30, 1984.

[38] 'On Afghanistan War, American Terrorism, and the Role of Intellectuals', Noam Chomsky interviewed by Suzy Hansen, 16 January 2002. Available, http://www.chomsky.info/interviews/20020116.htm

[39] Counterterrorism blog: Event Transcript: The Evolution of U.S Counterterrorism policy) counterterrorismblog.org/2008/02/event_transcript_the_evolution.php

[40] National Archives and Records Administrations

[41] Salmon Rushdie observed that the only instance in which the Muslims are not averse to accepting modernism is in the area of technology

[42] Annual Claremont Institute Dinner in honour of Winston Churchill, 17 November, 2007, http://www.claremont.org/events/pageID.2525/default.asp

[43] Pakistan has been double-dealing US for years": Former CIA analyst, Indo Asian News Service 28 December, 2008

[44] www.speaker.gov/blog/?p=877

[45] Pakistan's ISI aiding Taliban in southern Afghanistan: NYT 26 March 2009, PTI. Available at http://timesofindia.indiatimes.com/Paks-ISI-aiding-Taliban-in-southern-Afghanistan-NYT/articleshow/4317121.cms

[46] State Department Counterterrorism Coordinator's Integrated Approach', Michael Kraft. Available on counterterrorismblog.org/2007/12/state_department_countertterro.php

[47] Islamists poised to seize Somalia again in setback to U.S.', McClatchy Washington Bureau, 18 November 2008. Available on http://www..mcclatchydc.com/homepage//story/56097.html

[48] 'Beyond Al Qaeda: Global Jihadist Movement- Part 1', Angela Rabasa, et.al., Avaialble at www.rqand.org/pubs/monograph/2006/Rand_MG429.pdf

[49] Carrie Wickham 'Moderate Islam is the Mainstream', Emory Report, 9 September 2002, http://www.emory.edu/Emory_Report/

[50] ibid, Wickham

[51] 'AHPC to boycott Kashmir elections later this year, Pakistan Times, 5 November 2008.

[52] 'Bush is Conciliatory in Accepting Victory of Hamas', Glenn Kessler, Washington Post, 27 January 2006. p.A15, washingtonpost.com washingtonpost.com/wp-dyn/content/article/.../26/AR2006012601009.htm

CHAPTER II

ISLAMIST TERRORISM X-RAYED

Religious terrorism on the ascendance

The virulently radicalised form of Islamist terrorism that we have come to know in the last two decades (thanks to the Afghan jihad), has changed the course of terrorism, further away from the secular political variety that was dominant for well over hundred years. Prior to this, it was the PLO (Palestinian Liberation Organisation) that served as a focal point for modern terrorist activities since its formation in the 1960s. In one important respect, the PLO chapter had been a watershed in the history of terrorist movements as it significantly impacted the scope of terrorism by lending it a trans-national dimension. Henceforth, terrorism would recreate itself on foreign soils through the export of terror tactics employed by the PLO to espouse the cause of the Palestinians in various parts of the world (for example, Article 2, 15, and 23 of the Palestinian National Covenant or Charter adopted on 28 May 1964, highlighted its objectives by claiming Palestine, as it *existed* under the British mandate, while seeking to prohibit the 'existence and activity of Zionism' in Palestine).

It is over this issue of anti-Israelism in their overall nationalist-political agenda that the mother organisation suffered schism, just a few years after its formation. For example, the 1974 Ten Point Program that advocated the formation of a secular democratic bi-national state, created rifts within the organisation and resulted in the breaking away of the Popular Front for the Liberation of Palestine (PFLP) and the PFLP GC (General Command) from the PLO. The PLO, under Arafat, subsequently revised its anti-Israeli and anti-Zionist stand and admitted the right of Israel to exist as an independent state. However, other factions of PLO never relinquished their anti-Israeli activities. No doubt, latter day Islamist terrorism had its seed in the anti-Israeli agenda of Arab politics.

A few years later, the Iranian revolution in 1979, at Ayatollah Khomeini's behest, and its aftermath, lent a religious orientation, more specifically, a fundamentalist colour, to the hitherto secular-political movements in the region. This led Nasr Vali, adjunct Senior Fellow for Middle Eastern Studies, to comment that the Iranian revolution had transformed Islamic fundamentalism into a political force from Morocco to Malay.[1] Bernard Lewis wrote that the Iranian revolution expressed itself in the language of Islam.[2] The non-terrorist nature of the Iranian revolution of the initial years took a more violent turn in the latter years, and became, what Walid Phares called, one of the two 'trees' of modern jihadist movement.[3] In that respect, the Iranian revolution was another milestone in the history of terrorist movements in this region.

However, it must be mentioned that religious terrorist movements were not absent prior to the 1980s, for example, those inspired by the ideologies of Muslim Brotherhood. Neither were suicide missions the forte of religious terrorists alone. Suicide bombers or suicide squads existed in earlier times as well. The killers of Czar Alexander I in the 1880s were on a suicide mission. So was the assassinator of Archduke Ferdinand of Austria. The chief characteristic of modern Islamist terrorism is that it draws extra inspiration and adrenalin from religion because of the simple fact that religion and politics happen to be inseparable for Islam. This very inseparability of politics and religion leads one to conclude that religion could very well be used for political purposes.

In the recent past, religious terrorism (including major religions and various religious sects and cults) has come out with a vengeance to re-establish its supremacy over other forms of terrorism. It has registered a phenomenal rise in its numbers, from 11 to 16 out of a possible 49 identifiable international terrorist organisations in 1994, and to 26 out of 56 in 1995, then dropping to 13 out of 46 in 1996.[4] This reduction in numbers may be attributed to some strict counter terrorist measures and peace processes initiated by the United States in Bosnia, Middle East, and Ireland in the

1990s. However, Hoffman points out that even in 1996, religious terrorists carried out as many as 10 out of 13 most lethal terror attacks. Thereafter, religious terrorist strikes have been on the rise, especially, in the Middle East and Africa, culminating in the 9/11 attack on the WTC Twin Towers. To this must be added the casualties in ethno-religious conflicts in various parts of the world, in which various Mujahideen groups took part, during the entire decade of the 1990s.

In this connection, it must be remembered that even terrorists with secular objectives may use religious means, for example, Ireland, where both the Republicans (Catholic) and the Loyalists (Protestant) used religious rhetoric to undermine one another. Yet their objective remained political— whether the North would maintain its independence and join UK or whether it would form a unified Ireland by merging with the South. Thus, religious elements might figure in secular political terrorism, as in the above Irish case, while political elements may be present in religious forms, for example, al Qaeda's Pan-Arabism. The Center for Defence Information (CDI), in a study, tried to explain religious terrorism from various angles and concluded that both the secular and the religious forms share some common elements. This study further stated that the political element may be present in every religious form but it is more pronounced in the case of Islam.[5] What is more, with frequent interactions— a defining feature of contemporary terrorist movement— the borderline between both the secular or the religious terror groups has become narrower. That divide has become more meaningless, these days, as various terrorist groups with disparate objectives, strive to expand the horizon of their interactions with anti-social and criminal groups, as is discussed below.

More about Islamist terrorism

Islamist terrorists do not exist in vacuum. They can be apprehended, their activities can be largely neutralised with better intelligence; they are not all-powerful. Besides arms and money, they need an ideology, right or wrong, to motivate them. Much of the glamour, awe, and charisma surrounding them and with which they hope to influence the common masses, is owed to their 'ready-to-sacrifice for the cause' approach. Islamist terrorists use religion as that cause. Nevertheless, the 'glamour' attributed to freedom fighters or left wing communist guerrillas differ from that of the jihadists. The former never indulge in indiscriminate killings of innocent civilians and hence are far from being anti-people, but the latter are simply mindless murderers. It would be unthinkable for secular political terrorist groups to open fire on innocent commuters in a railway platform like the jihadists in the 26/11 Mumbai carnage.

The common man in a crowded meeting place may not be aware of their eerie and chilling presence, standing beside him, and breathing on his neck. The terrorist conducts himself like any other person and pretends to visit a particular public place, perhaps, out of 'curiosity'. Yet ruthless and cold-blooded killers are not like ordinary murderers. Terrorists come in small batches with detailed planning about the place and nature of their operations. Their presence, say, in Liaquat Ali Park, totally betrays the trust of common people standing next to him in full confidence that they (terrorists) are like other spectators who have come to have a glimpse of, say, the popular PPP leader Benazir Bhutto. Or, take the case of one such small terror group riding on cars and bikes on the high streets of Islamabad city alongside other vehicles, with the difference that the cars they are driving contain huge amount of deadly explosives, once again betraying the faith of common boarders in, say Hotel Marriott, who have no idea what is going to happen, next moment. By the way, my selection of targets in Pakistan confirms the fact that Pakistan itself is not immune from terror attacks. But that does not prove that it is no sponsor of terrorism. This is discussed in detail in Chapter VI dealing with state sponsors of terrorism. The all important fact is anyone playing with fire stands a greater chance of getting burned.

But there is no reason to assume that such killings are without purpose. These terrorists are trained, armed, provided with all logistical information, and sent to their destined location at an appropriate time, fully 'charged' to execute their intended operation in a mindless and mechanical manner. Yet, the bottom line is that these terrorists are mere human beings and it is their 'distance' (in every aspect) from the general public that evokes a 'particular' interest in them. They stay, for the most part of their existence, underground and occasionally surface very close to their intended targets stealthily. It is simply impossible to know, without some robust network of intelligence, when, how, and in what disguise they will carry out their campaigns.

One compelling reason why jihadists kill innocent civilians is that they are afraid of people. This simply means they already know that the common masses abhor their ways and views of life. By their mindless killings, they simply generate intense public hatred. Recently, a woman passenger in a Howrah-bound bus in West Bengal screamed at the sight of two 'women' clad in burqas and whispering in male voices, to draw public attention. The fellows in burqa immediately alighted from the bus and ran. The main difference between radical Islamist terrorists and other terrorist groups is that they do not hesitate to commit mass murders while their secular-political counterparts have no such agenda. Bruce Hoffman explains this killer mind-set of the religious terrorists in the following lines: "The reasons why religious terrorism results in so many more deaths than secular terrorism may be found in their radically value systems, mechanisms of legitimization and justification, concepts of morality, and worldviews embraced by the religious terrorist.[6] This seems to be a vague generalisation in so far that it fails to explain the driving force of modern religious terrorism: jihad.

Yet, as referred above, it would be a folly to assume that they are simply ruthless killers and that their religion and world views lead them to act with no other purpose. No, they have definite plans and strategies. They are fired up in the flame of revenge against what they feel are acts of infringement on their religion, land, or brethren, especially, by foreign or alien powers, that is, the 'infidels'. Their purpose is to declare jihad against foreign occupation and foreign oppression. And towards this end, it is immaterial who the enemy is: the erstwhile Soviet Union or the super power of the contemporary era, the United States. Regional jihadists in the Indian sub-continent chiefly have one political objective and one target: the Kashmir issue and India.

Yet, the jihadists are not without cunning and patience. They use tact and intelligence to fool their enemies and know how to survive the relentless onslaught from a superior adversary.

Interaction between various terror groups and its implication for Islamist terrorism

Jonathan Fine rightly observed that tactical concerns necessitated the various terror groups to cooperate with each other. In this connection, he cited the May 1972 meeting of the representatives of the IRA, the Baadar

Meinhoff Gang, and the Japanese Red Army, in Northern Lebanon's Badawi Refugee camp, at the initiative of PFLP leader George Habash. On 31 January1974, PFLP took part in a Japanese Red Army (JRA) led operation on a Shell oil refinery. This was seen as a gesture of reciprocity and meeting obligations in response to a JRA attack on the Ben Gurion Airport near Tel Aviv.[7] The Rand Corporation, in one of its monograph series entitled, *Sharing the Dragon's Teeth, Terrorist Groups and the Exchange of New Technologies,* revealed the results of three case studies in Mindanao, the West Bank and the Gaza Strip, and southwest Colombia. The study concluded that at least 11 terrorist groups in these three areas exchanged technologies and knowledge that proved mutually beneficial for these groups.

In another instance, the study found that the al Qaeda related Jemmah Islamiyah (JI) and the Hezbollah had given training and equipment to Fillipino and Palestinian militants, at the turn of the new century. Both these recipient groups learned the art of preparing Improvised Explosive Devices (IEDs), remote-detonation devices, and handling the Katyusha rockets, in lieu of providing safe haven and access to alternative sources of funding and arms procurement to their 'trainers'. [8]

The Provisional Irish Republican Army (PIRA) offered the same help to the Revolutionary Armed Forces of Colombia (FARC) that included remote detonation technologies, Mark 18 "barracks-buster" mortars, and guerrilla warfare tactics.[9] In exchange, the groups providing such assistance, for example, the JI and PIRA were believed to have gained safe haven and access to new avenues of finance, that is, smuggling routes. The Rand Study concluded, "In fact, the increased possibility for the exchange of technology and knowledge between groups, both because of and despite ideological persuasion, makes the designation of terrorist groups as 'local', 'regional', 'global' less relevant."[10] More ominously, such forging of alliances on a transnational level enhances the capabilities of concerned terrorist groups and gives a new lease, not only to these groups but also to other groups which were hard hit by the War on Terrorism. But these are not without stakes.

Such mutual arrangements of 'convenience' may both be the cause and consequence of gradual commercialisation of terrorism. While the need for arms and finance necessitate alliances between disparate groups, like the Islamist terrorists and the criminals, the simultaneous development of sub 'industrial' activities definitely results in greater commercialisation of terrorism. For example, the recent admission, following the arrest (March 7, 2009) of a Lashkar terrorist and an explosive expert, of Abu Taher, alias, Muhammad Zakaria, by the Indian Special Task Force, confirm my above claim. Abu Taher has revealed during police interrogation that he can prepare Improvised Explosive Devices (IEDs) and has given training to various terrorist organisations on how to use them and he has also been a supplier of IEDs to various groups. He even owned a plant to manufacture explosives in Rajshahi district in Bangladesh. He has helped the Jamat-ul-Mujahideen in Bangladesh in carrying out the recent serial blasts in several Indian cities. As the element of money making enters into the terrorist's calculations, wittingly or unwittingly, the focus on ideals may suffer, particularly for the jihadists.

Ideology may also become secondary as more and more terrorist groups interact with each other for varying interests. The issue of 'survival' (because of vigorous anti-terrorist and anti-drug trafficking campaigns) drives Islamist terrorist groups and criminal gangs these days, to form alliances. Consequently, it makes the job of the authorities easier to club these terrorist groups and criminals in the same bracket. Needless to mention, one of the chief aims of the War on Terror is to deglamorise the jihadists and to throw them from their present 'charismatic' heights, if any, into the dungeons of the criminal world. More importantly, the interaction between Islamist terrorists on the one hand, and criminals and drug peddlers on the other, clearly shows that religion, especially Islam, does not quite guide the activities of the jihadists since Islam forbids association with anti-socials and criminals. Moreover, the missing link between anti-Americanism and jihad remains a problem for the jihadist leaders. How can the political demand of 'America hands off from the Middle East' be transformed into jihad against the US, when the latter offers safe abode for Muslims from other countries and when it, instead of maligning Islam, respects it as is evident from the former American President Bush's speech in the wake of 9/11?

Political Objectives

There is little reason to believe that jihadists are not motivated by political objectives. Otherwise, why did some religious terrorist groups go back into their shells following the Middle East peace initiatives between the PLO and Israel in 1993? Some of these terror groups even took part in that peace process. These groups simply tend to use religion and religious rhetoric to swell the ranks of their recruits, in order to reach at a bargaining position vis-à-vis their adversaries.

One misconception about Islam that has great bearing on this discussion is that it endorses suicides and hence suicide missions. Koran does not condone suicidal acts. I have shown in the previous chapter that suicide missions were indeed carried out by other terrorist organisations, irrespective of their ideology. Robert Pape, the Chicago University professor and a political scientist, made an unbiased and an in depth analysis of the relationship between suicides attacks and religious terrorism. He prepared a data bank with detailed information regarding each individual suicide bomber in the last couple of decades or so, and his findings were that Islam, and for that matter religion, had not much to do with suicide bombing. Robert Pape felt that it was not religion but it was tactics and political objective that motivated these Islamist terrorists in their jihad against the 'infidels'.

Suicide bombing may be a potent tactic and hence it could be used in any kind of war situation. Suicide missions require an external target and also serve as an inspiration for other members belonging to the group. There would be no occasion for such self-sacrificial acts without an external target. That target may be religious or political. It may be mentioned here that in sectarian violence in Iraq, both the sects indulged in mutual killing sprees and not without suicide attacks. Even two days prior to the destruction of the famous Shia shrine in Samarra, a suicide bomber blew himself up in a bus in the Shia stronghold of Khadamiyah in West Baghdad. As for political targets, these happen to be primarily American and Israeli. This they call 'Lesser jihad' and Qital. After all, one cannot commit suicide to cleanse one's inner self. Inner defects and perverted thoughts have to be cured through a series of 'internal' struggles, for example, Greater jihad.

Robert Pape observed that almost all such attacks had a common secular and strategic goal— to compel modern democracies to withdraw military forces from territories that the terrorists consider to be their homeland.[11] In order to further disprove the connection between Islam and suicide missions, he has shown that there was no strict correspondence between social status or age groups and suicide attacks. Contrary to the popular notion that most of the 'fidayeens' happen to be under the age group of twenty, Professor Pape, basing his research on 315 attacks and 18 campaigns spanning over a period of two and half decades (1980-2005), has shown that while the average age for the Hezbollah *shahid* hovered around 21.1 years, it was 26.7 and 29.8 years in the case of the al Qaeda and the Chechens, respectively. Pape concluded, "The bottom line then is that suicide terrorism is mainly a response to foreign occupation."[12]

All said and done, every activity, including suicide bombings, is situation-specific. For example, Aisha, the third wife of the Prophet, once asked the Prophet if females could participate in jihad to which the Prophet told, 'There is jihad for them in which there is no fighting".[13] Notwithstanding, even a radical organisation like the al Qaeda has not refrained from employing female suicide fighters, in recent times, because of time and situation[14]

Suicide and jihad are often viewed as complementing one another. So, it is necessary to have a correct interpretation of the term 'jihad'. Jihad comes from the word 'Jahada' that simply means striving or struggling towards improving one's self through "self corrections", and, thereby, improving one's surrounding, since an individual happens to be a part of the society. He needs others in his group and society to observe righteousness and piety and, without his community, his efforts and strivings have little meaning. This is what the Koran demands. This is known as Greater jihad.

Jihad happens to be a political concept on two counts: first, Islam makes religion and politics inseparable and secondly since the terrorists carry out their armed struggle, this is a kind of war, Lesser jihad. Where there is war, we have got to remember the famous saying by the great martial genius Clausewitz that war happened to be the continuation of politics by other means. By that logic, even if one fights to defend one's religion, it is first of all a political affair because waging a war requires arms and funds above all and these can be had from political and state sources only. Even infighting between two factions of the same religion, like the Shias and Sunnies, may not necessarily take place on religious lines but may depend on external factors, like spreading mutual 'spheres of influence'. It may also be the handiwork of agent provocateurs or even state agencies employing such means, for example, the CIA role in Lebanon. Further discussion on Jihad could be found in the section dealing with 'how Islamic is Islamist terrorism' of this chapter. More discussions on jihad is done in the section dealing with 'How Islamic is Islamist terrorism', below.

Koran on the use of force and violence

Islam, like any other religion, happens to be a social concept in that there is little value to a religious theory or doctrine unless it is accepted by a broad section of the masses.[15] In this connection, it is worthwhile to remember a famous saying from the great Hindu spiritual guru, Ramkrishna Paramhansa, that nobody would have cared for God if human beings did not invent and elevate Him to that position. In other words, what he meant was that God owed his existence to human beings. That means that God, or for that matter religion, exists in and through human beings. It cannot be denied that any concept that has its source and proliferation in and through human beings has to be, primarily, a social concept. It is equally true of Islam since it puts emphasis on translating Koranic teachings into practice. Likewise, morality and ethics also have their taproots in social practices. What the Prophet meant by strict adherence to Allah's verses was that, human beings would only be spared of unwarranted distractions and superficialities that led to greed, avarice, power craze, and petty interests by focusing on these core concepts alone. It is only through a collective adherence to these original Koranic verses, that it would be possible to create a well knit society and a righteous commune based on the concept justice.

Koran and the Apostle's teachings underline the importance of community and society. Since Islam demands submission of the will of people to God's will, and since God has created male and female from a single root so that successive generations of mankind may get to know each other and cohabit in a spirit of cooperation and peace, it is obvious that Koranic verses are not simply concerned about the individual, but have a macro dimension. For example, according to a Koranic verse:

...if any one slew a person, unless it be for murder or for spreading mischief in the land, it would be as if he slew the whole people: and if any one saved a life, it would be as if he saved the life of the whole people.

[Al-Qur'an 5:32]

So, the sustenance and welfare of the community is at the heart of Islam. Once that is done, it is necessary to protect that community from wrongdoers within and outside. Hence the need is felt for the presence of laws and law enforcing agencies, to translate Islamic teachings into reality. Islamic law or the Sharia, serves that purpose. Yet what is needed is not a half hearted reference to such laws but their *incorporation* (italics mine) into the laws of the land, that is, the Constitution. The law enforcing agency happens to be the state and that state must be an Islamic state. However, for Islam, state is just a means towards a higher goal, that of the establishment of the Ummah, to ensure a happy, equitable, peaceful, free, and prosperous life for every member of the Muslim community.

Islam also maintains that while laws can be used for domestic purposes, external enemies have to be combated through force and war, provided they prove hostile and intransigent. Koran makes allowance for saving and protecting the lives of even the vanquished who would be willing to return to the path of peace.[16] The Prophet himself, on numerous occasions, pled that mercy be shown towards those willing to make amends and return to the path of righteousness. Many of the misconceptions surrounding Islam are unfounded and emanate from Western propaganda, based on a wrong perception of Islam. Needless to say, every religion sanctions the use of force for the purpose of self-defence, whether Hinduism, Christianity, or Islam.

Koran hardly condones violence and murder. Koran holds human life precious. It is here that the fundamentalists and the radical elements within Islam deviate by transcending the basic premises of Islam. Can these radical groups deny the fact that Muslims from various parts of the world live in large numbers in the US? There are many 'multicultural' families within the US, as mentioned by the US Consul General of Chennai in a discussion on Terrorism and jihad, initiated by the Islamic Research Foundation. It is this consideration that had led bin Laden to retract from his earlier fatwa directed against American citizens. Laden also issued a statement asking the American people to rise up against their 'rulers'.

The crux is that nothing tangible can be attained without US mediation in any conflict situation in any part of the world. That is why Laden was appealing for a change in the American ruling circle through the force of public opinion. Does this not mean that the jihadists, led by Laden, have a political objective which guides their terror ideology? As for peaceful coexistence of religions, the Prophet himself was against any use of force unless compelled by the other party to do so. Let the readers take a look at some of the original verses from Koran that has relevance for the above analysis.

...take not life, which God hath made sacred, except by way of justice and law: thus doth He command you, that ye may learn wisdom.
[Al-Qur'an 6:151]
Islam, like any other religion, speaks for the whole community and hence there is nothing unusual in its advocating self-defence, especially to protect the community, when wronged or attacked. It all started with the war on Mecca when the Prophet was driven away and humiliated.

Fight in the cause of Allah those who fight you, but do not transgress limits; for Allah loveth not transgressors.
Surah 2, verse 190, Abdullah Yusuf Ali

Again we find in Surah 4, verse 75,

And why should ye not fight in the cause of God and of those who, being weak, are ill-treated (and oppressed)? Men, women, and children, whose cry is: Our Lord! Rescue us from this town, whose people are oppressors; and raise for us from thee one who will protect; and raise for us from thee one who will help!
[Al-Qur'an 4:75]

Let me now examine why some of the deviations of the jihadist groups from the original teachings of Islam create problems for them and harm their causes. First, since their objective is to establish the supremacy of Islam on a global scale, (Koran never favoured forcible expansion of that religion) they run the risk of having to contend with other religions or religious groups, ideologically as well as physically, that is, war on cultural fault lines. Secondly, they have to fight off challenges from the law enforcing entities like the state, because the jihadists can't do without recourse to unlawful and violent means. Thirdly, they may have to confront the US, the sole super power standing like an insurmountable rock before them should they prepare to launch a second Great Crusade. Fourthly, they need the support from the followers of Islam in other parts of the world, who find it difficult to comprehend why all this is necessary when their religion, Islam, is in no way attacked or threatened and it enjoys the same freedom and respect from the rest of the world as any other religion. Fifthly, since religious terrorists are accountable to some degree of 'internal constituency', there are bound to be various interpretations and differences precipitating factional or sectarian divisions within that religion.

The very fact that modern Islamist terrorism is anti-Western and anti-American in nature, alone proves that such types of terrorism are far from being purely religious in nature. Prior to the birth of Israel as a separate state, anti-Americanism was at its lowest, even in Muslim states. Incidentally, radical Islamic movements have always been *relative* in nature, waxing and waning in proportion to the appearance or disappearance of a target or issue. Islamic fundamentalist movements often went back into their shells when the opponent was too strong, in terms of physical or ideological power, for example, the reign of Kemal Pasha and Gamal Abdul Nasser in Turkey and Egypt, respectively, or even communism that had kept ethno-religious issues on a tight leash for almost four decades after the Second World War.

Negotiations and political interventions have always proved handy in diffusing conflicts between groups and states, in which religion played a part, for example, Pope Leo I, accompanied by Avienius, an expert negotiator and a man of consular rank, and the Roman prefect, Trygetius, around 453 A.D. met the Hun emperor Attila near Mantua and prevented the fall of Rome. The Hun emperor reportedly listened to the Pope's advice and agreed not to attack Rome, of course, not without an enormous dowry (bribe?) from Princess Honoria.[17] Even Christianity had to depend on the political blessings of Constantine for its phenomenal ascent from virtual obscurity. Conversely, when religion gets the better of politics, chaos and disorder reign supreme, for example, the First Great Crusade. It is clear from the above that the curve of religion is dependent on state and politics.

Can there be a compromise with the Islamist groups?

Since every other major power, more or less toes the US line and since many countries, not excluding the Islamic ones, have demonstrated their fascination for American globalisation, democracy, and liberalism, there is virtually no player at the other end of the spectrum. So, these Islamist radicals deem it their bounden duty to bell the American cat through various terror tactics aimed at harassing and undermining that great power. Their purpose is twofold: to carry on their tirade or jihad against American values and ways, and to reduce Israel to a mere ethnic group, bereft of nation state status, under the command of the Arabs and the Palestinians. They lay the blame on the secular character of nation states that have given rise to a materialistic/hedonistic culture everywhere

It is important to examine what the word Islamist stands for. The term Islamist was adapted from the French word Islamiste, replacing the term Islamicist that was previously used in the English language.[18] According to Olivier Roy, the Islamicists look upon the state as the chief vehicle of reislamisation and thus seek to capture state power, build a 'true Islamic constitution', a 'true Islamic economy', and 'Islamic social justice'.[19]

While the Islamists are believed to endorse progressive ideas in keeping with modernity, the fundamentalists favour a return to the roots and they tend to reject the incorporation of new ideas on the ground that these are imported from the west. The paradox is that there are fundamentalists and moderates amongst the Islamists. For Islam, the term fundamentalist is a broad one that may cover extremists, radicals, and conservatives. Fundamentalists have differences within their ranks. For example, according to Robin Wright, fundamentalist movements also incorporate a great deal of modernity and innovation.[20] Ali Abootalebi wrote, "In any case, the classification of Muslim movements into traditionalist/fundamentalist and Islamist/reformist can be confusing, since Islamic doctrine itself allows for different interpretations and therefore different opinions on Sharia and its principles."[21] This is also the view Professor Gunaratna, who holds that due to the endless disputes over the basic concept of Sharia, there is no single, united perception among Muslims of what the Sharia is, what its content is, or how it should be applied. This alone has been the source of so many disagreements, debates, intellectual and clerical discourses and interpretations, thereby resulting in the proliferation of a wide range of Islamic movements, over time.

This discussion is extremely relevant in order to have a proper understanding not only of Islam but also of what goes on within that society when faced with modern ideas and developments. For example, al Qaeda had some initial success in organising jihadist movements in Algeria, Yemen, and Saudi Arabia, following the US misadventures in these countries. Now, these are the very countries that are experiencing a rise in revisionist doctrines. For example, Sayyid Imam al Sharif, one time head of the dreaded terrorist group, Islamic Jihad, had written a couple of books in the 1980s that were regarded as manuals for al Qaeda. Since 2007, he has forsaken his jihadist manifesto and called on young people to not be deceived by Internet heroes.[22]

There are other issues too. For example, the hard liners within Islamist groups have to maintain their radical image to score over other factions, for example, the Hamas vis-a-vis the Fatah. The Hamas, unlike the PLA, still believes in the liquidation of Israel and it advocates the internationalisation of Islam. The Hamas covenant clearly states that the struggle against Jews is 'very great and very serious'. It considers its electoral victory as but a step in that direction and that it would need 'more and more squadrons from this vast Arab and Islamic world to conquer and destroy Israel.' According to the Hamas and the Islamic Resistance Movement, the land of Palestine happens to be an Islamic Waqf and not a property, even of any Arab, Islamic, or the Palestinian organisations or sovereigns. Hence the Hamas pledges that no part of that Holy land will be squandered.[23] Similarly, notwithstanding the good work done by them in the sphere of social services, like education and healthcare, the group displayed its true colour when its cadres, in some recent past, overtook west Beirut through the sheer power of the guns.

But this is not to say that democracy, the availability of economic opportunities, and prosperity, do not temper cultural conflagrations. Persuasion and perseverance can shape the views of even hardened terrorists, depending on the above conditions. It is one of the basic assumptions of the US policies to empower the moderates and to geld the extremists within Islam.

How Islamic is Islamist terrorism?

Readers may note that in order to avoid some confusion, I have preferred to use the term Islamist terrorism throughout this book and not simple 'radical/fundamentalist Islamic terrorism'. These radical groups or their leadership, not necessarily religious figureheads, feel qualified to speak on behalf of the entire Muslim community. They espouse a more aggressive or a newer interpretation of Islam in a bid to cleanse Islam from the 'viruses' contracted by insincere and infidel Muslim rulers in the Middle East through their contact, contamination, and submission to 'corrupt' and 'perverted' Western values. However, not all the fellow Muslims, either in the Arab heartlands or elsewhere, subscribe to this view.

If one is to accept the English translation of the Arabic word jihad to mean 'holy war', this concept, interestingly, has no place in the entire Koran. According to Koran, *Jihad fi sabil-illah* is the way of Allah or striving in the name of God. This striving might mean waging war on oppressors under certain circumstances. However, instead of using the word *Harb*, a common Arabic term for war, Koran uses the word *Qital* to describe jihad by sword. Noted writer and journalist, Sultan Shaheen wrote, "*Qital* is predicated upon conditions and circumstances and it is, therefore, necessarily ephemeral. Jihad is ceaseless, it never stops. Jihad extends to each and every kind of Islamic endeavor; big or small; physical or material; moral and intellectual."[24] Daniel Pipes in an interview to a Hindi news portal Lokmanch, on January 6, 2009, brilliantly summed up that terrorism happened to be one of many forms that jihad may assume. According to Walid Phares, "The term 'Jihadist' is another, mostly American, equivalent of Islamism, a term used in Europe and in the Middle East to define radical Islamic Fundamentalists."[25] Of the two branches of jihadist movements, that is, the Salafists (Wahhabis in Arabia, the Muslim Brotherhood in Egypt, and the Deobandis in the Indian subcontinent) and the Khomeinist, this book is concerned with jihadists belonging to the first group. Needless to mention, within the first category belong both the global (al Qaeda and its 'nebula'. the numerous local organisations) and the local, the various Islamist groups in the Middle East and in the Indian sub-continent. The al Qaeda and its various associated groups together symbolise what Torres, Jordan, and Horsburgh believe a Global Jihadist Movement (GJM)[26]

It is this global jihadist movement that has become the centrepiece of modern Islamist terrorism spearheaded by neo-fundamentalist groups like the Salafi and the Wahhabi. Yet jihad, as interpreted by traditional Muslim law, ought to be territorial and under the guidance of political and religious leaders and hence not an individual obligation. The shift to global jihadist movement is interesting and important. Earlier, jihad stood for a long drawn process of indoctrination and penetration of societies. However, the concept underwent some change in the 1990s when the Mujahideen returnees from the Afghan front chose to go global and engage directly with foreign forces in various parts of the world, like Chechnya, Sudan, Algeria, Bosnia, etc. The al Qaeda leaders thus succeeded in converting the earlier 'collective' obligation into an 'individual' obligation to carry on a permanent jihad on a global scale.[27] This, in short is the evolution and trend in global jihadist movement. But it must be remembered that traditional territorially bound jihad is also prevalent alongside the GJM. Incidentally, GJM members are extremely heterogeneous and rootless fighters whose interests range from individual salvation to individual material gains.

Bernard Lewis thought that although Islam as a religion did not endorse terrorism, both the traditional and the fundamentalist followers of Islam accepted God as the 'sole source of sovereignty'. He concluded, "God is the head of the state. The state is God's state. The army is God's army. The treasury is God's treasury, and enemy, of course, is God's enemy." [28] It would be important to note that Koran views an enemy as one who repeatedly attacks God and his Messenger. Koran even advocates mercy on the lesser transgressors.

It is here that the missing link in the emergence of fundamentalist theories in Islam can be traced. For example, right from the Egyptian Muslim Brotherhood founder, Hasan al Banna, and its theoretician, Sayeed Qutb, down to Ayatollah Ruhullah Khomeini, bin Laden, and his deputy Ayman al-Zawahiri, every radical and fundamentalist writer has stressed that Islam and its followers were being tortured, exploited, and persecuted by the 'infidels' for over centuries. So these infidels ought to be treated as enemies and hence, God's enemies, and it is thus necessary to carry on jihad against these 'infidels'. Incidentally, one must remember that it is only when Muhammad was persecuted, blamed, his followers driven out of

Mecca and asked to leave their Prophet and his religion, that God or Allah gave permission to fight. The English translation of Surah [22:39] reads, *Permission is granted to those who are being persecuted, since injustice has befallen them, and God is certainly able to support them.*

In Sura [22:40], we find, *They were evicted from their homes unjustly, for no reason other than saying, 'Our Lord is God.'*

According to the Holy book, if it were not for God's support to some people against others, monasteries, churches, synagogues, and masjids—where the name of GOD commemorated frequently—would have been destroyed. But the jihadists fail to make a sober estimation of torture, danger to Islam and humiliation of its followers. This creates confusion among the ranks of common peace loving Muslims.

The HRH Crown Prince and Deputy Premier Abdullah Bin Abdul Aziz, reminded the audience in his keynote address[29] of a verse from Koran, already referred above, "O mankind! We created you from a single (pair) of a male and a female and made you into nations and tribes, that ye may know each other (not that ye may despise (each other). Verily, the most honored of you in the sight of God (he who is) the most righteous of you. And God has full knowledge and is well acquainted (with all things)." [Al-Qur'an 49: 13] What can be a better example of human tolerance and universal brotherhood than this?

Even if we are to accept American atrocities in Iraq and Afghanistan, tacitly admitted even by Obama[30], there remains enough room for doubt regarding the accusation that the US policies are unfriendly and hostile to the followers of Islam, when so many Muslims reside in that land, peacefully. Moreover, does America actually intend to drive away Muslims from either Iraq or Afghanistan? And finally, has the US harboured any such idea or destroyed any religious place of worship for the sake of humiliating another religion. The answer ought to be a big No. This is the missing link that I referred to above. It is well to remember a famous quote from Mao Zhe Dong (Mao Tse Tung) who said, "know thyself and thy enemy". While Koran, as discussed above, had clear guidelines regarding the nature of the enemy, can the same be said about the leaders of radical extremist groups when they brand the US as evil, even though none of the Muslim states seem to think so?

In this connection, it would be interesting to have a look at bin Laden's *Letter to America*, in which he spelt out his views about the Western society and its values. He said, "We call you to be a people of manners, principles, honor, and purity; to reject the immoral acts of fornication, homosexuality, intoxicants, gambling, and trading with interests...You separate religion from politics...."[31] Yet the stark reality is that so many Muslim states interact with America in the sphere of trade, culture, and politics.

On the hand, one has to take into account the genuine grievances and hatred, accumulated over centuries, as a result of the neglect and deprivation of the Muslim population, especially in this part of the world. It would be a folly to deny Laden the credit of internationalising his call for "jihad", thanks to the space allowed him by American policy blunders, especially of the Bush administration. The fact is that both the US and the al Qaeda feel that they have truth and justification on their side and it is this reality that is going to make the War on Terror a protracted one. There are only two possible ways to a resolution of the GWOT— force or negotiations. The all important question remains, at what cost? The day promises to be long and sacrifices many. Given the scale of indoctrination that the children undergo in various Madrassas in the Arab world, and given America's highhandedness in Iraq, any resolution of Islamist terrorist threat hinges on American withdrawal from Iraq and Afghanistan, at least in the short run. As for scale of indoctrination and the need to counter terrorism in the intellectual level, Alexander Yonah said, "I would say, we have to touch the children. In other words, we're late for the next 100 years". He was referring to the education that Palestinian and Arab children receive in schools in Palestine.[32]

Islam or any other civilisation, for that matter, doesn't enjoy the unique advantage that America has— super power status. That means, the US can't be oppressed by any other power and hence it has a 'license' to use force when and wherever it wants. That way, it would be a folly to generalise that Islam as a religion endorses the use of violence and terror without taking this perspective into account.

It is said, 'cometh the hour, cometh the man'. Perhaps, there would have been little occasion for a leader like bin Laden to make his mark in the international political firmament had the earlier US administrations been more pragmatic, a bit tolerant and more understanding about Muslims, and, most importantly, if the US had refrained from bombing innocent Iraqi and Afghan people merely to oust and capture Saddam or Laden? The US still has time to make amends before it is too late. This it should do urgently, otherwise, it would be advantage to the Islamic terrorists and, yes they (the jihadists) can make it if the United States through its indiscretion allows them that room of manoeuvre.

What went wrong with Islam after the Prophet?

According to the Koran, God sent the Prophet to establish 'Justice' on earth. Mohammed did so in his life time by founding Islam and unifying the various warring Arab tribes under a single religious faith, transcending earlier tribal bonds. So, the establishment of the Ummah, a unified community having its identity in common religious faith, offered a model for establishing God's will or justice. Earlier, and by its very nature, the Ummah had to be territory-specific. Later on, under the impact of western scientific and political ideas and developments, coupled with modern day interaction between nation states, the cyber world provides the territorial limits of the Ummah. Internet and various web sites now provide a 'virtual' territory for the consolidation of the Islamic community and faith on a global scale. One offshoot of this development is the spawning of individual leaders who make their own interpretations of Islamic laws. In the absence of a consensus on this subject, individual interpretations, theories, and doctrines are often challenged and replaced by other such doctrines complicating the tasks of the jihadists farther.

What does the concept Justice exactly mean as that concept lies at the core of all Islamic laws and social values? According to Koran, "We sent aforetime our messengers with clear Signs and sent down with them the Book and the Balance, that man stand forth in Justice" (*Al-Hadith 57:25*). This means not only establishment of justice by ending injustice perpetrated by tyrants but also disseminating justice to ensure equality amongst members of the community as per the Divine Law. But who was authorised to interpret the laws, that is, the Sharia, after Mohammad's death? It is on this point that Islam got divided into two sects soon after the Prophet's death. The Sunnis maintained that the successor ought to be chosen from Mohammad's tribesmen and that such a successor would have political and military command but not the Prophet's religious authority, which ought to devolve on a community of scholars, the Ulema. The Shi'ites, on the other hand, felt that the successor should come directly from Muhammad's lineage with all the three authorities, political, military, and religious, vested in the same person.

This failure on the part of Islam to come to a common consensus on such an important issue all but doomed this marvellous religion and triggered off tribal infightings and internal power struggles. The situation worsened further as external enemies like the Huns, the Turks, and the Mongols, unleashed repeated attacks on the declining Arab empire, from which it never recovered. The nadir of this downhill was reached in the nineteenth and the early twentieth century when the 'Muslim community experienced its darkest hour' through political fragmentation, economic deprivation, and subservience to Western colonial rule.[33] The successors of Mohammad, in the latter centuries, got more concerned with the issue of heirs and the riches of the vast empire. Politics got the better of religion.

It is undeniable that Mohammad's successors, other than the four right guided Caliphs, Abu Bakr, Umar, Uthma, and Ali, lacked that magic and authority to galvanise various factions into a powerful and unified community and to further consolidate the empire. Several objective conditions that had helped in the rise of the nomadic Arabs from their oblivion under Mohammad's leadership, no longer existed—a political vacuum following the weakening of both the Persian and the Byzantine empires through repeated wars, a novel kind of fighting technique by the Arabs suited to desert conditions, motivation and incentives the warriors enjoyed through sharing of booties from plunders, and their simple food habit, like eating of desert plants and shrubs that made them less dependent on supply lines.

Instead, the later day Arab rulers degenerated into corruption and luxurious living, like the later Abbassid rulers, as that empire sunk into the overstretch syndrome. Europe as a civilisation, under the banner of

Christianity, was fast emerging to replace the Arab civilization. This meant that the proponents of Islam were required to display dynamism and imagination and avert leadership problems, in order to preserve the unity of Islam, which was crucial to withstand the onslaught of the emerging western civilization. However, that was not to be.

The Prophet, during his reign, used to consult his companions and other members of his group to resolve practical and social issues, thereby, basing the Islamic polity on consensus and democratic principles. His immediate successors and companions, the Islamic Commonwealth, also adhered to the same practice. However, social and political issues grew vastly in size as the memories of initial decades of the Arab empire faded over time. The Prophet's instructions of not questioning the divine law and of basing the Islamic polity on the Sharia, required the later Islamic scholars to formulate a large body of new interpretations of the Sharia, since the latter was not supposed to cover every future issues. For example, while Sharia served as the only reference point in every doubtful circumstance, the Prophet also urged that specific problems must be resolved by later generations of Islamic scholars, taking into consideration the changes in time and situation.

However, later Islamic scholars found themselves rather overwhelmed by the enormity of issues, small or big, confronting them. They focused their attention more on problems at hand and less on the original verses of the Koran. Ziauddin Sardar commented that such a reductionist approach towards problem solving on political and social issues tended to shift the focus away from the 'absolute', 'unchangeable' and 'inviolable' aspects of the law, and rendered the concept of the Islamic polity more relative. This created a peculiar problem for Islam. On the one hand, there was Islam's glorious heritage that acted as a source of tradition, on the other hand, the acceptance of the western materialistic culture and science by many Muslims led the established Islamic clerics and the Ulema to conclude that changes cannot be ignored and that they have also to adapt to modernism.

This is only half the story. There was another undercurrent flowing simultaneously. Some Muslims, not necessarily religious personalities, rather, technical persons, blamed the deviation of the Muslims from the core principles of Koran and the Divine law, as the sole reason for the humiliation of Islam. They pointed to the medieval Sunni scholar Ibn Taymiyya's reasoning that jihad could even be carried out against fellow Muslims, like the Mamluks of Egypt did against the 'apostate' Mongols since the latter permitted some tribal laws to continue alongside the Sharia. The latter day proponents of Salfism used Taymiyya's reasoning as the reference point for reformation, and even purging religion from the deviations of the earlier period (like the relative and subjective interpretations by the medieval Islamic scholars) and, particularly from the baneful influences of the west.

The radical and revolutionary reformists demanded a return back to earlier days of Islam, that is, those of the Prophet and his companions. They reasoned that any deviation from the Islamic core robbed the religion of its spiritual content, so needed for the development of appropriate intellectual capacity to confront the viruses of western civilisation. Usually, radical and revolutionary reforms don't turn backward to the fundamentals of any ideology, but not so with Islam. Readers have to keep this important point in mind in order to have a better understanding Islam. Another goal for these jihadists is to rid the Muslims in the Middle East of the corrupt materialistic and cultural influences of the West by driving away these foreign powers from the Arab heartlands, through use of force. Yet, the crux remains—the issue of disunity within Islam that continues till this day, in one form or other.

Christopher Henzel highlighted one such division while tracing the origin of rifts within the Sunni Islamic movements. He suggested that the US must avail of the schism between the Sunni clerical establishment and the Salafist al Qaeda, in order to marginalise the latter. Incidentally, this policy has yielded some results in the recent 'surge' movement in Iraq. But this may not work in Afghanistan. The Iraqi and Afghan situations differ in respect of socio-cultural and political perspectives. The latter society lacks a definite national identity, being itself guided by tribal kinship rules, while the people of Iraq have long tasted the fruits of modern development. The tribes in Afghanistan are primitive and war-savvy and their terrain offers an ideal landscape for guerrilla warfare. That is why, the Taliban spokesperson, Zabihullah Mujahid, dared to rebuff as 'lunatic', US Secretary of State, Hillary Clinton's offer of an 'honourable form of reconciliation' with those Taliban members who left fighting against the US.[34] However, Henzel cautioned that any hint or idea that the US was creating such divisions within the Sunni ranks merely to destroy and thence to remake the Muslim culture could backfire. Henzel concludes, "At that point the world really would see the clash of civilisations sought by both al Queda and some US pundits".[35]

Yet, disunity within Islam happens to be the main disadvantage for its followers. Bob Waldrep writes that the followers of Islam today speak in different voices and there is no 'able leader who can call Islam into a united holy war'.[36] This argument gains further ground when we see that the Middle East, the spiritual centre of Islam, contains lesser number of Arab Muslims (the ones who volunteer to spread Islam to other parts of the world). Of the 1.2 billion Muslim world population, only 1/8 resides in the Middle East while the ratio of non-Arab to Arab Muslims comes roughly to 2:1. Incidentally, India, Indonesia, Pakistan, and Bangladesh have the largest concentration of Muslim populations.[36] It is here that the US has an edge over the jihadists.

There are two aspects to the discussions in this chapter. When I say that the jihadists have a political agenda instead of a religious one, I mean this in the context of Islam only and one must not view Islamic political concepts through the western eye of secularism, nationalism, democracy, liberalism, and free market mechanism. This is not so. Sharia happens to be the soul of Islam and binds politics inseparably with religion. Moral beliefs and ethics form the political foundations of Islam, in contrast to the western political thought that relies on the free choice of people. The real source of sovereignty in Islam emanates from the will of God through the Sharia.[37] According to the Koran, God, the Lord of Sovereignty, only exalts those whom He pleases and abases those He pleases.[38] The second aspect relates to cleaning and purging Islam and its lands of the harmful influences of the 'infidels' within and without (the apostate Muslim rulers, America and Israel), through jihad. When I suggest that negotiation or compromise is possible, it is within the context of the jihadists' main demand— the US withdrawal from Arabia. This point must be kept in mind since the concept of politics in Islam flows from the almighty alone and is hence based on equity, righteousness, and forbidding of the wrong. That is, it is based on absolute moral and ethical values instead of people's free choice, which it discards as merely relative and hedonist concepts.

Political and strategic reasons behind the rise of Islamist terrorism

Way back in history, rulers used to hire 'terror' groups or even irregular armies, not only to fight external enemies but to quell local rebellions. For example, the Roman army in its latter days incorporated even the Vandals, the Goths, and other warring tribes in the army to maintain internal order and to fight enemies at the fringes of the empire. The Chinese communists made use of the armies of warlords or compromised with them in certain localities during their revolutionary days. However, such ploys often backfire as these 'terrorist' outfits exploit the very powers that had made use of them. The American plight in letting the genie of Islamic fundamentalism out of the bottle during the Soviet-Afghanistan war is fresh in our memories. The United States is now learning it the hard way that it was better to have a rival superpower than to live under constant and unpredictable terror threats by non-state actors, like the jihadist groups.

The tone was set during the days of Soviet occupation in Afghanistan, when at least,three countries, Saudi Arabia, Pakistan, and the United States, with moral and arms support from Iran, China, and Egypt, trained the Mujahideen[39] group, an extremely dedicated fundamentalist conglomerate, to fight the occupying Soviet forces. Lots of money and arms flowed into one of the largest ever US backed covert operation since World War II. According to US officials, in all, the US funnelled more than$ 2 billion in guns and money to the Mujahideen during the 1980s.[40] No wonder such a great 'extravaganza' converted the decade long war into a business entailing so many actors and war materials.

Bin Laden had described such robust war activities in the following lines: "In spite of the Soviet power, we used to move with confidence, and God conferred favours on us so that we transported heavy equipment from the country of Two Holy Places (Arabia), estimated at hundreds of tons altogether that included bulldozers, loaders, dump trucks, and equipment for digging trenches".[41] The Maktab al-Khadamat (MAK) or the Afghan Services Bureau, set up by Laden and Azzam during the course of the Soviet-Afghan war to raise funds and recruit foreign mujahideen, generated sufficient wealth. Azzam wanted to install a pro-Islamic government in Afghanistan after the end of the war.[42] Al Zawahiri, the leader of the Egyptian Islamic

Jihad (EIJ) had other ideas— to use MAK assets to fund a global Jihad and the overthrow of governments in Muslim countries deemed un-Islamic.[43]

With substantial resources— men, arms, and money— at their command, the Mujahideen leaders and fighters might have been looking for another enemy and another theatre of operation. Subsequently, Afghanistan got embroiled in a protracted civil war after the Soviet withdrawal. Bosnia, Chechnya, Tajikistan followed suit, not to speak of Kashmir. One of the chief reasons for this development was that the Mujahideen outfits that had fought against the Soviets simply lost their 'jobs' after that war. In Bosnia, they seemed to have regained their jobs. According to the London based journalist, Brendan O'Neill, "Washington helped to create the gateway between the Middle East and Bosnia, protected the supply of funds to Bosnia by bin Laden and others, and secretly armed a Bosnian army that kept Mujahideen in paid employment (otherwise, knowing as war-mongering), after the Afghan-Soviet war came to an end."[44]

Mujahideen infiltration in Kashmir, at ISI's behest, injected into a hitherto religiously indifferent freedom movement in Kashmir, the virus of sectarianism and fundamentalism, thereby setting the stage for 'jihadi' battles in the subcontinent.[45] It was again strategic considerations that led the United States to support Bosnian Muslims during the 1992 Bosnian crisis. In a 2001 interview, Holbrooke had admitted that Bosnian Muslims "wouldn't have survived" without the help of al Qaeda militants.[46]

During the Afghan civil war, the United States preferred to keep a low profile in respect to the Mujahideen, as the latter had done the bulk of the fighting against the Soviet occupying forces. Moreover, the United States had little time to pay any serious attention to the developments in Afghanistan, as it was faced with the uphill task of managing world affairs single handedly, in the absence of the other super power. In 1996, the Taliban, aided by the Pakistani army, consolidated their grip on a civil war weary Afghanistan. The Taliban restricted all individual freedom in Afghanistan. Bin Laden, after being extradited from Sudan, took refuge in the Taliban dominated Afghanistan, during this period.

Next, the US attack on Iraq in the 1991 Gulf War generated great suspicion and hatred amongst a large section of the Muslim community despite the fact that such an invasion followed Iraq's unlawful occupation of Kuwait. During the Cold War period, both the superpowers carried on 'proxy wars' in the Middle East. But the first Gulf war touched a raw nerve as the inhabitants of the Middle East viewed the American move through an anti-Israel prism. They thought that they now had to face a single military colossus which could make other powers do its bidding. Since the balancing power of the Cold War days was absent, Islamic militants, extremists, and even terrorist groups had no other option than to intensify their surprise and clandestine attacks directed at the superpower's soft belly. These militants comprised militia from various Middle East countries, like Saudi Arabia, Yemen, Egypt, Palestine, etc.

Time and again, Islamic militant groups have forced the mighty United States to withdraw, for example, from Lebanon in 1983 and Somalia in the early 1990s. They kept on increasing the tempo of that pattern. All these were not helped by the repeated and relentless month-long American attacks on Iraqi targets in 1998 or Sudan and Afghanistan, the same year. Muslims were angered and the hard liners grew more determined to carry on their terror attacks on American targets. The US support for the Bosnian Muslims in the Balkan crisis was overshadowed by the formers' Middle East misadventures. Whatever the American policy makers had in mind, right or wrong, the rest of the world, especially, the Muslims living in the Middle East didn't like the American bullying in the Middle East. They thought that they were virtually served with a fait accompli.

Moreover, the inaction or silence of other major powers, including China and Russia, with only occasional venting of displeasure, against the American unilateralist approach, definitely sent a wrong message to the Muslims in that region. These two erstwhile communist giants might have their own perceptions, calculations, tactics and long-term strategies of meeting post Cold War realities. However, Muslims, especially the radicals and the fundamentalists, had no need for such considerations as they got more resolved, and even issued fatwas to carry on terrorist strikes on US targets in various parts of the world. I have already mentioned that the lack of a balancer in international affairs, unlike in the last one hundred years, made radical Muslims fall back on clandestine and subversive activities. The state of unipolarity in international affairs thus has been the strategic reality of the post Cold War era which was responsible for resurrecting Islamist terrorist movements from near oblivion.

Driven by the same geo-strategic compulsion, the United States tried to make the most of its good time, in its capacity as a super power. History has catapulted the United States into a situation that every other great power coveted but failed to hold on— the possession of the extremely strategically important Middle East and its energy reserves. While the United States had succeeded in occupying and installing a government in Iraq that it hoped would ensure regular oil flows from the second largest oil reserve region, this was only short lived, as the post Saddam Iraq soon plunged into unprecedented chaos and anarchy. Suicide bombers and IEDs virtually took hold of the streets of Iraq's main cities. The local 'warlords' saw their chances of fishing in the troubled waters of the Euphrates and the Tigris in order to hold Iraq to ransom. Iraq now remains the most fragile state, ever on the edge of fragmentation, despite the formation of the Shia-led coalition government. The main beneficiary of the war on Iraq has been the al Qaeda who entered the country through various transit points at the borders as early as 2004. Even the former US President Bush, in his various addresses admitted that al Qaeda had a good presence in Iraq.

Once again, due to time constraint (since occupation of Iraq had to be swift, thereby, ensuring an unlimited and smooth oil supply) and geo-political considerations, the Bush administration displayed a sense of paranoia in respect of Iran and North Korea. One of the major blunders that the United States did commit at this point was to issue warnings to North Korea and Iran with 'dire consequences' should they not behave like other law abiding states. This alarmed not only the Muslim community but also other major powers like China, Russia, and the EU. Doubts and suspicions started to creep in the minds of other democratic and secular states. Russia, India, and China declared their intentions to form a strategic alliance to counter American unilateralism. The EU also went out of its way to enter into negotiations with Iran and North Korea, bypassing the United States.

The United States found itself in a situation in which the number of hostile states kept increasing and allies portending to alienate. The emboldened Iraqi 'freedom' fighters or the jihadists, whichever way one may choose to call them, simply increased the tempo of snippings and suicide attacks on American targets. Iraq proved to be another Vietnam for America and, importantly, another safe haven for dreaded Islamist terror groups like, al Qaeda. Neither did Iran lie low, as it had always been the chief source of funding and training of some notorious Shiite Islamic terrorist groups that threatened to rip Iraq apart.

From a seemingly invincible power, the United States has now been reduced to a despondent and shock stricken nation. Mr. Bush's unpopularity touched a new low at home and abroad, and an Iraqi journalist even dared to hurl shoes at him during a press conference in Baghdad. Iran's move was clearly to get America bogged down in Iraq and to divert the American attention from Iran. All the above objective conditions in international politics simply helped in the proliferation of radical Islamist terrorist groups, especially, al Qaeda. Jessica Stern, an NY Times Reporter, in an article in August 2003, observed that the US attack on Iraq had turned a non sponsor state of terrorism to one serving as a focal point for the spread of terrorism to various other parts of the world.

The paradox is that greed and power have corrupted the vision even of the most intelligent and pragmatic leaders of America. The United States had information from the CIA during the 1991 Gulf War that Iraq might sink into anarchy and civil war if Saddam was overthrown. The United States heeded that advice because it was then heading a multinational 'mission' and stopped short of overrunning Baghdad. But it could not resist the temptation to destabilise Iraq by invading that country on false charges, in 2003. The inevitable happened and the United States was made to realise that it was playing with fire. The United States is now looking for an exit strategy in Iraq and Afghanistan and this time at the cost of another Islamic country, Pakistan.

References

Nasr Vali, The Shia Revival, Norton, 2006, pp.121.

[2]Bernard Lewis, 'Islamic Revolution', 21 January 1988.The New York Review of Books, Vol. 34, Number 21&22. Available at http://www.nybooks.com/articles/4557

[3]Walid Phares, 'The Jihadist Movements Dual Nature'. Available at http://www.ifri.org/frontDispatcher/ifri/publications/actuelles_de_1_ifri_1197584475485...5/12/2009

[4]Bruce Hoffman, 'Old Madness, New Methods: Revival of Religious Terrorism Begs for Broader US Policy'. Available at www.rand.org/publications/randreview.

[5]Explaining Religious Terrorism— Part 2: Politics, Religion, and the Suspension of the Ethical, August 3, 2004. Available at www.cdi.org.

[6] ibid., Hoffman.

[7]Jonathan Fine, 'Contrasting Secular and Religious Terrorism', Middle East Quarterly, Winter 2008, http://www.meforum.org/article/1826

[8]Rand Study 'Sharing the Dragon's Teeth: Terrorist Groups and the Exchange of New Technologies, Rand Corporation Monograph Series, prepared for the Departent of Homeland Security, by Kim Cragin, Peter Chalk, Sara A. Daly, Brian A.

[9]ibid,

[10]ibid,

[11]Robert Pape, Dying to Win: The Strategic Logic of Suicide Terrorism, Hardcover,Random House, 2005

[12]ibid, Pape

[13]Abdel Bari Atwan, The Secret History of AL-QA'AIDA, Paperback, ABACUS, 2007, p 108.

[14] (Ibid, Atwan)

[15] Muhammad Asad, The Principles of State and Government in Islam, Islamic Book Trust, Kualalampur, 1980.

[16] Dr. Zakir Naik, Terrorism & Jihad: An Islamic Perspective, IRF.

[17]Edward Gibbon, The Decline and Fall of the Roman Empire, Ch.XXXV.

[18] Trevor Stanley, Definition: Islamism, Islamist, Islamiste, Islamicist, Perspectives on World History and Current Events, July 2005. URL: http://www.pwhce.org/islamism.html Downloaded: 26 June 2009

[19] ibid, 'Globalization and Islam', Conversation with Olivier Roy by Harry Kreisier, January 25, 2007,

p.3, Islam and Ummah', globetrotter.berkeley.edu/people2/Roy/roy-con0.html

[20] Ali R. Abootalebi, Islam, Islamists, and Democracy. Middle East Review of International Affairs, Volume 3, No. 1 - March 1999

[21]ibid,

[22]The new jihadists: hotspots The National Staff, updated 7 March, 2009, UAE

[23]'Hamas Covenant, Avalon Project', Documents in Law History, and Diplomacy. Complete transcript of The Covenant of the Islamic Resistance Movement, dated 18 August 1988. avalon.law.yale.edu/20th_century/hamas.asp 'Hamas Covenant, Avalon Project', Document on Law, Politics and History. GIVE FULL REFERENCE, PUBLISHERS DATE, ETC.

[24]'Jihad: A Battle for peace and Justice', Sultan Shaheen, 23 December1999. Available at http://www.jammu-kashmir.com

[25]Walid Phares, The Jihadist Movements' Dual Nature,Jihadist Movement sWorldwide, http://www.ifri.org/frontDispatcher/ifri/publications/actuelles_de_l_ifri_1197584475485/ publi_P_actuelles_mib_walid_phares_1216047300844

[26]'Analysis and Evolution of the Global Jihadist Movement Propaganda', 2006, Torres, Jordan, and Horsburgh, Terrorism and Political Violence, Routledge, 18:399-421.

[27]Conversations with Olivier Roy (2007), p 5. Available at, http://globetrotter.berkley.edu/ people2/Roy/roy-con5.html

[28]Bernard Lewis, 'Islamic Terrorism?', 1987, in Terrorism: How the West can Win, edited by Benjamin Netanyahu, Farrar, Strauss, Giroux, p.66)

[29]Final Report of the Counter-Terrorism International Conference Riyadh, February 5-8, 2005 ICT/ SUMMARY REPORT/2005 www.ctic.org.sa/CTIC-Final Report(Summary).doc

[30]US President Obama tacitly acknowledged this when, in answer to a question put forth by a journalist, during his maiden Press Conference as the US president in Washington, he remarked that his administration didn't approve torture and humiliations inflicted on other people.

[31]'Islamic terrorism', Wikipedia: the free encyclopedia. Available at http://wikipedia.org/)

[32]Event Transcript: The Evolution of U.S. Counterterrorism Policy, Counterterrorism Blog. Available at http://counterterrorismblog.org/2008/02/event_transcript_the_evolution.php.

[33]Samuel P. Schlorff, 'Muslim Ideology and Christian Apologetics', in Understanding Islamic Terrorism, Bob Waldrep, www.wfial.org/index.cfm?fuseaction=artTerror.article_2

[34]'U.S. Reconciliation offer "lunatic"-Taliban Spokesman', Reuters, 1 April 2009.

[35]Christopher Henzel,Origins of al Qaeda's Ideology: Implications for US Strategy [Long] Parameters, US Army War College Quarterly, Spring 2005, www.freerepublic.com/focus/f-news/1385306/posts.

[36]Bob Waldrep, Understanding Islamic Terrorism, www.wfial.org/index.cfm?fuseaction=artTerror.article_2

[37]Mohammad Asad, The Principles of State And Government In Islam, Islamic Book Trust, Kualampur, papaerback, 1999, p.39

[38]Koran, 3: 26

[39]Mujahideen means one who carries out jihad. Initially they were loosely formed fighting tribal groups in Afghanistan but the term is broadly applied these days to any Muslim in any part of the world carrying on war against the 'infidels'

[40] 'Anatomy of a victory: CIA'a Covert Afghan War', Steve Coll, the Washington Post, 19 July 1992. Available at http://www.globalissues.org/article/258/anatomy-of-victory-cias-covert-afghan-war.

[41]Transcript of Osama bin Laden's interview by Peter Arnett. Available at http://www.anusha.com/osamaint.htm.

[42]Allen Charles, God's Terrorist, 2006, pp. 284-5.

[43]Wright Lawrence, Looming Tower, Knopf, 2006, pp.130

[44]'Brendon O'Neill, Bosnia, Hysteria Politics, and the Roots of International Terrorism', July 30, 2008. Available at antiwar.com.

[45]Ayesha Jalal Partisans of Allah , Jihad in South Asia, Harvard University Press,

[46] ibid, Brendal O'Neill

CHAPTER III

SINEWS AND ARMS: THE LIFEBLOOD OF TERRORIST ORGANISATIONS

Islamist terrorist groups and how they secure funds

Terrorists need funds and arms for sustenance and propagation of their groups and activities. These are their oxygen and life support systems. Some experts even compare terrorist funding with water taps that need to be turned off. In her recent visit to India, just after the 26/11 Mumbai massacre, Dr. Condoleezza Rice, in a press conference, cautioned not to *underestimate* the role of finance in sustaining terrorism. Any discussion on how to stop the flow of funds to terrorists ought to focus on two aspects: (1) locating the various sources of funding, visible or 'invisible', and (2) the earnestness with which the international community wage this 'financial' war against various terrorist groups.

First, it is necessary to briefly identify the various Islamist terrorist organisations and to have a firsthand knowledge of how they secure funds. For the purpose of this book it would suffice to mention only a few major terrorist organisations that are still active one way or the other on a transnational scale. The US State Department has an elaborate list of banned Foreign Terrorist Organisations (FTO) and their activities, enabling it to impose sanctions against various terrorist groups.

It won't be out of place to mention that the PLO, once the mother of all terrorist organisations in the Middle East, used to carry out most of its activities against Israel and its citizens, besides fanning out its activities in other parts of the world, through its associate groups for the first two decades since its inception in the mid 1960s. The PLO no longer indulges in direct terrorist actions in any part of the world, but its surrogates like the Palestine Islamic Jihad (PIJ) and the Popular Front for the Liberation of Palestine (PFLP) still do. Although PLO now operate in their new designation as the Palestine Authority (PA), some of the older bodies of PLO still exist, but only those that are in accord with the 1993 Oslo Agreement.

PLO received, and still receives, financial assistance not only from many of its original patrons, like Egypt, Syria, Iraq, Saudi Arabia, and Kuwait, but also from the United States and Europe. PLO, with an estimated asset of $10 billion, has an annual inflow of $2 billion from 'charitable Islamic donations, OPEC funding, American and European Union aid, extortion, payoffs, illegal arms dealings, drug trafficking, money laundering, and fraud'.[1] According to a 1999 Daily Telegraph Report, PLO has worldwide investments worth $50 billion. As per the PLO records, made public in 1988, Saudi Arabia has donated $855 million over the previous decade while the Kuwaitis have given $2 billion over 26 years. Furthermore, the US Congress apportioned $900 million (not accounted for) to PLO till 2000, in the wake of the Oslo Accord, in order to moderate its activities and to keep it away from the Hamas.[2]

Al Qaeda, like the PLO, has a global reach. They raise their funds through contacts with the drug cartels and illicit traffickers, underworld mafia, smugglers, non-banking channels like 'hawala', legal money transfer channels, exploitation of loopholes in financial systems and poor banking regulations in several other states and regions, individual donors, various charitable organisations, alms, and sponsoring states. According to an October 2002 report by the Center for Defence Information, al Qaeda derived its funds from at least four sources: inheritance and investments of bin Laden, direct funding from Arab supporters of al Qaeda, contributions through Islamic charitable organisations, and criminal activity.[3]

It is difficult to give an exact estimate of bin Laden assets from his inheritance and investments in various bank accounts, open or secret, legal or illegal, in the current atmosphere of strict financial counter measures. With increased vigilance and tighter banking regulations on the part of the international community, the al Qaeda, these days, relies more on 'unconventional' channels. So, it is difficult to gather updated records of

Laden's total assets or to get any idea about his current earnings. Neither is it clear, how much financial assistance al Qaeda and its various affiliates receive from Laden. Nevertheless, the same CDI report puts the figure at $250 to $300 million while the donation from al Qaeda supporters has been estimated to be around $16 million.

The Hamas receives its funding, partly from Iran and partly from the donations of Palestinian expatriates residing in various parts of the world, including the Arab states. Hamas also raises funds in Western Europe and North America. Hezbollah gets financial backing, training facilities, supply of weapons and explosives, as well as political, diplomatic, and organisational support from Iran. Religious donations and proceeds from legal and illegal businesses constitute the group's other sources of finance. Incidentally, Iran also imparts training to the activists of several other terrorist organisations and even supplies them with weapons.[4] Another radical Islamic organisation in South East Asia, Jemaah Islamiya (JI), meaning 'congregation of Islam', which has its root in a radical movement in Indonesia in the 1940s, seeks to establish an Islamic state, incorporating Indonesia, Malaysia, Singapore, Southern Philippines, and Brunei. JI had been banned in 2002 as per the UN 1267 Committee's list of terrorist organisations linked to al Qaeda and Taliban. It was believed to be behind the Bali car bombing in 2002 that resulted in the killing of hundreds of civilians. JI has its own contacts and patrons in the Middle East and in some other non-governmental organisations that provide it the necessary ideological, financial, and logistical support.

The Islamic Union of Uzbekistan (IMU) had its roots in a rebellion by a handful of Muslim youths led by Tohir Yuldeshev and Jumaboi Khojaev. They were members of the Islamic Renaissance Party (IRP). It all started with their demand for a piece of land for the erection of a Mosque that culminated in the formation of the IMU in December 1991. IMU's demands include the formation of an Islamic state, first in Uzbekistan and then a greater one including Central Asian Muslim states. The US intelligence sources believe that it was al Qaeda that has helped formation of the IMU through funding, in order to secure a foothold in Central Asia where Laden had little base.[5] Besides al Qaeda, IMU receives financial support from a large Uzbek Diaspora, Islamic extremist groups, and patrons in the Middle

East, Central Asia, South Asia, and Saudi Arabia, including some sources close to Prince Turki-al-Faisal, the head of Saudi Intelligence. According to Pakistani intelligence sources, IMU might have supplied fissile material needed to manufacture improvised nuclear devices, to al Qaeda.[6]

Harkat Ul-Mujahedin (HUM), another dreaded Islamic militant group based in Pakistan, is funded by donations raised from wealthy and grassroot donors in Pakistan, Kashmir, Saudi Arabia, and other Gulf states, besides soliciting donations through magazine ads and pamphlets. Two other Islamic militant organisations that have been in operation for quite some time are the Jaish-e-Mohammed (JeM) and the Lashkar-e-Toiba (LeT). Both these organisations have al Qaeda links but they operate from Pakistan and carry out attacks on India. Harkat-ul-jihad-al-Islami (HuJI) happens to be another militant organisation that seeks to 'free' Kashmir from India's hold. All these three organisations have common sources of funding, mainly Pakistan, and are also believed to receive financial aid from al Qaeda.

Al-jihad (AJ), an organisation responsible for the assassination of the former Egyptian President Anwar Sadat in 1981, happens to be another dreaded Egyptian extremist group whose goal is to establish an Islamic state in Egypt. AJ is under the banned list of the UN and many states, including Russia. AJ gets its funds from al Qaeda with whom it has merged in 2001. AJ also raises funds from Islamic non-governmental organisations and through criminal activities.

The list may go on endlessly but it would suffice to say that the sources of finance are mostly common and this makes the task of choking the supply line of terrorist funding easier.

Why the terrorists need funds?

It is not difficult see that terrorist funding, like in the case of every other group, have to be divided and allocated into various parts. First, a substantial portion of the 'booty' has to be kept for the maintenance and luxurious upkeep of the leaders, at home and abroad, evident from their properties and life-styles. The terrorist leadership has to maintain a 'safe' distance from and pay 'infrequent' visits to the lower tier members in order to keep a high profile image as well as to escape getting identified. Interestingly, a highly placed Pakistani government spokesperson revealed before the media that Mohammed Masood Azhar, the founder of Jaish-e-Mohammad and implicated in the 26/11 Mumbai incident, was apprehended and kept interned in his own luxurious and multi-storied house in Karachi! Although this report was later denied, what remained unchallenged was the possession of a very luxurious and multi-storied building in Pakistan by a terrorist leader.

One of the reasons why some of the lower level terrorist activists feel motivated to carry on terror campaigns, is that they know that, like, their leaders, they too can enter the heaven here, in this land of the living, someday. Of course, it must be remembered that not all lower level activists can attain that status because they are supposed to sacrifice their lives for a cause. Recently, the Sri Lankan army has discovered a fully air conditioned bunker in which the LTTE supremo Prabhakaran used to stay during the Sri Lankan army offensive against the LTTE in the occupied areas. However, it would be a folly to put all the terrorist leaders in the same bracket. There are always exceptions. For example, bin Laden himself leads a very austere and nomadic life in the jungles and caves in uninhabitable mountainous regions in the Afghan border.[7] There may also be other top al Qaeda leaders who lead humble life styles, but they are not many in numbers. According to the Indian national news channel, Hurriyat leaders had luxurious life styles prior to their recent set back over the Kashmir election issue. These Hurriyat leaders are now running short of funds from their patrons, far and near, and are going through hard times due to the recent global recession. Their offices remain empty these days and their life styles have become far more moderate.

Another portion of terrorist funds has to be earmarked towards bearing the costs of actual operations. This operational phase has several stages (the captured terrorist in the Mumbai mayhem has given detailed information about this) leading to the ultimate terror strike, from recruitment, training, arming, ammunitions, and maintenance-clothes and costumes, to other necessaries like dry foods, tooth paste and brushes, mobile phones, rucksacks, etc. Next, this core group has to be familiarised with logistics, detailed knowledge of the exact location of their intended targets, possible routes, how to get into appropriate positions, one after the other, at important points (for which they have to bribe local accomplices) so that one miss doesn't spoil the year long preparations.

Lastly, the remaining portion has to be kept for the upkeep of family members of the terrorists who get killed or captured during operations, and other propaganda purposes like TV ads, distribution of flags, and banners among the primary members, supporters and sympathisers. The quantum and duration of assistance for the family members of slain terrorists may vary, although most of these terrorists are either disowned by their families, or they happen to be orphans or have little family attachments.

Although bin Laden's al Qaeda abhors the capitalist system based on 'usury', ironically, it is the radical Islamist terrorist groups that are now absorbing the vices of the capitalist financial system based on profit and interest, as they now tend to interact with other underground and illegal organisations in their bid to procure arms and funds. Conversely, terrorist exploits of the loopholes in the conventional banking and financial sector definitely highlight the limitations of the capitalist system.

Modern capitalist financial system is still insufficiently equipped to cover the loopholes in many parts of the developing and the underdeveloped world, which have weak financial and political infrastructures. To be more specific, the United States, in the post Second World War era, created an international financial architecture to benefit its business and military interests, primarily in those regions where well developed financial and infrastructural facilities already existed. Of course, it sought to create both these facilities in many erstwhile third world countries, through its surrogates, the IMF and the World Bank, towards the closing decades of the Cold War. Nevertheless, the United States still needs more time to modernise the vastly untapped regions in many other parts of the world that are supposed to serve as potential markets for American business barons. Underworld financial activities, of which the terrorist groups are the latest additions, have exposed, intentionally or unintentionally, the loopholes in the US led global financial order, by activating 'Trojan' horses' or hidden demons, like unaccounted channels of financial transactions, money laundering, etc. *In a word, it would not be easy to disown the charges against the evils of the US led capitalist liberal financial order, once the prime target of the communists, and now exploited by Islamist terror groups, like al Qaeda.* One such example is drug trafficking which acts as reliable anchor for money laundering activities.

Drug Trafficking and terrorist funding

The terrorist groups collect funds from various legal and illegal activities like drug trafficking, video pirating, internet hacking, collections from various travel agencies and cell phone distributors, businessmen, groups or individuals.[8] These are among some of the alternative financing mechanisms to earn, move, and store assets as the space for use of formal banking and conventional financial systems gets continually narrowed because of stringent counter financial measures by the international community.

As far back as November 2003, the US Government Accountability Office (GAO) submitted a report to Congressional requesters seeking the nature and extent of terrorists' use of alternative financing mechanisms in respect of earning, moving, and storing of terrorist assets and about the challenges that the US would face in countering such alternative finance mechanisms. The GAO found that terrorists earned assets through selling contraband cigarettes and illicit drugs and through misuse of charitable organisations that collect large donations. They use both these as means of earning and moving of funds through informal banking systems, like hawala. Terrorists also make use of commodities like precious stones and metals to move and store their assets.[9]

Thanks to some effective financial countermeasures by the United States and the international community, referred above, jihadist groups, like al Qaeda, have fallen back on a more resourceful and lucrative source of earning, drug trafficking, from production to distribution. Although the massive American bombings of Afghanistan in the initial months of the War on Terror were supposed to burn away all poppy fields and render the soil barren, recent spurt in the smuggling of opium, hashish, etc., from Afghanistan to various Central Asian and other routes, highlights that the revenues accrued from the sale of drugs form an important source of funding terror campaigns. The highly remunerative nature of the drug trade, supported by a stable and ever increasing demand on a global scale and the existence of an already well established distribution networks, have made it an important source of terrorist funding in recent years. The mountainous peripheries of the Golden Crescent comprising Pakistan, Afghanistan, and Iran provide a safe haven for the production and distribution of opium. Recently, the US diplomat in charge of South and Central Asia, Patrick Moon, held talks with the Iranian Deputy Foreign Minister, Mehdi Akhundzadeh, at the Russian initiative, in Moscow, since the drug traders find it lucrative to use Iranian trade routes. Even Akhundzadeh told delegates that narcotics posed a 'serious threat' to Iran and the problem could not be solved by a single country. He reported that Iran seizes three tons of opium on its borders every day.[10]

Although it is the end use that separates the drug cartels from those of the Islamist terrorist organisations, there is enough possibility of the one 'vitiating' the other. This also happens to be one vulnerable area for the Islamist terrorists. CIA has notorious records, especially, in Latin America, in ruining the image of progressive governments during the cold war era. No other agency has any better information and data bank regarding these drug traffickers than the CIA. It would be difficult for the jihadist groups to prevent criminalization of terrorism as the terrorists interact more and more with drug cartels. Drugs are dangerous things and it is a potent weapon to undo any organization or even a country's social fabric, for example, the opium trade in China, in the mid-nineteenth century. A more recent example had been the demoralizing effect of opium and other drugs on the Soviet army as the soldiers came into contact with the captives and thence with the drug agents.

Religious terrorist groups, these days, have developed an increasing preference for combining smuggling and drug trafficking with terrorist activities, for example, the IMU (Islamic Movement of Uzbekistan). Initially the IMU had a purely political ideological agenda, but in view of recent financial restrictions, IMU had to look elsewhere, viz., drug trafficking. This terrorist-drug mafia-smuggler chain now covers most contemporary terrorist groups from the 'leftist guerrillas to the right wing extremists, and from the secular nationalist group (like the Kurdistan's Workers' Party or the Basque ETA) to Islamist organisations such as the Hezbollah and the IMU'.[11] The author herself admits in pointing out that besides the usual sources of funding, the Islamic groups (although she calls it exception) take advantage of the geography (proximity to and along the long borderline of the poppy fields) and weak legal infrastructure of some state borders to resort to drug trafficking.[12] According to Stepanova these groups were initially ethno-political in nature but later became Islamized and are also to be found in areas once dominated by moderate Islam and in the Balkans and North Caucasus. However, she feels that repressive government measures and civil wars may also be responsible for this change, for example, to a new hybrid type of criminal Islamist group. Mr. Michael Kirk also believed that due to increased activities of the Drug Enforcement Administration (DEA), the terrorists and the drug cartels have shown trends towards forming a hybrid organization: part terrorist, part drug cartels. The terrorists also raise taxes from drug traders in lieu of guaranteeing the security of drug laboratories and airstrips. The bottomline is that it is not so much ideology or religion but materialistic compulsions that could well shape the future of even the jihadist movements.

Such interactions also occur in other regions and between two terrorist groups with different objectives: religious and secular political types. Such a swap between religious and secular objectives could even be found in the case of a single terrorist group, in two different periods. For example, the Islamic militants believed to be fighting in Kashmir for their independent political rights, in the 1980s, had purely secular political objectives till the infiltration of Wahhabist elements from Saudi Arabia transformed that movement into a more radical and religious one. Thereafter, once again, politicisation of religious terrorism took place as the ISI and the Pakistan army regulated the movement to their advantages in the mid 1990s. So, it is difficult to see how terrorist groups, having no independent and fixed base of operation and while being pursued by the international community, could hold on to their original ideologies for long.

According to the 2005 United Nations World Drug Report, the total value of illicit drugs produced in the year 2003 was estimated at US $13 billion. The respective figures for wholesale and retail sales, including the values for the amount of seizures, had been put at US $94 billion and US $322-$400 billion respectively. Heroins yield some 8 to 10 times higher revenue than those yielded by the same quantity of cocaine. As far back as 2004, Mark Steven Kirk, Illinois Republican, told in an interview that al Qaeda was reaping $28 million a year from sale of heroins.[13]

According to a recent UN estimate, international drug trade yields $322 billion per year. The Drug Enforcement Administration has linked 19 of the 43 designated terrorist organisations for engaging in illicit global drug trade and 60 per cent of terrorist organisations with illegal narcotics trade.[14] Despite seizures and restrictions, there has been no fall in the drug trade volumes. What is most alarming is that this growing nexus between terrorist organisations and various drug cartels, smugglers, illicit traffickers, etc. enables the terrorist groups to conduct their operations in such a stealthy manner that it becomes increasingly difficult for the authorities to identify the exact nature of transactions made by the terrorist groups. Thus the need for stringent financial countermeasures is urgently called for to cut this vital taproot of terrorist funding.

In this connection, it is worth mentioning that the United States happens to be the largest consumer of drugs. President Bush specifically mentioned this in his post 9/11 speech when he appealed to the Americans to relinquish drugs in order to deny the drug traffickers an important source of revenue that made its way into the terrorist hands. Lamond Tullis had shown that the US consumer expenditures in the late 1980s varied from $100 billion to $300 billion, and it ranked second only to weapons trading in terms of cash volume. There is not much reason to assume that the statistics would speak differently in the recent years.

Readers would remember how some of the terror groups like the IRA had private transport monopoly in Belfast, and of PLO's share of the Hashish and Cannabis trade in the Bekaa valley. The Scotland Yard detectives had a crack down on IRA-PLO money laundering operations around the early 1990s. European police uncovered a 300,000,000 pounds' worth of these forbidden drugs transported from Lebanon in two freighters chartered by the PLO.[15]

Two associates of Laden, Yousef Nada and Idris Nasreddin, used to run joint trade empires in the decade of the 1990s, in various fields ranging from real estate to fishery worth crores of dollars, spread over Europe and Africa.[16] The yearly turnover of businesses of the terrorist-criminal-illegal activists, taken together, in the first five years of the first decade of the new millennium, was estimated to be something around $1.5 trillion. Interestingly, such sums often spill into the western financial institutions through money laundering operations and keeps the liquidity flowing into the economies of the US and Europe![17] Loretta Napoleoni revealed another startling fact that even the US government's effort to stake its claim in the business of terrorism through a 20 months online futures market speculation project on assassinations, coup and acts of terrorism, had to be abandoned because of pressure from the US Congress and the Senate. This is all what goes on in the name of war on terror: commercialization of terrorism!

Problems with the Charities

Charitable organisations belong to a gray area since much of the funds raised by these organisations, especially, the Islamic ones, for humanitarian purposes find their ways into terrorist channels. That is why GAO in its above report emphasized the non transparent nature of these charitable organisations. Many of these organisations are based in the United States. Daya Gamage of the Asian Tribune, in a July 2007 report, mentioned insufficient progress made by the Interior Revenue Service of the Treasury Department in respect of tax exempt charitable organisations having possible links to foreign terrorist organisations. Gomez further felt that such organisations might also play a crucial role in helping terrorist organisations not only to carry out their attacks through financial support but they might also be used to provide logistical support to the terrorists in carrying out international operations.[18] The Treasury Department Reported that a staggering 1.6 millions of tax exempt organisations in the US alone (excluding churches) with $2.4 trillion in assets and $1.2 trillion in annual revenues, exist in the United States.[19]

If this happens to be the case with the United States, the plight of other countries can be well imagined. Many Islamic countries, for example, those belonging to the Gulf Cooperation Council, have little urge or interest to expose clandestine financial transactions between the radical Islamic terrorist organisations and the wealthy businessmen in the region. For example, despite repeated complaints by the United States about the workings of the UN designated Islamic International Relief Organization (IIRO), the latter still has many branches in several countries. IIRO had long been accused for its alleged support of six al Qaeda training camps in Afghanistan implicated in the 1998 bombings of US Embassies in Kenya and

Tanzania. The US intelligence agencies have strong evidence that another charitable organization, the Blessed Relief, help finance the al Qaeda. The operations of the Haramain Charitable organization having branches in many countries and serving as the ideological bulwark of the jihadists (through opening of schools etc) are too well known. Most of these Muslim charitable organisations have Saudi officials in the influential positions. So it requires tremendous clout and evidence to get them identified and designated.

One reason on the part of these Islamic countries' reluctance to nab the officials or take appropriate actions against these charitable organisations diverting funds to terrorist groups, especially, al Qaeda, is that these charitable organisations perform social and development works for the Muslim community, at home and abroad. Since charity forms a key component of Islamic society, it is extremely difficult to separate and distinguish between the workings of genuine and fake organisations. There are even instances when the donors may not be aware of the diversion of funds to terrorist groups. However, it could turn out to be a grave issue if the average Muslim makes it obligatory on their part to help in the process of microfinancing the charitable organisations, irrespective of their affiliations. Recently Professors Toga Kokar and Carlos Yordan of the Drew University have tried to explore the reason behind average Muslim supporting such kinds of financing. The Paper entitled, "Microfinancing Terrorism: a Study in al Qaeda Financing Strategy", published by the Social Science research Network concludes that despite other sources of funds, al Qaeda relies heavily on such charities since "individual donations are a key source of financing because it is a steady flow of funds."[20] According to this paper, it is rather the social pressure that leads the average Muslim to help finance the cause of terrorism. Religion and religious practices are central to every Muslim. Common Muslims may thus suffer from a guilt feeling that while they can't actively take part in jihad, they may do so, indirectly. It is here that al Qaeda has been largely successful in mobilizing public opinion in its favour.

As already stated, charitable organisations happen to be the second largest source of financing jihadist groups. No country can put a lid or even restrain the activities of organisations, such as the Arab League or the International

Islamic Relief Organization or those charitable organisations that continue under the guise of 'dawa'. To complicate the issue, ready replacements are always forthcoming once some organisations gets identified and banned, thereby, keeping the FBI and the other American investigative agencies on a state of permanent alert. One top American expert in the field of terrorist financing admitted that although constant tracking and subsequent blocking of the activities of many such charitable organisations had yielded encouraging results in stopping the flow of money into the hands of various terrorist groups, the terrorists are still ahead of the investigative agencies in adopting newer tactics to raise funds. Senator Charles E. Grassley of Iowa remarked, "We are simply not prepared right now to keep up with them and put them out of business once and for all."[21] This is extremely worrying. If the established financial experts and institutions fail to track the available and potentially new sources of terrorist finances, then it is not hard to imagine that these terrorist organisations must be making use of or hiring 'ex-experts' belonging to traditional financial institutions. Moreover, it's a near shame that a clandestine group or groups, mostly mobile, can garner such expertise and resources that their traditional and more established counterparts can't.

US counter terrorism financial measures, success, and problems

After the 9/11 incident, the US woke up to the reality of the dangers posed by the jihadists, spearheaded by the al Qaeda. It has since employed stricter countermeasures to combat terrorist funding, which have yielded significant results. For example, roughly $121 million worth of terrorist assets were frozen on a global scale in the year following 9/11, more precisely, November-December 2002. The first three months alone, that is, the last quarter of 2001, accounted for more than 80 per cent of this, while in the next eleven months, less than 20 per cent of that amount was seized. "Of the total $121 million blocked worldwide, more than 75% reportedly has been linked to the Taliban and al Qaeda and the rest to other terrorist entities."[22] However, the success from such financial counter measures pertained to a few countries including the United States.

Since 9/11, the Treasury Department had publicly designated 500 individuals and entities as terrorists with al Qaeda connections, in some form or other. Numerous individuals and entities have been prosecuted by the Justice Department under the 'material support' statute for aiding various terrorist groups.[23] Asset freezing has taken place in other countries, too. The action plan framed by the G7 Finance Ministers soon after 9/11 stressed the commitment of their respective countries to abide by the various UN resolutions, establish financial intelligence units, and get financial supervisors and regulators to ensure that the terrorists don't make inroads into the private sector. Notable was the action plan issued in 2001 by the G20 Finance Ministers to "deny terrorists and their associates access to, or use of, their financial systems, and to stop abuse of informal banking networks".[24] The efforts of the United Nations, (Resolutions 1267 and 1273) and those of Financial Action Task Force (FATF) have lent further credence to the international drive to choke the financial pipelines of various terrorist organisations.

However, the tempo of such anti-terrorist financial campaigns that had started with great gusto in the initial months after 9/11, slowed down in subsequent years. Obviously, when the countermeasures (most of which existed much prior to 9/11) were enforced strictly after 9/11 in order to plug the loopholes in the existing rules regarding illegal financial transactions, including money laundering, drug trafficking, narcotics, smuggling, freezing of terrorist assets, criminalising etc., there was still some room for seizing and blocking a number of such transactions that had escaped the net, earlier. Thereafter, the addition of the 'terrorism' factor into ordinary criminal financial conducts and calculations called for fool proof countermeasures. Once some of these counter measures were in full operation, the flow of funds from usual channels for various terrorist organisations dried up substantially. As a result, there set in a general slackness in counter terrorism activities in respect of terrorist funding. The second reason for this slackness is that the terrorists, by then, resorted to newer ways to keep their supplies flowing.

However, there are still problems with enforcing stricter counter financial measures on a trans-national scale because of the differences in perceptions between the US and other countries. Even the EU countries don't entirely concur with the US on the issue of terrorism and terrorist financing since they have their own priorities and interests. Dr. Rachel Ehrenfeld remarked that many EU states didn't even feel the need to prohibit the various Europe-based subsidiaries of Hamas operating as its front organisations (already shut off in the USA) from sending funds to the West Bank and Gaza. Her new book, *Funding Evil: How Terrorism is Financed and How To Stop It*, threw some light on many of the unlawful and clandestine ways by which these terrorist organisations raised funds. However, Ehrenfeld's proposals to stop these avenues of clandestine financing suffer from one limitation: the United States can request but it can't force other countries to take up the issue of stopping such funding with the same determination and zeal that it does. For example, Saudi Arabia spent $87 billion in the last decade for spreading Wahhabism and it is still the weakest link in the chain of countering terrorist finances.[25] On top of it, many counter terrorist campaigns and undertakings overlap and more often cut both ways, as will be discussed below. Eradicating terrorism or even reining it may thus prove to be a Herculean job. There are wheels within wheels and this leads us to some important findings.

Following the famous law of economics that money changes hands, it is virtually impossible for the United States to fully block all the financial routes leading to terrorist funding. Added to this is the fact that every group or organisation has *some support base*. Secondly, as mentioned above, domestic, social, religious, and geo-political interests of individual nations vary. Take the case of the Sri Lankan Tamil Tigers, the Liberation Tigers of Tamil Eelam (LTTE) that resorted to violence to attain their sole objective—an independent state for the Tamils living there. The Sri Lankan government may not like (as I write this, the SL army has succeeded in eliminating the LTTE from its soil) this but the LTTE, reportedly, had its supporters in India, especially, in Tamil Nadu, who have, for long, provided moral, financial, and political support to the organisation. Likewise, the Islamist terrorists may seem abominable to the United States, but many Islamic states in the Middle East and many Muslims across the world empathise with the al Qaeda and other radical Islamist terrorist groups.

The United States has, time and again, encountered such uncomfortable situations whenever it tried to impose economic sanctions on other countries that it felt, had violated certain norms in international relations. However, in most cases these sanctions have proved counterproductive because other countries didn't feel the same way and there was opposition within the US on this issue.

Another problem area is the lack of proper administration in conflict prone areas to guarantee that the relief aid offered by various agencies *reach* their intended targets. Many relief agencies working in Afghanistan or Iraq, or even in the conflict prone regions of the sub-Saharan Africa, the Balkans, or the Middle East, find that the funds meant for humanitarian purposes are being pocketed by various warring factions, militant ethnic groups as well as terrorist organisations. Many a times they are even forced to donate large sums to these organisations. For example, the United Nations Relief Works Agency (UNRWA), the organisation that oversees and facilitates aid to Palestinians, gave away $521.7 million to the PLO authorities to alleviate the plight of the average Palestinian. Most of that money slipped back into the pockets of the leaders and their terrorist associates.[26] According to the same source, the UNRWA is staffed by so many Hamas members that it is nicknamed the "Hamas Union". How frustrating it must have been for the United States to discover that the Palestine Authority (PA) chief, Yasser Arafat, had prior knowledge that some members of the banned Al-Aksa-Martyrs Brigades had their names on the payroll of the PA. Classified sections of US Congress September 11 report alleged a 'web of connections among Saudi businessmen, the royal family, charities and banks that may have aided al-Qaeda or the suicide hijackers'.[27] Not long ago, Mr. Stuart A. Levey, a Treasury Undersecretary, told a Senate Committee, "Saudi Arabia today remains the location where money is going to terrorism, to Sunni terror groups, and to the Taliban than any other place in the world."[28]

The American counter terrorism efforts in regard to terrorist financing have three aspects: (1) implementation and enforcement of stricter domestic financial legislations; (2) removing the hindrances in the way of implementing these rules, that is, disagreement among various investigative and law enforcing agencies of the government, and (3) dependence on other countries, that is, the sincerity and seriousness with which other nations and other organisations, like, the United Nations, the IMF, the World Bank etc., frame and amend their laws to suit counter terrorist financing.

As referred above, the US efforts, domestic as well as international, to counter terrorist funding in the wake of 9/11, were focused mainly on tracking and freezing the assets of terrorists. Significant gains were made in this regard immediately after 9/11. Immediately after 9/11, the former Secretary of Treasury, Paul O'Neill said that the administration sought to starve the terrorists of funding and close down the institutions that supported or facilitated terrorism.[29] However, a year later, the CDI Primer on terrorist finances concluded that despite the identification of over 240 terrorists and freezing assets worth $112 million belonging to terrorists, "the efforts of hundreds of top financial investigators and the resources of the world's financial and law enforcement institutions have seemingly come to naught." The Report observed that the "range of financial resources" at the disposal of the terrorist groups, and the "array of the means they use to channel and meld these resources" were the areas where the counter financial measures failed in arresting the flow of terrorist finances.

Thomas Kean, the Chairman of the 9/11 Commission felt that although a lot of energy of the government had been spent on drying up the sources of terrorist funding, it lagged far behind in following the money. Many other experts in the area of terrorist financing have made the same observations. Dr. Rachel Ehrenfeld, Director of the American Center for Democracy & the New York City Center for the Study of Corruption and rule of the Law (CSC), New York, USA, also pointed to the need to follow this money trail of the terrorists when she remarked, "...to confront global terrorism, especially Radical Muslim Organisations, we need to cut off their money. Thus we must also fight their support systems: criminal organisations, money launderers, and illegal drug producers and traffickers."[30] Former President Bush admitted, "al-Queda continues to adapt in the face of our global campaign against them." Lauretta Napoleoni writes "terrorist financing mutates continuously," which generally keeps terrorists a step ahead of the authorities.[31]

The US government passed the Bank Secrecy Act (BSA) in 1970 to combat the threat of money laundering—legitimizing 'dirty' money earned through various illegal activities by diverting them into conventional channels of regular financial institutions (another way of making black money white). According to this Act, domestic financial institutions have a great responsibility to collect information on each financial transaction in excess of $10,000 limit set by the Secretary of Treasury (in the case of suspicious activities the limit is $5,000), keep a record and pass on information to federal officials, as per the Currency and Foreign Transaction Reporting Act (CFTRA). CFTRA requirements also extend to transactions involving foreign financial agencies and to exporters and importers where the monetary instruments exceed $10,000. The BSA was subsequently amended to include criminal and terrorist activities. In 2001, Congress brought terrorist financing, even if they are legally derived funds, under the purview of the BSA.

The US Congress had long tightened its legal noose round money laundering activities with the passage of the Money Laundering Control Act in 1986. That Act aimed at declaring three types of money laundering illegal: domestic, international, and attempted money laundering, as part of an undercover 'sting operation'. To top it up, the Congress, in 1992, passed the Annunzio-Wylie Anti-Money Laundering Act that sought to counter violations of anti money laundering laws by the depository institutions through higher penalties, and more significantly, empowering the Office of the Comptroller of Currency (OCC) to revoke the Charter of National banks, should they be charged with money laundering offences.

Already, with the enactment of the International Emergency Economic Powers Act (IEEPA) in 1977, the US president had assumed broad powers to seize foreign assets, prohibit any transactions in foreign exchange and payments between financial institutions involving foreign currency and the import and export of foreign currency. This Act, as per the Executive Order 13224, allowed the president to authorise the Department of Treasury to designate individuals and entities as terrorist financiers, thereby, keeping the latter out of the US financial system. IEEPA can be construed as an extension of the 1917 Trading with the Enemy Act that authorizes the US president to declare national emergency.[32]

The Uniting and Strengthening of America by Providing Appropriate Tools Required to Intercept and Obstruct Terrorism Act (the USA PATRIOT Act), passed in the wake of 9/11, serves several purposes: combating financing of terrorism (CFT) and its emphasis on anti-money laundering, expanding the horizon of law enforcement, emphasis on financial information sharing and facilitating terrorist investigations abroad. Banks belonging to other countries having corresponding banking accounts or doing business with the US banks, are required to upgrade their AML/CFT process. At about the same time, a multi-agency task force, the Green Quest, was set up for the purpose of countering terrorist funding. It has a comprehensive checklist that reminds one of the days of licenses and control, a few decades back. However, the complex issue of ensuring safeguards against small groups or individuals who support terror campaigns out of their earnings continues to torment American financial experts. This will require stricter domestic legislation that might infringe on civil liberties.

Another area of concern is that terrorist groups often resort to electronic money transfer facilities and commodity trading in diamond, gold, etc. The Dubai based Multi Commodities Centre (DMCC) and the Commodity Futures Trading Commission (CFTC) had already issued alert notices in respect of the latter type of transactions. Post 9/11, futures trading in the United States has either been proscribed or severely restricted. As mentioned earlier, besides trading in commodities (illicit drugs and counterfeit goods), terrorist organisations make use of the remittance system involving bulk cash, charities, and informal banking systems for the management and movement of their assets.[33]

Peter Brookes highlighted al Qaeda's increasing reliance on commodity trading in gold, gems—including diamond trading from various conflict zones in Africa— weapons, and drugs, to earn and move money.[34] Besides, he provides some important information on the working of some Islamic charitable organisations, like the al Taqwa, a large financial outfit that operates in the Middle East, Europe, and the Caribbean and has funnelled tens of thousands of dollars to al Qaeda, Hamas, and other terror groups through various other Muslim charities. Another big Muslim charitable organisation, happens to be al Haramain Islamic Foundation, which operates by constantly changing names, sometimes at different places within a single country.[35]

As early as 2004, The Council on Foreign Relations Task Force had proposed several measures to combat terrorist funding. Its recommendations included the need to establish an international organisation to combat the financing of terrorism, blocking donations to charities suspected of aiding terrorists, tackling money laundering, and arresting the trade in gems and metals.[36] Other recommendations included expanding the budget for the

Treasury Department's Office of Technical Assistance in order to provide better training and expertise to foreign governments to enable them to implement and update regulatory and enforcement measures, both in respect of financial institutions and charitable organisations. Another important recommendation was to strengthen intelligence agencies with proper "linguistic, financial, and cultural expertise to investigate and combat Islamic terrorist financing effectively." The task force emphasised the need to implement background investigations on institutions, corporations, and non-governmental organisations receiving US government grants, in order to ensure that money is not diverted into terrorist hands, and to tie the IMF assistance to individual nations' success in implementing strict anti-terrorist financing laws.

However, despite the US government's continued effort to narrow the space for terrorists in respect of raising funds, not much headway could be made in this direction because of the alternative remittance systems that terrorists make use of. On top of it, the age old problem of red-tape and lack of coordination between different branches and agencies pose real hindrances for successful implementation of financial counter measures. Another problem area highlighted by Lee Hamilton in his testimony before the Senate GAC, is the lack of transparency in respect of resource allocation for these agencies. Hamilton also stressed the need for greater Congressional oversight in assessing the performance of the Executive in countering terrorist financing.[37]

The problem of regulating alternative remittance practices is like separating a needle from a haystack. Terrorists take advantage of the political and cultural sensitivities attached to such types of remittances. For example, charitable organisations serve as mediums of fund raising for social and development purposes. They carry a lot of community sentiments. Moreover, terrorists find it more convenient to divert funds through such channels because a large part of this sector is unaccounted for and many of them cater to the needs of the immigrant community. It is not easy to close any charitable organisation, yet, something needs to be done to keep terrorists from using them. Limiting terrorist financing becomes all the more difficult if there are too many considerations, like safeguarding rights enshrined in the American Constitution and other democratic values, continuing with a lenient immigration policy, ensuring that usual transaction procedures like remittances and other regular banking habits don't suffer because of a few, maintaining ethnic and community harmony, sticking to the arduous job of separating extremist, fundamentalist, and terrorist factions from moderate ones, and above all securing international consensus on the implementation of financial counter measures.

Any discussion in countering terror financing would be incomplete without reference to international efforts. Since such funding and its various taproots cannot be cut without active help from other countries, the United States has worked through both the United Nations and other multilateral and bilateral bodies to enable and promote international standards and protocols. The job of designating bin Laden, al Qaeda and members of Taliban has been entrusted to the UN 1267 Committee, that requires all UN member states to freeze assets of the designated entities, as soon as these are posted on the UN web site.

Another multilateral body, not based in the United States, is the Financial Action Task Force (FATF) that looks after and formulates anti money laundering policies. On 31 October 2001, FATF had made eight recommendations—ratification of the UN International Convention for the Suppression of the Financing of Terrorism and implementation of relevant UN Resolutions in this regard, criminalising terrorist acts and funding, freezing and confiscating terrorist assets, requiring financial institutions to report suspicious transactions linked to terrorism, imposition of anti money laundering requirements on alternative remittance systems, and ensuring that non profit organisations are not be misused for financing terrorism. In 2002, the FATF Working Group on Terrorist Financing, in collaboration with multilateral bodies like the UN, the IMF, and the World Bank, has already identified a number of countries that would receive technical assistance in order to enable them to comply with its above recommendations.

Procurement of Arms

Like funding, the jobs of procuring and ensuring uninterrupted arms supplies happen to be equally important for every terrorist organisation, big or small. In the absence of regular arms supplies, terrorists get despondent and demoralised like a fish out of water situation. The fire and spirit, fervour and zeal, light and heat, so necessary to maintain a group's unity tend to evaporate fast. Fear of insecurity begins to creep in. The risk of being apprehended increase exponentially. Differences of opinion arise within the ranks of various terrorist groups and with it the possibility of a split. Thus, counter terrorist policies primarily aim at putting an end to terrorist activities, global, regional, or domestic, chiefly by choking the two life support systems: finance and the flow of arms. Other benefits from counter terrorism policies follow, as a matter of course. Incidentally, one of the chief reasons for the demise of the LTTE was the significant drying up of its funds and arms supplies following the adoption of strict counter terrorism financial measures by the international community. The issue is simple: no finance, no arms; no arms, no terrorism. It is extremely important to know how terrorists procure arms.

Being non-state and amorphous groups— already on the run and being hotly pursued by various state authorities—it is not possible for terrorist groups to set up factories for arms production independently and without the help of sponsoring states. The usual practice, whether in national liberation and anti-colonial struggles or political and ethno-religious conflicts, is to seek arms from outside the group, at home or even from other states. Since it is always their goal to inflict as much damage as possible in a single operation, terrorists are after those kinds of weapons that are light and portable with great lethal power and, importantly, easy to operate from a distance. Terrorists also try to stay abreast of time and they learn from previous engagements and mistakes. Each successive operation is meticulously planned, but plans can be successfully carried out only with appropriate weapons. Moreover, arms suppliers or agents are only too keen to provide latest and sophisticated weapons in the interest of their business.

The armoury of the contemporary terrorist groups, generally consists on the one hand of explosives like land mines, IEDs, pipe bombs, molotov cocktail, fertilizer truck bombs, barometric bomb, triacetone triperoxide (TATP) bombs, RDX and nitroglycerines, and hand and rocket propelled grenades. On the other hand, small and medium sized weapons like AK-47, T56, Grail SA-7, RPG-7, Stinger missiles, rifles, and limitless supply of ammunitions comprise the rest of their arsenals. All these can be acquired only through illegal ways as the sale and possession of these weapons by individuals and groups cannot take place in the open market. Anyone who has visited Afghanistan and its border towns, and the tribal areas of the FATA in Pakistan, might easily have come across arms bazaars where these weapons can be found in abundance.

Not long ago, Indian intelligence sources, acting on an information provided by the Interpol, seized ten trucks carrying 150 rocket launches, 840 rockets, over a million rounds of ammunitions, 2000 launching grenades, 250000 hand grenades, and 1700 assorted assault weapons.[38] This largest arms haul was worth $4.5-5.7 million. According to revelations made by two of the accused in the 2004 Chittagong arms haul case, Hafiz-ur-Rehman and Din Mohammad, it was the United Liberation Front of Assam (ULFA) chief, Paresh Barua, who along with another accomplice had gone all the way to Chittagong to collect these arms in 2004. Jane's International Review, a defence journal, held Mr. Paresh Barua and the National Socialist Council of Nagaland Chief Procurement Officer, Mr. Anthony Shimray, responsible for this arms trafficking incident. These arms arrived from China and, as per the confessions of the two accused, the entire operation was in the full knowledge of top Bangladesh politicians at that time.

The above episode convincingly bears out the claim that various terrorists groups cooperate with each other, and that they have state sponsors. India has, for long aired its grievances with the Bangladesh Government for providing a safe haven to the insurgents from the North East. Incidentally, In April 2006, coalition forces in Baghdad recovered large caches of weapons from suspected terrorists. A look at their weaponry reveals the kind of weapons that are in vogue in the terrorist arsenal. These were AK-47 assault rifles, sniper rifles, pistols, 81.75 mm and 85 mm projectiles, 82 mm illumination rounds, 90 mm high-explosive rounds, 100mm heat projectiles, rocket propelled grenades, homemade rocket launchers, 55 gallons of home-made explosives, pressure plates, artillery shells, a 7-foot missile, a 14.5 mm Dishka heavy artillery machine guns, and anti-tank missiles.[39] Both the above cases simply give an idea of the preferred weapons of various terrorist groups.

It may thus be safely assumed that terrorists depend on some agencies and even some states that provide them with arms, training, and safe havens. Terrorist groups indeed find it extremely difficult to operate from their hiding, particularly from remote and inaccessible regions, for long. Since most of the terrorist groups these days are interconnected, their modus operandi in securing weapons happens to be the same.

Needless to say, arms tend to flow where there is money and vice versa. For arms 'trade' to take place, there must be a demand for arms in bulk quantities and demands arise only when there is occasion. No group or state would purchase and collect arms without purpose. As mentioned above, terrorists in every age have resorted to the state of the art technology weapons. Modern terrorist groups rarely use swords or knives when guns and rifles are easily available. There may be some time lag due to this availability factor. For example, many of the explosives used for military purposes might be available some years after they had been regularly put to use by the armed forces. Nevertheless, leakage may take place either at the end of returning soldiers or the arms dealers.

Till a couple of decades ago, arms dealers and agents had to acquire sophisticated and lethal weapons in clandestine ways. It happened to be the two super powers during the Cold War era that catered to the demands of weapons across the globe over a host of issues. Since the two super powers never came to actual blows during the entire Cold War period, they found other ways to 'test' these weapons, that is, supplying arms to rival groups and warring states in the Gulf and the Middle East, in Afghanistan, in Vietnam, Laos, and Cambodia, in the Horn of Africa, and in various other conflict zones of Latin and Central America. Yet, both the super powers followed some restraints, and made sure that the proliferation of such arms did not lead into the wrong hands. For example, the United States had some long standing export control and licensing on the sale of arms.

Even this thin curtain of restriction fell once the Cold War ended. The United States, on its part, found that the ever increasing stock of its conventional weapons needed to be eliminated or reduced, partly because of the Conventional Forces in Europe (CFE) treaty with the erstwhile Soviet Union, and partly due to the absence of major wars. Simultaneously, it became necessary to upgrade, replace, and replenish many such conventional weapons to keep pace with developments in arms technology. The sale of such weapons offered the only outlet under the circumstance. Conventional military equipments that are sold to states usually include heavy weapons like tanks, artillery, and aircrafts, etc. Yet, there is another side to it. Military spare parts for these weapons could well be used to manufacture small arms and light weapons that are needed, mostly in low intensity wars. Interestingly, the Soviet-Afghan war saw both these types of weapons in operation.

The end of the Cold War and the Soviet-Afghan war had several side effects. Both were responsible for the proliferation of ammunitions, small arms, and spare parts in the hands of the various warring groups in so many areas of conflict. What is more ominous is that the easy availability of such spare parts provides the requisite material that can be used as means to produce small arms in limitless quantities. It should be noted that the United Nations, after the first Gulf War, barred member states from supplying even those spare parts to Iraq that was supposed to enable it to produce for these weapons. Another fall out of the end of the East-West conflict was that there were many surplus weapons left in the hands of the OSCE (Organization for Security and Cooperation in Europe) countries and adjacent states. This large supply of light weapons resulted in the aggravation of tensions in regions sensitive to ethno-religious conflicts, by converting them into virtual war zones. Secondly, it also turned the relatively peaceful zones under OSCE into zones of unrest. The breakaway states from the erstwhile Soviet Union, in the 1990s, became the foci of illegal arms supplies to rogue states and to various rebel factions. The net result of all these was the unprecedented escalation of conflicts over ethno-religious issues, irredentism, and even terrorist activities in various parts of the world during the entire decade of the 1990s.

It is well known that such light and portable weapons are in great demand, especially among terrorists. It won't be wrong to say, that the recent spurt in terrorist activities, whether religiously motivated or with secular political agendas, has mostly been due to proliferation of light weapons. A report in the Dawn (14 January 2003) clearly revealed that the ratio of legal to illegal weapons possessed by individuals in Pakistan alone was 1:3. The paper reported that according to Interior Ministry officials, there were about eighteen million illegally held weapons in Pakistan. The newspaper further goes on to claim that in 2003, in Peshawar alone, the police had seized 3,900 weapons comprising Kalashnikovs, rifles, shotguns, pistols, stenguns, cartridges, and rocket launchers. Another startling revelation was that even a US firm had placed a $120 million order for guns from the "Darra arms dealers and manufacturers, reputed worldwide for their fine imitations of vintage weapons including pistols and rifles."[40]

Another important development of the post Cold War era was America's shift from national security concerns to open encouragement of arms trade. Consequently, most of the restrictions on arms trade were relaxed. The United States has now virtually become the leading nation in advocating 'liberalisation' of arms trade. With the threat of communism gone, the United States was in a hurry to open its conventional arms market to the rest of the world. After all, it took the United States a full four and a half decade since 1945 to capture one of the most lucrative export markets, the arms market. Moreover, the American effort to tie (and hence enslave) every other state to its sophisticated weaponry (don't forget how the United States imposes arms embargo to bring its deviant 'subjects' to book) had another important objective— to capture and monopolise arms markets, not only of the developing world but also of other developed countries. Efforts in these directions gained momentum with the onset of the post Cold War era as the numerous tentacles of the US military machine made deep inroads into the defence structures of so many countries (not to forget the joint military exercises that provide vital intelligence information to the lone super power or the merging of big American arms manufacturers with those of its EU counterparts).

According to a reliable estimate, the US based firms enhanced their profit margins from an average of 30 per cent earned during the Cold War period to 55 per cent in 1995 to 1997, alone. This was because a majority of countries that were blacklisted during the Cold War era from having access to sophisticated US arms and technology became eligible to receive them. Since 9/11, besides selling arms to India, Pakistan, Tajikistan, Azerbaijan, Armenia, and Yugoslavia, the United States made arms deal with Oman (fighter jets and missiles) and Egypt (missiles). According to a report titled 'Shattered lives' the United States, during this period, sold weapons or imparted training to nearly 90 per cent of the countries believed to be harbouring terrorism, in order to better prepare them to fight the war on terrorism![41] One observer had compared the reach of American 'arms' business in the post Cold War period with those of McDonald's and Coca-

Cola. Thus, one of hidden agendas behind the US declaration of War on Terror could well be to promote its weapons market, globally.

Besides capturing most of the world's arms markets, the United States has another goal— to prolong that position by focusing on continuous research activities through government investments in R& D and encouraging arms export promotional efforts, for example, financial support and tax breaks, at the same time. The tone was set during Bill Clinton's presidency when arms transfer deals were linked with US economic interests. Countries receiving American arms were obligated to give priority to American 'interests' in other sectors of their economies, too. Needless to say, some European countries, like Britain, followed suit. Prominent government officials of UK, like their US counterparts, now plead on behalf of their respective arms companies to secure orders from other countries. Way back in 1976, Jimmy Carter in his Presidential address remarked, "We can't have it both ways. We can't be both the world's leading champion of peace and the world's leading supplier of arms."[42]

The Control Arms Campaign, which is run jointly by Amnesty International, Oxfam, and International Action Network on Small Arms (IANSA), in the same report titled *Shattered Lives*, has highlighted that unlike the WMDs, conventional arms trade did not attract any bans. As a result, quite a few countries find it convenient to produce and trade in small arms. The report concludes that arms easily fall into wrong hands through 'weak controls on firearm ownership, weapons management, and misuse by authorized users of weapons.'[43]

Another noticeable effect of this globalising of the US arms trade is the offsetting and outsourcing of jobs and production abroad. For example, Turkey and South Korea can now produce F-16 fighter jets all by themselves while Turkey even made attempts to export 46 jets to Egypt. All these lead to unbridled proliferation of lethal conventional weapons, light weapons, and explosives, to every part of the world and thence to the terrorists.[44]

Terrorists everywhere, find it very convenient to rely on small and light arms, and find the use of explosives extremely handy in inflicting as many casualties as possible, in men and material. Such tactics suit their hide and seek approach since the last thing a terrorist would want is to be captured alive. Rohan Gunaratna had observed that, of late, the terrorists were shifting their weapons preference from standard weapons like the AK-47, T56, G3, or M16 to stand-off weapons like rocket- propelled grenade launchers (RPGs), light anti-tank weapons (LAWs), surface –to-air missiles, and mortars.[45] Now the terrorists have another potent weapon at their disposal— IEDs— which they use besides these standard weapons, as they did in Iraq, Afghanistan, the recent Mumbai blast, the Lahore attack on a cricket team, and in the recent clashes between Indian security forces and the terrorists near the Pakistan-India border. The satellite pictures of India and the USA, show how every Taliban member lives and sleeps with assault rifles, like the Huns who never alighted, even for a moment, from horseback.

One notable feature of the post Cold War era is that most of the low intensity wars, like ethnic conflicts, irredentism, and other politically motivated conflicts in various parts of the world, make extensive use of small arms and light weapons (SALW) only. Professor Michael Klare of Hampshire College observes, "Modern small arms—especially assault rifles like the Soviet/Russian AK-47 and the U.S. made M-16-have played an especially conspicuous role in recent conflicts, accounting for anywhere between 35 and 60 per cent of all deaths and injuries in warfare since 1990." Professor Klare found that all but 3 of the 49 conflicts after1990, were fought with SALW.[46] This clearly shows that the traditional major wars, based on heavy weapons, are being replaced by low intensity wars, at least, for the time being.

This link between small arms and low intensity conflicts in the post Cold War era was highlighted in the 2001 UN Conference on Small Arms, where many delegates concurred that the global trade in illicit small arms and light weapons preponderated in Africa. The report mentioned that in West Africa alone, some 7 million of those deadly weapons could be found and that such a high concentration of small arms was brought about by the incessant civil wars that engulfed the continent for the whole of the 1990s.[47] No less a personality than the then UN Secretary-General compared the effectiveness and destructiveness of small arms with those of weapons of mass destruction and lamented that these weapons claimed more lives in a single year than those brought about by the nuclear bombings in Nagasaki and Hiroshima! Little wonder that Africa should serve as a conduit for proliferation of small arms into the terrorists' hands. The preparatory Committee for Review

Conference on Illicit Small Arms Trade in 2006 discussed issues ranging from brokering, arms transfer both to state and non-state actors, and also possession and management of ammunition stockpiles.

The rational for the above discussion lies in the fact that terrorists also swim with the currents of time and they too have taken a leaf out of the pages of other conflicts in various parts of the world. The bottom line is that the choice of arms is dependent not only on the prevalent techniques but also on the various other contemporary conflicts, including terrorism, and that means that they are interdependent, at least, in use and application of weapons. The recent 26/11 Mumbai massacre has clearly demonstrated how assault rifles and hand grenades could cause mass casualties and immense problems for the security forces. These two weapons have become the defining features of modern terrorist campaigns. Even the FBI chief, Robert Muller, in a speech at the Council on Foreign Relations admitted, "The Mumbai attacks illustrate, the simplest of weapons can be quite deadly when combined with capability and intent."

Very recently, in early January this year, the Indian Security forces had a nine-day long engagement with terrorist outfits from LeT and JeM in the dense jungle in Doda district in Kashmir. The engagement was reminiscent of the 1998 Kargil War when dreaded Pakistan sponsored jihadists occupied an unassailable, but inhospitable height, to fight the Indian army. The security forces, found well-constructed bunkers in the rocks littered with ration and tea pouches that showed how these terror outfits made preparations for a prolonged engagement. Their strength lay in unlimited ammunitions, missile launchers, and assault rifles that they carried with them or had an assured supply of these weapons from their associates hiding nearby, or from across the border. The bottom line is that these terrorists would lay their hands at anything they can, from spare or broken parts of a gun to snatching of weapons from the security forces in combat operations.

Thus the American view that state-to-state arms distribution needn't be regulated because these are not going to fall into the hands of the terrorists sounds hollow. Moreover, American duality stands exposed when it fears that while WMD or the nuclear weapon/material could be procured by terrorists from the failed, weak, or rogue states, these are unlikely to happen in the case of conventional and even portable items. However, the United States has agreed to support many recommendations of the above Conferences and that is a good thing. The United States has also taken several initiatives to arrest the flow of illicit arms and arms trafficking. According to a State Department Fact Sheet, the United States took a lead role in concluding the Inter-American Convention against the Illicit Manufacturing of and Trafficking in Firearms in 1997, the first international agreement of the Organisation of American States (OAS), designed to prevent, combat, and eradicate illicit trafficking in firearms, ammunition, and explosives. It is a party to the United Nations Protocol to Combat the Illicit Manufacturing of and Trafficking in Firearms. It has contributed experts and funds to destroy small arms, light weapons, and ammunition in Liberia, Haiti, and the former Yugoslavia. It has enhanced its vigilance at the borders to check such flows besides engaging in international diplomacy with many nations and international organisations on reduction and destruction of illicit small arms.[48]

A representative of the Million Mom March said that majority of American citizens favoured better regulation of guns, including closing the gun-show loophole that allow criminals and minors to get weapons. "The American public was learning that guns purchased in legal markets in their country often flowed into the global illicit market for small arms."[49] Terrorists may even take advantage of the recent rise in killing sprees in schools, colleges, and universities in the US because of the easy availability of small arms to American individuals. Recently, the Pakistani Taliban chief, Baitullah Mehsud, has claimed responsibility for the killing of thirteen people in a New York building by a couple of gunmen.

Terrorists take full advantage of all the benefits of modern civilisation, that is, trade liberalisation, globalisation, improvements in modern communications. Incidentally, Salman Rushdie had remarked that while Islamic fundamentalists abhor western democratic values, they are not loath to adopt western technology. Terrorist groups have little problem either in carrying weapons in their own chartered ships that bear flags of legitimate operators and traders, or in using their front organisations and cells for securing the end-user certificates needed to collect weapons they direly need. Thus Professor Gunaratna rightly feels that "bilateral and multilateral mechanisms, such as monitoring the transfer of funds, movement of officers and crew, and tracking arms carriers, are of paramount importance to control the threat."[50]

Indeed, one can't have the full cake after eating half of it. The United States feels that it alone has the right to initiate or complete any action it deems fit, as it has the necessary power and resource to quell any attendant consequences. It is the same geo-political interests and super power hubris that have led the United States to simultaneously supply arms to rival states like India and Pakistan, Palestine and Israel, Iran and Iraq. It acts in a heedless and uncaring way when it supplies sophisticated weapons to major sponsoring states of terrorism, for example, Pakistan and Saudi Arabia. The same contradiction haunts the United States when it keeps the option of supplying arms and sinews to rebel groups fighting for national liberation or even a dictator repressing genuine rebellions, in American interest.

I have decided to club the two vital lifelines of terrorism, fund raising and arms procurement in a single chapter because of the fact that almost all US counter terrorism policies are based on the omnibus US criminal legislation, Anti terrorism and Death Penalty Act of 1996 (AEDPA) (discussed in detail in a later chapter) and both these lifelines overlap constantly. Legislations and their enforcements still comprise the bulk of US counter terrorism measures. But unless these laws are made fool proof and implemented in all seriousness, the US efforts in choking the above two lifelines of terrorists might end in a wild goose chase. They may require either a choice between sacrificing some civil liberties of the American people or a drop in the standard of living consequent on American retreat from the Middle East and elsewhere.

References

National Criminal Intelligence Service report, 1993.
[2]Palestinian Facts, Israel 1991 to present PLO Finances. Available at www.palestinefacts.org
[3] The Terrorism Project, CDI Primer: Terrorist Finance.
[4]Country Reports on Terrorism, Office of the Coordinator for Counter terrorism, 30 April 2008, Chapter 3 -- State Sponsors of Terrorism Overview
[5]CDI, Terrorism Report, In the Spotlight: Islamic Movement of Uzbekistan (IMU), 25 March 2002. Available at http://www.cdi.org/terrorism/imu-pr.cfm
[6]ibid.
[7]Abdel Bari Atwan, 'The Secret History of Al-QA'IDA', Abacas, 2007
[8]Funding Evil: How Terrorism is Financed-And How to Stop it, A Meeting with Dr. Rachel Ehrenfeld, 16 September 2003, The Nixon Center, Washington DC., www.nixoncenter.org.

[9]Terrorist Financing, www.gao.gov/cgi-bin/getrpt?GAO-04-163

[10]'US and Iran open Afghanistan peace talks', Times Online, 29 March 2009. Available at http://www.timesonline.co.uk

[11]Eaterina Stepanova, 'Illicit Drug Trafficking and Islamic Terrorism as Threats to Russian Security: The Limits of the Linkage', PONARS Policy Memo No. 393. http://www.csis.org

[12]ibid.

[13] 'Heroin Traffic finances bin laden',Rowan Scarborough of the Washington Times, 6 December, 2004. www.washingtontimes.com. Also available at www.mafhoum.com/ press7/218E61.htm

[14]Michael Braun, 'Drug Trafficking and Middle East Terrorists: A Growing Nexus?', Special Forum Report # 1392, Policy Watch, 25 July, 2008, Washington Institute, http://www.washingtoninstitute.org

[15]Congressional Record, 'The World's Largest Drug Field', Hon'ble Robert K. Dornan in the House of Representatives, July 27 1990. Available at http://www.fas.org/irp/congress/1990_cr/h900727-syria.htm.

[16]Loretta Napoleoni, '10 Things You Don't Know About Terrorism', Special Guest Article, The Progress Report. Available at http://www.progress.org/2004/napo03.htm).

[17]ibid,.

[18]'Foreign Terrorist Charitable Fronts in US Left Undetected Due to Limited Scrutiny, Reveals Government Report', Asian Tribune, 29 July 2007. Available at www.asiantribune. com.

[19]Ibid.,

[20]'Islam and Charities in the USA'. Available at www.creepingsharia.com,

[21]'Saudi Arabia is prime source of terror funds, U.S. says', Josh Meyer, the LA Times, 2 April 2008.

[22] CRS Report RL31658, Terrorist Financing: The US and International Response, pp.1.

[23]'Extremism's Deep Pockets: The Growing Challenge of Fighting Terrorist Financing', Michael Jacobson, The Politic, 17 February 2008, The Washington Institute for Near East Policy, http://www.washingtoninstitute.org

[24]Ibid.

[25] 'Turning Off the Tap of Terrorist Funding', A briefing by Rachel Ehrenfeld, 19 September 2003, Middle East Forum,

[26] ibid.

[27]' 9/11 hijackers linked to Saudi government', Press Trust of India/Associated Press, 2 August 2003. Available at www.expressindia.com.)

[28] ibid, Josh Meyer, the Los Angeles Times, 2 April, 2008.

[29] Statement of Secretary Paul O'Neill on Signing of Executive Order Authorizing the Treasury Department to Block Funds of Terrorists and Associates, 24 September 2001, Terrorist Financing: Current Efforts and Policy Issues for Congress.

[30] 'Funding Terrorism: Sources and Methods, Rachel Ehrenfeld

[31] Daily Analysis, 'Rethinking Terrorist Financing, Council on Foreign Relations', 31 January 2007.

[32] Terrorist Financing: U.S. Agency Efforts and Inter-Agency Coordination, www.fas.org/ sgp/crs/terror/RL33020.pdf

[33]AML-CFT, India, 'Are commodity markets funding terrorist activities?', Sreekumar Raghavan, Commodity online aml-cft.blogspot.com/2008_11_01_archive.html.

[34] al Qaeda's cash, Peter Brookes, The Heritage Foundation, 29 December 2003.

[35]ibid,

[36] 'Terrorist Financing, Report of an Independent Task Force Sponsored by the Council on Foreign Relations, www.cfr.org/pdf/Terrorist_Financing_TF.pdf

[37] Lee Hamilton, Testimony before The Senate Governmental Affairs Committee on Reorganizing America's Intelligence Community: A View from the Inside, 16 April 2004.

[38] Complicity of State Actors in Chittagong Arms Haul Case Revealed, Sreeradha Datta, 9 March, 2009, Institute for Defence Studies and Analyses.

[39] Terrorists Detained, Weapons Caches Uncovered, American Forces Press Service, DefenseLink News Article, 23 April 2006. U.S. Department of Defence, Available at http://www.defenselink.mil/news/newsarticle.aspx?id=15380

[40] 18 Million Illegal Weapons in Country: Small Arms Survey, 2002, Global Policy Forum, Dawn, 14 January, 2003

[41] The Arms Bazzar, Shattered Lives, Ch. 4, pp.54, Control Arms Campaign, October 2003, www.amnesty.at/controlarms/cont/report/cover_contents.pdf

[42] ibid.

[43] ibid.

[44] Ibid,

[45] Rohan Gunaratna, 'Terrorism and Small Arms and Light Weapons', Symposium on Terrorism and Disarmament, 25 October 2001, United Nations, New York.

[46] Small Arms Proliferation and International Security, prepared by Professor Michael Klare, Hampshire College, Amherst, Mass, USA, PAWSS/Conflict Topics-Small Arms.

[47] Disarmament Diplomacy, Issue No. 59, July-August 2001.

[48] U.S. Comprehensive Initiative on Small Arms and Illicit Trafficking, Fact Sheet released by the Office of the Spokesman U.S. Department of State, 23 February 2000.

[49] Disarmament Diplomacy:- Documents and Sources, Issue No. 59, July-August, 2001

[50] Ibid, Gunaratna, Terrorism and Small Arms and Light Weapons'

CHAPTER IV

INDIA IN THE EYE OF TERRORIST STORM

Mumbai Mayhem of 26/11

26 November 2008, was like any other day and it was business as usual in Mumbai. Like, in New York and Washington eight years back, nobody in that Indian commercial city had the slightest idea that death was just moments away; that the flow of life and society depended not on any regular rhythm of usual social interactions in which incentives and hopes abide but on the mercy and whims of merchants of death from across the border who relished in using foreign cities as the testing grounds of their newly acquired training and skill. About ten terrorists (the exact figure is still unknown, though the then Maharashtra Chief Minister, Vilas Rao Deshmukh, in a press conference on 27 November put the figure around 20-25) took off from a Pakistani city, Karachi (as per the accounts given by the lone captured terrorist, Azmal Qasab, during the course of police investigations, and later corroborated officially by the Pakistani Interior Minister), to let loose a carnage carried with an intense hatred for human lives. The noise of their guns was a wake-up call for citizens of every civilized society. The international community realised that only a full-scale and a proactive commitment coupled with a fool proof security system are what is required to counter such violent and mindless acts, in future.

The details of that terrorist campaign are now known, especially from the confessions of the only terrorist captured alive that night, and corroborated by other investigative agencies from other countries, above all, by the Pakistan government. The attackers came in a ship all the way from Karachi through the waterway leading to Porbandar, Gujarat, changing boats several times in mid sea. They took a fishing trawler named Kuber mid sea, to get near the shore of Mumbai. In the process, they reached the Gateway of India embankment riding on two dinghies. As they left Kuber, they killed the only witness, the Kuber pilot. Interestingly, they left some vital clues in the same trawler, like 15 tooth brushes, winter jackets, and a satellite phone, which helped a lot in subsequent police investigations.

There is no consensus on when they actually arrived in Mumbai as the accounts of various 'eye' witnesses varied. But it can be safely said that they might have alighted at two locations around 8.30 p.m., that fateful evening. However, an eye witness had said that she had seen ten men get off from a boat that evening (it is difficult to make out how she felt the need to count these heads and, that too, in the darkness). From there, these ten fellows dispersed into groups to carry out the carnage in at least ten places in various parts of Mumbai. The attackers marauded the crowded Leopold Café, Chatrapati Shivaji Terminus (CST), Metro Cinema, Cama hospital, Vidhan Bhawan, Girgaum Chawpatty, Taj and Trident-Oberoi hotels, and Nariman House, abode to a Jewish minority group. During the course of operation, a taxi containing RDX blew up at Ville Parle and there was another explosion near the Mazagaon dock.

At every point during the encounter, though ill equipped and ill prepared, the Mumbai police confronted, and even killed and injured, a few terrorists. While the brave police personnel drove out the terrorists from public places (note the contrast with the recent Lahore terror attack on cricketers, when the Pakistani security personnel failed to kill or injure even a single terrorist, let alone capture them), these terrorists took refuge in three buildings, the Taj and Oberoi hotels, and Nariman House, believed to be their main targets. It was not until the morning of 29 November that these buildings were given 'all clear signals' by the army, the police, and the National Security Guards. It took nearly 60 hours to flush out the terrorists, dead, from these three buildings. In all, over 160 civilians (30 foreign nationals from 10 countries including Britain, the United States, France, Israel, Australia, and Japan), were killed and more than 350 people were injured. At least, 14 policemen laid down their lives, including three top cops of the Mumbai police. One member of the European Parliament, Erica Mann of the social Democratic

Party of Germany had come to Mumbai to have trade negotiations. She later told: "I am sure there were more than three terrorists in the Taj -- we ourselves saw quite a few." Also she feels that there may have been more victims than the government allows: "We saw so many bodies taken out."[1] According to CNN IBN source, two NSG commandos were killed in the whole operation. The bodies of 9 terrorists were found, while one was captured alive. But that does not account for 15 tooth brushes that they had left in Kuber.

The terrorists opened random and indiscriminate fire, on both security forces and unarmed civilians, using their AK-47 rifles and they hurled countless grenades during the entire operation. Eyewitnesses say that some of them were even smiling while shooting. One security guard said afterwards that the terrorists looked 'determined and ruthless'. Some other eyewitnesses reported that they were young and even looked innocent and amiable! Some other 'on-the-spot' witnesses even recounted that they were shouting '9/11' as they kept pumping bullets into innocent civilians. It is thus difficult to make any accurate estimation from post facto eyewitness accounts.

Nevertheless, 26/11 provides ample evidence of the real intentions of the jihadists and how they carry on their operations. All of these need to be analysed seriously. But before I do that, let me mention the name of these ten terrorists as announced by the Mumbai police. All of them were around twenty years, smart and wore jeans and black T-shirts and carried back sacks laden with grenades, and other materials They were, Azmal Amir Qasab from Faridkote, (the only terrorist who had been captured alive), Abu Ismail Dera Ismail Khan from Dera Ismail Khan, Hafiz Arshad, Babr Imran from Multan, Javed from Okara, Shoaib from Narowal, Nazih and Nasr from Faisalabad, Abdul Rehman from Arifwalla, and Fahad Ullah from Dipalpur Taluka. Azmal Qasab and Abu Ismail Dera Khan unleashed most of the open attacks that took place in the Leopold Café, the CST, Cama Hospital, Metro cinema, Vidhan Bhawan, and Girgaum Chawpatty. Four others went to the Taj Hotel and two each into the Trident-Oberoi, and Nariman House.

According to some sources, these attackers may have taken cocaine and LSD as syringes were found lying next to their dead bodies. Subsequent medical tests have found traces of drugs in their blood. These drugs, along with steroids, were presumably consumed to keep them awake and to keep their performance/energy level high so that they could *fight* off their 'adversaries' in longer encounters. Also, the intake of such drugs was supposed to obviate the need for food. According to security sources, the terrorists in the Taj and Oberoi hotels even took naps, evident from the intermittent stoppage of gunfire.

Jean-Louis Bruguiere, a retired French counter terrorism expert and top official in Trans-Atlantic Terrorist Finance Tracking Program said, "We have never seen instances of operatives using drugs in attacks before, but we've also never seen the kind of open-ended, insurgent-style strike of civilian targets by Islamists prior to Mumbai."[2] Indeed, the Mumbai terror attack has brought to light so many truths about the workings of Islamist terrorists, which even cumulative evidence of the last four decades could not. Any attempt to undermine 26/11 would be naïve on the part of the international community.

Azmal Qasab told the police that the terrorists made long-drawn and arduous preparations for 'mission' Mumbai. He also disclosed that they underwent rigorous training, which lasted over a few weeks, in a camp based in Muzaffarabad in Pakistan occupied Kashmir (PoK), under the guidance of a leading Lashkar-e-Toiba (LeT) commander, Zaki-ur-Rehman Lakhvi. The training comprised intense shooting practices from assault rifles, hurling of grenades and rocket launchers, preparing and hurling of bombs, swimming and rowing in rough waters in Kashmir, acrobatics, and other physical exercises, fasting and getting used to low food intake, practicing how to stay awake, etc. These terrorists were also trained to engage security forces in prolonged encounter. The Union Minister Mr. Kapil Sibal told a private TV channel that the terrorists set up their own control room in the Taj and Oberoi Hotels, to coordinate their activities and to contact their masters in Pakistan! It was quite likely that they had real time information of when and where the Indian Commandos were being dropped, during the flushing operation. Mr. Sibal suspected that they might have undergone training lasting over months to execute such a carefully designed plan. Incidentally, a recent BBC probe, shown on BBC television, Monday, 29 June 2009) revealed the startling information that the 26/11 attackers might have been aided by local Lashakar cell members in Mumbai who relayed the precise police positions to their leaders in Pakistan during the course of entire operations. These leaders, in turn, guided the actual attackers through 'minute-by-minute' directions over mobile phones.

In another shocking revelation, the police learnt from eyewitnesses and various other sources, including employees of Cama hospital, that female terrorists wearing *burqas* fought alongside their male counterparts the same night! This suspicion gains more credibility from a recent report from Iraq about a female terrorist, Samira Ahmed Jassim, a 51-year old lady belonging to a Sunni Arab militant Islamic group. She used to recruit young females as suicide bombers in Iraq. According to an Iraqi spokesperson, Major General Qassim Al Moussawi, Sameera confessed having trained 28 such terrorists who carried out suicide bomb attacks in various parts of Iraq[3]. It is easier for women in *burqa* to fool security forces and carry weapons.

Qasab further told the investigating authorities that two other members of his group had stayed in Taj Palace Hotel for four days prior to 26/11. He also mentioned that a few others might have stayed for, at least four months in Mumbai and made a thorough survey of their target areas as a run up to the final assaults.[4] He admitted that two of them had worked in Cama hospital— as a chef and a table boy.[5]

According to a Daily Mail report, 29 November 2008, the fund for the Mumbai terror massacre was raised in Britain by a banned Islamic terrorist group. Qasab himself claimed to belong to the Lashkar-e-Toiba (LeT) and his links with LeT commander Lakhvi. Intercepts from telephonic conversations clearly point to a Pakistani link, which has been confirmed by the US intelligence agencies investigating the matter. Only recently, the US has furnished the Pakistani authorities with proofs of LeT's involvement in the Mumbai massacre.

Mark Steyn, the author of *America Alone*, feels that attacks such as the one in Mumbai, may take place in any second-tier democratic city, in any part of the world. But he asserts that we must not to miss the wood for the trees. He feels that the main motivation for Islamist terrorists has always been Islamic ideology, seeking to establish Islamic rule on a global scale. He feels that the outcome would be ultimately decided by the acceptance level among common Muslims. However, I think that he has completely misread the Mumbai terror saga. These terrorists were simply programmed by their masters in Pakistan and were told to unleash a reign of terror in Mumbai. It may also be the handiwork of Dawood Ibrahim, bent on taking revenge on Mumbai, the city he lived in and from which he was driven out. In any case, these terrorists were mere pawns. They never left any Islamic message in Mumbai. The only thought in their minds, as they left Karachi, was that life had little value and if *they (the terrorists) had to die,* then others had no right to live. The cruelty behind their killing can only be explained by a narrow and micro world outlook— others must follow what they (the terrorists) do and nothing else. Way back in the 1980s, young Khalistani brigades used to harbour the same attitude. Mark Juergensmeyer of the University of California, Santa Barbara, in a paper titled *From Bhindralwale to Bin Laden: the Rise of Religious Violence,* has given a detailed account of how they feel that their world views happened to be correct and exemplary. One terrorist even called him a 'sheep' for questioning him.[6] I'll return to the Mumbai saga a little later, but before that, it would be appropriate to have a look at the nature of terror attacks that India has seen in the recent past.

A litany of terrorist attacks in various parts of India

India has been the object of Pakistan sponsored terrorism for quite some time. In 2008 alone, quite a numbers attacks by terrorist groups armed and trained in Pakistan took place in various Indian cities. On 13 May 2008, Jaipur experienced serial blasts within the space of a few minutes, killing 68 people. On 26 July, there were a series of blasts at several points in Ahmedabad, killing 57 citizens. On 13 September, terrorist bombs killed 8 people in busy areas in Delhi. On 30 September, over hundred innocent people lost their lives in another serial bomb blast in the Capital.

Mumbai has experienced recurrent terrorist attacks since 12 March1993, when 257 people were killed in a serial blast brought about by 13 bomb blasts across the city. On 6 December 2002, a bomb blast in a Brihanmumbai Electric Supply and Transport (BEST) bus in Ghatkopar killed 2 people and injured 28. On 27 January 2003, a bomb placed on a bicycle in Ville Pearle exploded, killing 1 person and injuring 25. On 13 March the same year, a bomb went off in the compartment of a train near Mulund station killing 10 people. On 28 July, 2003, a bomb placed in another BEST bus in Ghatkopar exploded, killing 4 people and injuring 32. Nearly 44 people were killed and

150 injured in two blasts, one close to the Gateway of India and another at Zaveri Bazaar on 25 August 2003. On 11 July 2006, a series of 7 bomb blasts in several trains in and near Khar, Mahim, Matunga, Jogeswari, Borivali, and Santacruz took a total of 209 lives and left 700 injured.[7] The spurt in violence and terror activities in and around Mumbai since 1993 has been viewed by many as the handiwork of the mafia don Dawood Ibrahim. Dawood was driven out of the country and reportedly took refuge, first in Dubai and then in Pakistan. Dawood, according to Indian intelligence sources, has links with the al Qaeda and the LeT. Interestingly, all the above attacks were carried with bombs and explosives. Russian intelligence agencies claim that they have definite proof of Dawood's involvement in the 26/11 Mumbai massacre.

Delhi came under the terrorist radar when the terrorists had a go on the Indian Parliament on 13 December 2001. An explosives laden car failed to blow up due to some technical problems, much to the relief of Indian Members of Parliament. However, the terrorists, dressed in black commando apparels, hoodwinked the security staff by attaching the Parliament and Home Ministry stickers in their cars. They fired indiscriminately from AK-47 rifles, killing nine police and Parliament staff. All the 5 terrorists were killed in a 45-minute encounter. The open encounter by the jihadists on the Indian Parliament was a prelude to the kind of urban warfare that the terrorists unleashed in Mumbai on 26 November. New Delhi suffered another serial attack on 29 October 2005, when at least 60 persons were killed and 200 injured in three separate explosions.[8]

The fall out of the demolition of the Babri Masjid on 6 December 1992, finally culminated in the 5 July 2005 terrorist attack on the demolished shrine. The *gun battle* between the terrorists (believed to be sent by Dawood Ibrahim) and the UP police lasted for about two hours, killing all the 6 terrorists. Varanasi also became target for the terrorists when, on 7 March 2007, a series of blasts at various points of that holy city took a toll of fifteen lives and injured over a hundred people. Islamic militants responsible for this attack belonged to a dreaded Bangladeshi terrorist group Harkat-ul-Jihad-al Islami (HuJI), having links with the ISI.

Bangalore, which had hitherto remained safe from terrorist attacks, finally came under the terrorist scanner when several blasts occurred there, almost simultaneously, on 26 July 2008. Earlier, on 28 December 2005, the Indian Institute of Science (IISC) was targeted by terrorists. Another neighbouring state, Andhra Pradesh, home to the Naxal People War Group, mostly active in the Telengana region, has long been the scene of many left wing terrorist activities. Their objective is political ideological and they have close links with the Maoists in Nepal and the LTTE in Sri Lanka. They target the police and security forces. They have a formidable fighting capacity with more than a 1000 well-armed militia at their command.

North East India, the land of the seven sisters, has always been tense due to ethnic unrests. There have also been intermittent clashes between migrants, mainly, from Bihar and West Bengal, and the local people. This strategically important and vulnerable region has always been under constant threat from states like China, Pakistan, Nepal, and Bangladesh that act as state sponsors for various insurgent groups, home grown as well as foreign. What is more worrying is that some of the neighbouring states like Bangladesh even offer a safe haven and a meeting place for various terrorist groups. Indian intelligence sources have often forestalled their plans. Terrorists from Bangladesh use West Bengal and its border areas as transit points to fan out to other parts of India.

Mumbai Massacre analysed further

26/11 Mumbai terrorist episode has yielded some rare insights into what goes on in the world of the Jihadists. More importantly, it has great bearing on the direction of future terrorist activities. Making an in depth analysis of the nature and objective behind such attacks is worth the trouble. For one, the Mumbai plot— envisaged by the LeT chief Zakiur Rehman Lakhvi and other top master minds of associated terror groups, like the Indian Mujahideen and the HUJI, all at the behest of the Pakistani Inter Services Intelligence (ISI) — could be a dress rehearsal for some bigger event. May be it will supplement the hitherto 'hit and run' terrorist tactics with a limited dose of urban warfare, that is, shorter but direct engagement with security forces, especially, in crowded cities.

Taliban had made use of the both suicide bombing as well as limited 'open war' (the gun battle lasted for two hours) against security forces in connection with an attack on two government buildings in Kabul on 11

February 2009, in which at least 9 people got killed. The more recent Lahore terror attack on some cricketers also took the form of an open engagement with security forces. Some terror experts apprehend that such a shift in their operational activities may be a prelude to another 'surprise' strike at the heart of the United States and Europe by Islamist terrorists. Otherwise, how can one account for the extremely meticulous planning that only the best of brains in the army are capable of, behind the Mumbai terror attack?

As mentioned above, the Mumbai terrorists were let loose in India's commercial capital only after undergoing rigorous training. Much time and patience were trquired in designing such an 'urban' warfare. One important consideration in such planning is the 'flexibility' factor— to change, pre-pone, or post-pone the timing of the attack. Incidentally, this happens to be an important feature of jihadist attacks. 26/11 was no exception. Indian intelligence sources, like the Research and Analysis Wing (RAW), frequently send reports of probable attacks planned by terrorist groups on any Indian target, much in advance. Yet, many of these attacks either don't materialise or take place much later. For example, the Union State Minister for Home affairs told in the Parliament that, as early as mid 2007, he had warned the Maharashtra government that a terror group from Pakistan might enter through the waterways of the Arabian Sea and strike at crowded places in Mumbai. Security was tightened accordingly. The coast guards and the Mumbai police were put on high alert but nothing happened.

There are numerous such occasions when terrorists and their master minds prefer a wait and watch policy, based on information from various networks and local accomplices. They look forward to a more opportune moment. Indian intelligence sources have gathered that the Mumbai terror strike was originally scheduled to coincide with the Indian Prime Minister M.M. Singh's visit on 29 November (he was supposed to stay at the Oberoi-Trident hotel), but then it was pre-poned by three days. Who knows, they may even have access to government sources, days in advance, that even the media can hardly boast of?

It is extremely necessary to keep a safe data bank of these alerts and to open a special cell to follow them up and monitor the movements of terrorists and suspicious fellows. Extraordinary situations demand extraordinary measures and even extraordinary time may last long. There ought to be proper coordination between various intelligence and law enforcing agencies. The FBI has an enviable success record in this respect and they have succeeded, so far, in staving off any further attack on their homeland since 9/11. For India, this job is not at all difficult because the architects of these terror plots are known to reside in Pakistan. Moreover, various Islamic terrorist organisations and names of their members happen to be in the Indian 'watch list'. One may argue in this connection that the issue could be resolved easily by targeting Pakistan. However, that is not a wise option.

The point is that terrorists often change the timing but not their original tactics and modus operandi, on the basis of last minute information. After all, they will always have another occasion to 'test' those meticulously planned tactics. The Mumbai mayhem has clearly shown that even the *means and goals* in respect to specific mission may remain unaltered over a long period. There are reasons for this. First, it is not for nothing that their commanders arrive at a particular idea or a plan. Even, bin Laden admitted that much time and patience were required to plan and execute any big terror operation.[9] Secondly, each and every one of these ideas is important since they have a larger implication, as will be discussed below. These terrorists also desperately need certain 'operational' belief system and 'confidence' in their minds.

The underlying reasons for this set of beliefs or confidence are manifold. Some are imposed and even coerced, for example, a sense and feeling of trust on the leader are deliberately inculcated in the minds of terrorists, as a primary condition. Secondly, terrorists have memories of earlier successes and they know that they would succeed again, if they can wait for an opportune moment. Thirdly, each terror attack, especially the bigger one, generates so much interest in the media, and thence in the public mind, that terrorists' confidence levels are boosted tremendously. The stronger the adversary, the greater is the gain. Fourthly, and importantly, the longer a campaign endures, greater is the possibility of its taking root in the minds of common people and, for that matter, of the terrorists. All these plus points enhance the confidence of terrorists. Conversely, failures have the opposite effects. In this backdrop, the Mumbai mayhem has been a tremendous success story for these terrorists.

Besides arms and mone, jihadists have an additional advantage— their religious ideology. However, no religion endorses the killing of others. Islam is no exception, even though Islamist terrorist masterminds interpret various verses of Koran to justify the killing of enemies and infidels. After all, means will take care of the ends. The crux is— how far can one stretch the idea of justifying actions by misinterpreting religious scripts> Then there remains the all important question: who is better qualified to interpret God's justice and determine when and where that threshold is crossed? It is over this issue that the fundamentalist and the more radical elements within Islam flounder and find it difficult to preserve unity within and among their groups. Nevertheless, the excitement, promise, and lure of staying in the limelight are too irresistible for terrorist organisations. The Mumbai terror attack, carried out at the behest of the Lashkar-e-Toiba (LeT) had one such objective— to tell others what the terrorists are capable of doing and how long their arms' can reach. According to a recent US State Department source, LeT is now expanding its field of activity, which may also include the American mainland.

Indeed, Islamist terrorism at the behest of the al Qaeda or LeT, has crossed a definite threshold in the history of terrorism. Their leaders have come to accept the fact that a tremendous imbalance exists in the contemporary international order, in favour of the United States. Consequently, they have little option except resorting to frequent terror strikes, which happen to be their comparative advantage and which, ironically, work to the maximum disadvantage of their chief adversary, the United States. With battalions of 'holy' armies at their command to carry on the Lesser Jihad, these terrorist leaders know that they will not have to face any blame or backlash effect, since the followers of Islam are devout, their belief and allegiance to their religion and to their leadership unflinching, and their numbers are on the rise on a global scale. They believe that if they don't succeed now, their successors will do it someday, for sure. So, long live 'jihad'!

Undeniably, while the Mumbai terror attack was a sorrowful event for the civilised world, it was a bonanza for the terrorists. And this is what the terrorist leaders count on. 26/11 has undeniably spawned an awe-inspiring fascination in the minds of fellow terrorists for their slain comrades. As a result, the young brigades and followers of Islam feel encouraged to emulate the 'feat' of these 'heroes'. Besides, there might be a general public fascination, even in the target country as to how a handful of terrorists held out and fought against a regular battery of army, Marine Corps, police force, and Commandos, for days together. This huge psychological victory alone justifies the cool, patient and calculated planning of their leaders, besides adding to the terrorists' confidence and belief in the efficacy of terrorism. The 'martyrs' may even figure in the folklores of that particular culture. I have heard one eyewitness in the Leopold Café describing the terrorists in these words, "I have seen two of these fellows physically in front of me", as if he had a glimpse of angels! It is highly likely that many such descriptions in the coming days will be coloured with exaggerations.

Distance, indeed, lends enchantment to the view. These 'inaccessible' terrorists (because of the distance and barrier erected by the law enforcing bodies) might generate some pull on the common masses if such acts become fairly regular and frequent. That is why, I have stressed that the Mumbai terror campaign has virtually changed the face of modern international terrorism. Conversely, valiant members of security forces are not fancied as much because of the general impression that it happens to be their duty. However, the good news is that such moments of 'spell' are ephemeral and are inversely proportional to the frequency of attacks that might even out that 'surprise' element associated with the success of terrorists. Conversely, the bad news is that, as 26/11 becomes more distant, another terror attack may well revive those memories in the public mind. So, one crucial aspect of the global War on Terror, which may, to a large extent, determine the outcome of the war, is to choke and smother any possibility or recurrence of jihadist attacks.

Islamist terrorism, as we have seen in the Mumbai episode, is different from any other brand of warfare, including usual guerrilla warfare, because the latter does not have a religious agenda like the former. Radical Islamist terrorists have a unifying ideology that tends to bind and is less prone to division, unlike other terrorist or guerrilla groups. In the case of radical Islamist groups there is little scope for argument and the line of demarcation is very clear. It is based on the question of allegiance and fidelity. Those on the other side of the divide are simply infidels. But the guerrillas often suffer from leadership problems, especially, in the wake of failures.

The only captured terrorist in the Mumbai tragedy, Azmal Qasab, had disclosed that they were told by their leaders that they could be brought back. This means that they were given to understand that they didn't have a suicide mission and that their chief objective was indiscriminate killing of civilians and to engage the security forces in a protracted gun battle. So, there was always the scope for an exit route, especially in crowded cities, like the attackers on Sri Lankan cricketers did in Lahore. All of Qasab's other nine associates got killed and none of them committed suicide. It may, however, be argued that since they didn't hold hostages for ransom, they did not want to flee. However, this aspect is still unclear. First, the same News Correspondent, Mr. Richard Watson, who conducted the BBC probe that I have referred above, wrote that in other disturbing telephone calls, a terrorist leader cynically consoled the Rabbi's wife in Nariman House that she could live to enjoy the Sabbath if she cooperated by passing on demands to the Israeli consulate. Secondly, it may be that their masterminds did not want themselves to be identified, even though the actual attackers might have been unwilling to die. No doubt, the terror masters would do everything to ensure that *they, and for that matter their sponsors, don't get identified.* So the terrorist attackers must die. Also, the terror leaders would hardly like to miss any opportunity to denigrate their opponent.

Whatever be the case, one thing is clear: these attackers were programmed with hatred for the common people so much that they did not hesitate to kill Hindus, Muslims, or people belonging to any other religion. One important point to note is that, *they were not instructed from above to spare nationals belonging to particular countries or religion.* Another significant finding of the Mumbai mayhem is that future engagements with enemies would be a bit more open and direct, in contrast to the earlier hit and run guerrilla tactics. These smaller but open skirmishes will have a purely psychological bearing on the morale of the adversaries, conveying the important message that terrorism hasn't lost its charm and lustre. One other important point missed by terrorism experts, especially, in the Mumbai terror attack, was the use of mobile phones during the entire operation. Besides engaging in communications within themselves, the surprise finding is that there was a third vertex to this triangle—communication with their bosses stationed in Pakistan. What does it imply?

There may be several implications of this remote communication between the on-the-spot actors and their off-the-field masterminds. First, the master planners might have thought it appropriate to boost the morale of the actual actors, as well as to demonstrate to their adversaries that the terrorists were not alone in their mission. Secondly, the master planners and patrons of such operations might want to know the real problems faced by the terrorists during the course of operations. Were the weapons that they carried with them enough for such an operation? What was the morale of their opponents, that is, the Indian security forces, in the course of the combat operation? What about the selection of more appropriate locations from where the terrorists could have carried out their operations in a better manner? The terror masters wanted to get such feedback straight from the horses' mouth. Such information is vital in the backdrop of 9/11.

Terrorist masterminds focus a lot on psychological aspects, too. They have found out that while earlier types of operations, like sniping, hurling bombs from a distance, or placing bombs in bicycles and vehicles, might have resulted in quite a number of casualties, people might well get accustomed to these. Moreover, as referred to earlier, the terrorists stand a greater chance of being caught because of the heightened awareness among security forces and the general public. Terrorists do not want eyewitnesses. While fighting security forces at the Taj Palace hotel, they even hurled grenades at journalists and common people looking at them from a distance. A person who was closing his shop after day's work was shot as soon as he was spotted by a terrorist. It may be remembered how a photographer working for a TV channel was shot dead by a terrorist engaged in fighting the security forces in the December 2001 attack on the Indian Parliament.

Another noticeable phenomenon in Mumbai terror attack was that the encounters were of shorter durations with long pauses. This may not be without purpose— to deceive security forces into believing that they (the terrorists) are either finished or gravely injured, or that they have run short of ammunitions, in order to tempt the former to come within their range. I have already referred to a third possibility. They needed time to sleep. Another important feature of 26/11 was the agility with which these terrorists have changed floors through windows and balconies of upper floors (by knotting together drapers and bed sheets as climbing ropes) to fight security forces, underlining the fact that they had undergone rigorous training in their camps. In short, they simply tried to convey the message that they couldn't be dislodged as easily and as swiftly as the security personnel believed. It also turned out to be a battle for supremacy over their conventional counterparts and they have been largely successful in this, albeit for a brief period. This remotely controlled (based on the Pakistani soil) operation in Mumbai reminds us of a modified version of the first Crusaders who went on foot all the way from France to Levant. Today's Crusaders don't have to travel on foot. They make use of modern means of transport and communications. They definitely have an 'external' destination, like in the days of the Great Crusade. The modern 'crusaders' have, as their destination, Washington, New York, London, Frankfurt, and Mumbai.

As is evident from above, India happens to be one of those few countries that are at the eye of the terrorist storm. A 2007 Country Report, released in April 2008 by the US State Department, highlighted the fact that in 2007 alone, violence connected with separatist and terrorist related activities took a toll of 2300 lives across India.[10] Lisa Curtis rightly pointed out that over the past few decades, India has been the scene of many separatist and extremist movements, from the Khalistani movement of the early 1980s in Punjab and the JKLF led Kashmir separatist movements, to the ethnic separatist movements in entire North East. In this connection, the ever growing menace of the Naxals and Maoists in the central and eastern parts of India must also be mentioned.[11] All these insurgent activities continue to threaten the political, religious and social integrity of a multicultural nation like India. Although the Naxals are fast becoming a real threat to the country's stability (even the Indian Prime Minister, M.M. Singh has in a recent speech acknowledged this fact), Islamist terrorism portends the gravest danger for the Union's integrity because the Naxals don't enjoy the religious 'shield' of the jihadists. But any discussion on Islamist terrorism and their attacks on India would be largely meaningless if we don't understand the activities of groups responsible for perpetrating such attacks on Indian targets. This is discussed below. Needless, to mention, Islamist terrorism works on two wings mentioned at the outset of this book: jihadists with global reach like the al Qaeda and those engaged in local and regional issues. But together, they form a unit and that really complicates the task of the US policy makers in combating Islamist terrorism. This chapter deals with the latter group, that is, local and regional ones.

Lashkar-e-Toiba

The recent spurt in Islamist terrorism, fostered and abetted by the ISI in Pakistan, has, somewhat, eclipsed other forms of separatist and extremist movements, right or left, which plagued India so far. ISI offers training facilities, arms, and safe havens to various terrorist groups, mainly, in the Pakistan occupied Kashmir, in order to destabilise India.

The 26/11 Mumbai attack was carried out by one such banned terrorist organisation, the Lashkar-e-Toiba (LET), with its headquarters situated in Muridke near Lahore. LeT has worked under a different name, Jamat-Ud-Dawa (JUD). LeT was initially formed in 1990 by Mohammad Sayeed and Zafar Iqbal in the Kunwar province of Afghanistan and later shifted to Pakistan. Pakistani politicians claim that LeT is a humanitarian organisation that had served the earthquake victims in the 2005. According to a BBC news report, Lashkar had its collection box in every shop in the main bazaar of every Pakistani town for the purpose of raising funds.[12] LeT's views, ideology, and objective, as outlined in a pamphlet titled *Why are We Waging Jihad,* have been to install an Islamic rule in India, unite the Muslim majority regions surrounding Pakistan, and plant the flag of Islam on the soils of Washington, Tel Aviv, and New Delhi.[13] Besides, LeT openly advocates targeting of Indian, American and Israeli interests.

The LeT was set up to carry on insurgent and terrorist activities in Kashmir and to torment Indian security forces. It carried out some dangerous and daring attacks in the residential complex of the Border Security Force (BSF) in Bandipore on 13 July 1999, followed by another attack on 27 December 1999, on the headquarters of the Special Operations Group (SOG) at Srinagar. It advocates the idea of 'fidayeen' attack, which earned it a lot of respect from other terrorist organisations. According to the Indian national security adviser, Mr. Narayanan, LeT has become an international terrorist organisation that can match the al Qaeda in every respect. It has set up sleeper cells in Australia, the United Kingdom, and the United States, and provides training to terrorists from other countries. Very recently, a Times of India report on 4 July 2009 revealed that as per the UN

Security Council resolution, 29 June 2009, three LeT leaders, Arif Qasmani, Mohammad Yahya Mujahid and Abu Mohammed Ameen al-Peshawari were banned as terrorists allied to al-Qaida. Security expert B Raman feels that al-Qaida makes up for its difficulty in recruiting Arab as jihadists by relying on "LeT's extensive network of Pakistan diaspora jihadis, who are being trained and sent off on missions or as sleeper cells." Since 26 December 2001, it is in the banned list of the Foreign Terrorist organisations prepared by the US administration. The Indian government banned the organisation under the Unlawful Activities Prevention Act. The UN proscribed it in May, 2005. Britain banned it in March, 2001.[14]

A notable feature of LeT activities is the extreme brutality and hatred with which it carries its operations. Ajay Sahni recounts three occasions of such brutality perpetrated by LeT— cold blooded murder of 23 people in Wandhana on 23 January 1998, the massacre of a wedding party of 25 people in Doda, Jammu, on 19 June 1998, and murder of 35 Sikhs in Chittisinghpura on 20 March 2000, when the then US President, Bill Clinton was on a visit to South Asia. In the same year, LeT had carried out an attack on the army barracks at the Red Fort in Delhi. It was implicated in the October 2005 bomb attacks in Delhi, which killed 60 people. Earlier, on 13 December 2001, LeT, along with another terrorist organisation, Jaish-e-Mohammad (JeM), ventured to launch an attack on the Indian Parliament. Zarar Shah, a highly placed LeT member, reportedly confessed having masterminded the Mumbai massacre, along with Zakiur Rehman Lakhvi, a LeT Commander. Zarar Shah corroborated Azmal Qasab's confessions and said that his organisation gave training to these terrorists in the art of urban encounters. Pakistani authorities continued to deny the involvement of LeT in the Mumbai mayhem in November notwithstanding solid evidences produced by intelligence agencies of India, UK, and the United States. It was not until 12 February 2009, that the Pakistani authorities publicly acknowledged that a 'part' of the 26/11 plan was framed on the Pakistani soil. LeT is reputed for imparting a regular, two months training to its militant cadres in the handling of AK series rifles, LMGs, pistols, rocket launchers, and hand grenades.[15]

Indian Mujahideen and SIMI and Jaish-e-Mohammad (JeM)

In recent years, most of the terror attacks on India had been carried out by a relatively new terrorist group called the Indian Mujahideen, supposedly a surrogate of LeT, comprising young and lower-tier outfits from the Students Islamic Movement of India (SIMI) and the Harkat-Ul –jihad-e-Islami (HUJI). Indian Mujahideen claimed responsibility for a series of attacks in various parts of India, including Jaipur, Ahmedabad, New Delhi, Varanasi, UP, and even Assam. It lets its activities be known, through emails, just before each operation.

Students Islamic Movement of India was formed with an avowed objective to convert India into an Islamic state. SIMI was formed at Aligarh in the State of Uttar Pradesh on April 25 1977. Mohammad Ahmadullah Siddiqi, Professor of Journalism and Public Relations at the Western Illinois University, Macomb, Illinois, was its founding president. Having branched out from the student's wing of the Jamaat-e-Islami Hind, this organisation has already been declared banned by the Indian government under the Unlawful Activities (Prevention) Act, 1967. SIMI had carried out its terror strikes in various parts of India in retaliation of the Babri Masjid demolition in Ayodhya in 1992. The conflicting interest of Indian politicians has prevented the government from taking a firm stand in respect of SIMI.

Jaish-e-Mohammad (JEM), meaning Army of Mohammed, was founded in Pakistan in March 2000 by Maulana Masood Azhar, shortly after his release from a prison in India. The objective of Jaish-e-Mohammed (JEM) is to overthrow of Indian rule in Kashmir and the latter's integration with Pakistan.[16] JeM carried out suicide attacks at the gates of a local army headquarter in Badami Bagh, Srinagar, on 23 April 2000, and on the J&K Secretariat building in Srinagar on 28 June 2001. It carried out a car bomb attack on the State Legislative Assembly complex at Srinagar on 1 October 2001, which killed 38 people including four fidayeen.

Another Islamic terrorist group operative in the Kashmir valley is the Hizb-ul-Mujahideen (HUM), formed in 1989 to counter the more secular JKLF. The HUM was said to have collaborated with JeM in carrying out the Chittisinghpura massacre. At present, the HUM with its contradictory stand on the Kashmir issue, has only limited operations in Kashmir.

How India secures itself from terror attacks

The recent spurt in terrorist bombings in various parts of India led the Indian prime minister, M.M. Singh to announce new security measures, such as installation of closed circuit televisions in crowded places, like stations, airports, markets, and shopping complexes; increasing the size of police forces; and the creation of a research wing that would facilitate the country's Intelligence Bureau (IB). Counter terrorism experts in India suggest that the size of the police forces must be increased in order to combat this country-wide menace. The existing level of police and paramilitary officers, taken together, is insufficient compared to those in advanced countries. India has so far managed with 126 security personnel compared to 250 available per 1, 00,000 people in developed countries.[17] Incidentally, the international requirement or recommendation for peacetime policing stands at 222 per lakh. One disturbing feature of the recent terror attacks on Indian targets has been the complicity of local elements. I have already mentioned that attacks such as the one in Mumbai, could never have taken place without support from domestic elements. Some seasoned intelligence officers in India believe that the ISI tends to cash on the poverty and backwardness of Indian Muslims in order to woo them as recruits or to use them as sleeper cells to destabilise India. So, the government needs to pay urgent attention in this area by initiating measures that would alleviate the poverty and deprivation of the Muslim community, and tie them into developmental and democratic processes.

Like the United States, India, too, suffers from lack of coordination between its various intelligence and investigative organisations. Maintaining a comprehensive national database on crime and terrorism is a *sine qua non* for effective counter terrorism policies. Currently, the Intelligence Bureau oversees the job of an Interagency Counterterrorism Centre, entrusted with analysing intelligence information gathered from other organisations. Yet, it could make little headway due to lack of staff and resources.[18] Besides, the Central Reserve Police Force (CRPF), the Border Security Force (BSF), and the Director General of Military Intelligence, have their own collect intelligence networks in the border and disturbed areas. The Central Bureau of Investigation (CBI) looks after matters related to domestic criminals and national security. However, lack of political will and the divergent interests of various political parties hamper in the promulgation of stricter laws related to terrorism, for example, the controversy over the Prevention of Terrorism Act (POTA).

The government seems to have woken up to the gravity of the situation after the Mumbai terror attack, when it tabled a new bill for the creation of the National Investigative Agency (NIA) and another bill, The Unlawful Activities (Prevention) Amendment Bill, to tackle terrorism more effectively. These bills were passed subsequently. The National Investigative Agency Act seeks to set up an agency at the Central level,that would be empowered to investigate terrorist acts and other crimes which have national ramifications. The Unlawful Activities (Prevention) Amendment Act is supposed to expedite the investigation, prosecution and trial of terrorism related cases. The NIA has been placed in a concurrent jurisdictional framework, with provisions under specific Acts for conducting trials in terror related cases in special courts. The Home Minister said in this connection, "There have been innumerable incidents of terrorist attacks, not only in the militancy and insurgency affected areas and areas affected by left wing extremism but also in the form of terrorist attacks and bomb blasts in various parts of the hinterland and major cities."[19] Efforts are also being made at the state and national levels to secure India's internal waterways. Surveillance helicopters will keep a strict watch on the beaches and waterways, while coastal guards will monitor the presence and arrival of suspect boats and ships.

Mr. Ajay Sahni of New Delhi's Institute of Conflict Management, has rightly held India's crumbling political, administrative, and a 'terminally' ill justice system responsible for failing to provide appropriate counter terrorism guidelines, within a reasonable time frame.[20] Indian politicians, as I have referred above, suffer from conflicting interests and, perhaps remain in a mood of denial, which hinders the administration from pursuing any counter terror measure with seriousness. One outcome of this 'denial' mood is that by now, the Naxal 'red corridor' is closing in towards the Indian capital itself. Another problem is the government's (both at the state and the central level) dilemma in modernising the police forces because of the apprehension that superior weapons might make the police more arrogant, which could increase the vulnerability of political persons, the army, and common citizens, alike.

Thus the terrorists continue to enjoy the 'space between the army and the police'.[21] This dilemma has been highlighted by a security analyst at the Centre for Land Warfare Studies in New Delhi, who says, "We can't call in the Army because we're a democracy, but the police can't handle it".[22] The same dilemma of whether to use police or the army (and even where the police is deployed, whether to permit the police to resort to firing) has plagued every Indian state in combating armed rioters. The West Bengal government's lack of political will and ineptitude of the opposition parties has virtually reduced the police to the status of 'dummies'.

Ajay Sahni commented that the gravest threat to India's security may not come from Pakistan, or the ISI, or even the terrorists, but may be attributed to 'the limitless acts of omission, the venality, and ineptitude of the political and administrative executive, and the complete absence of accountability in the top echelons of the government'.[23] However, he is not always consistent on this point. On another occasion, (the train attacks in Mumbai on July 2006, during the rush hour), he had observed that this was part of an ongoing war against the Hindu dominated India by South Asian Muslims. He commented, "It is a continuous process of preparing for attacks and carrying them out."[24] Mr. B. Raman, another terrorism expert and a former Additional Secretary, Government of India, New Delhi, told in a web site that India, like Algeria, Spain, and Morocco, has become a victim of jihadists because of its foreign policies that cater to American interests.

On the other hand, Mark Sappenfield[25] lays the blame for such attacks on Indian home grown cells. Dr. Sahni also feels so when he refers to such attacks as the handiwork of the 'widely dispersed cadres, opportunistically drawn from different and often unconnected modules' and making use of locally procured explosives and materials.' Sahni concludes that this alone renders the job of tracing linkages backwards extremely difficult.[26] However, the presence of home grown cells never disproves the fact they are not sponsored by states on the other side of the Indian borders. Moreover, the all important question remains: how can the terror activities in the Kashmir valley by terror groups, aided and abetted by the ISI from the other side of the border, be explained, then? Readers may remember how Iraqi rebels used to carry out their campaigns based on homemade explosives and through home grown cells at the behest of al Qaeda. There are numerous independent home grown cells in America but the US administration never admitted that they had any links with al Qaeda. The presence of home grown cells, rather emphasises how the sponsors of terrorism, that is, Pakistan, devise newer ways to perpetrate terror attacks.

Pakistani profile to terrorist activities in India

Barring the ultra left Naxalite movements and the ultra right movement by Hindu fundamentalists, all other insurgent activities in India have been spawned, nurtured, and abetted by Pakistan since the 1950s. It all started with Nagaland when some rebel Naga group members received training, arms, and ammunitions in the Chittagong Hill Tracts (CHT), then under East Pakistan. The Nagas entered CHT through Mynamar. The Ne Win Government, on India's persuasion, virtually closed the Mynamar route for the Naga rebels, at that time. Thereafter, these Naga insurgents continued to receive training from China, not unlike the Mizo National Front (MNF), courtesy Pakistan. Both the Naga and the Mizo separatist movements suffered setbacks due to Indian victory over Pakistan and with the creation of Bangladesh. A few years later, China also reversed its policy of exporting 'revolutions' in other parts of the world, thereby dealing a final blow to these two insurgent activities.

In the meantime, the ISI got busy in two other key areas in India— Punjab and Kashmir, to foment and intensify separatist movements. When Ms. Benazir Bhutto became the Pakistani Prime Minister in 1989, she handed over documents relating to Khalistani activities that helped the Indian security forces to terminate that dreaded saga of violence in Punjab. Pakistan continued to support fundamentalist groups like the Harkat-Ul Mujahideen (then Harkat ul Anser) and the LeT, who had moved their bases from Afghanistan to Pakistan occupied Kashmir (PoK). Pakistan provided help only to pro-Pakistani groups in Kashmir, in order to marginalise the rather secular and independent JKLF.

With the installation of a 'friendly' Taliban rule in Afghanistan, Pakistan went from a passive helper to an active sponsor of terrorist groups in Kashmir. In the meantime, India tried to furnish solid evidence to the successive US administrations, under Reagan, then Bush Sr. and Clinton, to persuade it to declare Pakistan a terrorist state. But these requests were turned down. The reason was geo-political, since Pakistan had been a reliable ally of the United States during the entire Cold War period.

Economic interests were no less important. The United States helped UNOCAL, a US based company with substantial clout in the American ruling circle, to construct an oil and gas pipeline from Turkmenistan to Pakistan through Herat. The American grace smiled once again on the fundamentalist terror groups, HUM and LeT. These groups had helped Taliban gain control over Afghanistan. Later on, as Laden and the Taliban turned hostile to UNOCAL, that American 'grace' fast faded. The United States put pressure on both the Taliban and Pakistan to come down heavily on bin Laden and the al Qaeda. Would the United States have taken the course of chasing Laden only if the UNOCAL had its way in Afghanistan? This might also help explain why the American wrath fell on Afghanistan instead of on Saudi Arabia, despite the fact that at least 15 Saudi nationals took part in the 9/11 attack on America and despite irrefutable proof of Saudi funding of that attack.

Pakistan has now officially replied to the Indian Dossier on 26/11 and admitted that a 'part' of the 26/11 plot was hatched on the Pakistani soil, with links to LeT and its chief Zakiur Rehman Lakvi, The Pakistani Federal Investigation Agency (FIA) made a separate probe, based on the findings by the Indian side, and has revealed several new names. Six suspects were arrested. One man, named Hamad Amin Sadiq, allegedly from Punjab, was believed to be the main operative in coordinating the entire Mumbai terror attack. According to the Pakistani interior Minister, Rehman Malik, Pakistan had found that the terrorists made use of instruments of modern communication, like domain servers, cyber link, SIM cards, Voice Over Internet Protocol (VOIP), and other accessories, including, payment locations, that spanned several countries, Austria, India, Russia, Spain, Italy, and the United States. The engines of the Kuber trawler and of two other boats bore the name of a shop in Pakistan. As I write this, Pakistan had sought further clarification by putting 30 questionnaires to India. The Indian government has sent its reply to Pakistan, giving further proof in response to those queries. Pakistan got one Javed Iqbal, a Pakistani living in Barcelona, extradited and arrested, in connection with making payments towards the procurement of mobile phones, domain servers, etc. Italy happened to be the venue of money payment, according to Malik. Pakistan wanted India to answer how several SIM cards could be secured from India. Pakistan also expressed astonishment how the boat carrying the terrorists could get through the Indian waterways when it took its fuel near the Gujarat waterways.

Pakistan had lodged an FIR against all those terrorists who took part in the Mumbai carnage, under ATC, thereby admitting that these terrorists happened to be Pakistani citizens. But Pakistan's reply had no reference either to the role of ISI in arming and training these terrorists or in destroying terrorist networks and infrastructures in border areas in Pakistan.

References

Francois Gautier, '26/11: A Taj Survivor's Untold Story', 27 February 2009, Rediff News. Available at http://www.rediff.com/news/2009/feb/27-a-taj-survivors-untold-story.htm.
[2]'Were the Mumbai Terrorists Fuelled by Coke?', Bruce Crumley, 3 December 2008, Time in Partnership with CNN
[3]'Female suicide bomb recruiter' Samira Ahmed Jassim captured, Times Online, February 3, 2009, timesonline.co.uk
[4] 'I have no regrets: surviving Mumbai terrorist tells Indian Police', Victoria Ward, the Daily Record, 1 December 2008, DailyRecord.co.uk
[5]ibid.
[6] From Bhindranwale to Bin Laden: The Rise of Religious Violence', Mark Juergensmeyer, Orfalea Center for Global & International Studies, paper 20, 2004.
[7]Terrorism in India, Wikipedia, the free Encyclopedia.
[8]ibid.
[9]The Secret History of AL-QA 'IDA, Abdel Bari Atwan, Abacus, 2007, paperback
[10]US Department of State, Country reports on Terrorism 2007, April 2008.
[11]Lisa Curtis, 'After Mumbai: Time to Strengthen US-India Counterterrorism Cooperation', A Backgrounder, Published by the Heritage Foundation, No.2217, 9 September 2008.
[12]BBC News, Profile: Lashkar-e-Toiba.
[13] South Asia Terrorism Portal, SATP, Institute for Conflict Management, Lashkar-e-Toiba, 'Army of thePure', http://satp.org/satporgtp/countries/india/states/jandk/terrorist_outfits/lashkar_e_toiba.htm
[14]ibid.
[15]bid.
[16] In the Spotlight: Jaish-e-Mohammad (JEM), Terrorism Project, CDI, August 22, 2006
[17] ibid., Lisa Curtis
[18] ibid., Lisa Curtis
[19] PTI, The Hindu Business Line, 'Govt. introduces Bill for National Investigative Agency'. December 16, 2008, www.thehindubusinessline.com/businessline/blnus/14161682.htm
[20]ibid., Ajay Sahni.
[21] 'India Faced with home-grown terrorism', Mark Sappenfield, Christian Science Monitor, 26 September 2008, http://wwwcsmonitor.com.
[22]ibid.

CHAPTER V

TERRORIST ATTACKS ON THE UNITED STATES

Litany of terrorist attacks, at home and abroad,on the United States

9/11 must be viewed, not as a separate incident, but as the consummation of a series of previous attacks by some Arab Muslims, generated out of hatred for American foreign policies. The seed of that hatred was planted in 1947 when the United States took initiative in giving shape to the state of Israel through the United Nations General Assembly Resolution 181. The 'Partition of the West Palestine Mandate under the British' was adopted by a vote of 33 to13 with 10 abstentions. Incidentally, West Palestine consisted of the territory that remained after the British transfer of over 75 per cent of its Mandate of Palestine to Emir Abdullah, after the end of the First World War. Thereafter, the United States went on piling up more hatred on itself as it took Israel's side in the Arab-Israeli wars in 1948, 1967, and in 1973. For well over two decades after 1948, the Arab countries found it easy to target Israel rather than the remote United States because of geographical proximity

Things took a different turn with the setting up of the Organisation of the Petroleum Exporting Countries (OPEC) which enabled the various Gulf and Middle Eastern countries to accumulate petro-dollars that had twofold implications— to aid the Arab states and the people of Palestine in their fight against Israel and to weaken the American dollar empire by taking back control of most of the Gulf oil resources, then under Western control. The disaster in Vietnam and the breakdown of one of the twin pillars in the Middle East— Iran (with the overthrow of the Shah regime and its replacement by an Islamic Iran under Ayatollah Khomeini, in 1979)—added to American problems in the region. Conversely, with the liberation of various Muslim dominated areas in the Middle East and Africa from European domination, in the immediate post 1945 decades, the Arabs nations were able to take the cause of the Palestinians outside of the Middle East.

Little wonder that all these developments led the Arab countries to club the United States in the same bracket of 'infidels' as Israel. As a result, the United States came increasingly under the radar of these Islamic states, especially the fundamentalist elements in these countries. The first salvo in this regard was fired in the early 1980s when Ayatollah Khomeini declared the slogan "Death to America". Just prior to that, Iranian radical students seized the US Embassy in Teheran holding 52 Americans hostage for a period of 444 days. An audacious secret mission, Operation Eagle Claw, to rescue the hostages failed due to mechanical failures sustained by three of the eight helicopters deployed for the purpose. To add to the tragedy, eight US servicemen lost their lives as one helicopter rammed into a refuelling plane.

In May 1981, the US intelligence gathered the information that Muammar el-Qaddafi had plans to assassinate the US diplomats in Rome and Paris. That Libyan plot was forestalled. The US response was prompt. President Reagan ordered the closure of Libya's diplomatic mission in Washington D.C. and the expulsion of Libyan diplomats from the United States. Next, the militant Islamic organisation, Hezbollah, kidnapped thirty Western hostages, including a few Americans in Lebanon, in 1982. In one of the longest ordeals in international diplomatic history that continued till 1992, the CIA Station Chief William Buckley (kidnapped in 1984) either died or killed during captivity while some others, including Terry Anderson, were later released. This decade-long hostage crises led to secret arms sales to Iran (since Iran had complete control on the Hezbollah) by the Reagan administration to secure the release of hostages. The funds accrued out of this arms sales were diverted to the US-backed Contras fighting the Sandinista government in Nicaragua and the episode came to be known as 'Iran-Contra affair'.[1]

Meanwhile, Lebanon continued to remain the scene of recurrent terrorist strikes on American targets, till 1985. On 18 April 1983, 63 people, including 17 Americans, were killed in a suicide car bomb attack on the US Embassy in Beirut. The Islamic jihad or the Hezbollah was believed to have been behind this attack. On October 23, the same year, a Shiite suicide bomber blew up a truckload of explosives at a US military barrack at Beirut International Airport, killing 241 of the 1800 US marines sent there to help the multinational force in separating warring Lebanese factions. On 20 September 1984, a truck bomb again exploded outside the US Embassy annex in Aukar, North East of Beirut and took a toll of 24 people including two American military personnel. On 14 June 1985, the Hezbollah hijacked and took to Beirut, a TWA flight 847 en route from Athens to Rome and held it for 17 days. One US Navy diver was killed during the operation. The hijackers were demanding release of 700 Shiite Muslim prisoners from Israeli custody.[2]

In the meantime, Kuwait got involved in two incidents when on 12 December 1983, Shiite truck bombers attacked the US Embassy and other targets (the French Embassy, the airport control tower, a major oil refinery and another residential area), killing 5 and injuring 80. An Iranian backed group called Al Dawa was believed to have been behind these attacks. On 3 December 1984, a Kuwait Airways flight 221 bound for Pakistan was hijacked, reportedly, by Hezbollah, and diverted to Teheran. Two Americans were killed.

American soldiers and tourists were targeted in Spain (12 April 1985 bombing of a restaurant frequented by the US soldiers, killing 18 Spaniards), in the Mediterranean Sea (7 October 1985, one US tourist was killed when gunmen attacked an Italian Cruise ship, Achille Lauro), in Rome and Vienna (18 December 1985, when airports in both these capitals were bombed, killing 5 Americans), Athens (2 April 1986, when a bomb exploded aboard a TWA flight 840 en route from Rome, killing 4 Americans) and West Berlin (5 April 1986, when a bomb blast in a disco frequented by the US servicemen killed 2 and injured 230). Most of these attacks were blamed on Libya.

Then followed the great tragedy in 21 December 1988, when a New York bound Pan America Boeing 747 crashed, following a terror bomb explosion during the flight. The plane crashed into a small town, Lockerbi in Scotland, and killed 259 (35 Syracuse University students and many US military personnel on board, and 11 on ground). Libya admitted its involvement in that incident after 15 years and offered $2.7 billion to the families of the deceased as compensation. Another car bomb exploded on 13 November 1995, in Riyadh at the US military headquarters, killing 5 US military servicemen. Yet another truck bomb exploded on 25 June 1996 near the Khobar Towers military complex in Dhahran, Saudi Arabia, killing 19 Americans and injuring many. The act was attributed to bin Laden and his associates.

Back home, on 26 February 1993, a bomb placed in the basement garage of the New York World Trade Center exploded killing 6 and injuring about 1,040 people. The blame was laid on al Qaeda without any concrete evidence. On 19 April 1995, Oklahoma City experienced a car bomb explosion outside the Federal Office building killing 168 people and damaging more than 220 buildings. Convicts Timothy McVeigh and Terry Nicols were believed to be associated with an anti government plot to avenge the branch Davidian standoff in Waco, Texas.[3]

In Africa, on 7 August 1998, US embassies in Nairobi and Dar-es-Salaam were hit following truck bomb explosions, resulting in the death of 12 Americans out of 263 casualties and injuring over 5000. Bin Laden was again held responsible for this heinous attack that compelled President Clinton to order military strikes on terrorist facilities and hideouts in Afghanistan and Sudan. On 12 October 2000, the Navy destroyer, USS Cole, was hit by the explosion of a small boat in Aden while the destroyer was engaged in a refuelling operation. 17 soldiers were killed and 39 injured and once again bin Laden's al Qaeda was implicated. The American administration issued alerts for American tourists travelling abroad.

Then came the 9/11 terrorist attacks in New York and Washington. On that fateful morning, some 19 Islamic terrorists belonging to the al Qaeda group (though that group never directly owned responsibility), 15 of whom were Saudi nationals, hijacked four commercial airliners and crashed two of these airliners into the Twin Towers of the World Trade Center (WTC) in New York City, killing all the passengers on board and countless other civilians in the WTC. The third plane rammed into the Pentagon and a fourth missed its intended target, supposedly the White House, and crashed into a field in western Pennsylvania. Apart from the 19 terrorists, the total human casualties came to around 2,974. According to a study by the New

York City Partnerships and Chamber of Commerce the direct and indirect economic costs of the 9/11 destruction amounted to $83 billion, based on 2001 dollar rates.[4] The September incident led President Bush and his administration to reshuffle the government, create a separate Department of Homeland Security and the Office of the Director of National Intelligence for effecting better coordination and information sharing between various agencies, and importantly, to pass the USA Patriot Act.

According to the US Department of State, nearly 23 per cent of the terrorist attacks worldwide in 1995 involved US citizens and property. Yet, attacks on the US and European targets in the Middle East proved more lethal than in other regions. According to Daniel Pipes terror attacks by the jihadists claimed 800 American lives prior to 2001.[5] Terror attacks on American citizens and targets outside the United States never ceased despite the US declaration of War on Terrorism. In June 2002, a bomb exploded outside the American Consulate in Karachi killing 12. The al Qaeda was supposed to be behind this incident. Eight Americans were killed in a suicide bomb attack at housing compounds for Westerners in Riyadh on 12 May 2003. Saudi Arabia came into news headlines again, when, in May and June 2004, terrorists attacked the offices of a Saudi oil company and took foreign oil workers hostage in a residential complex. 22 people died, including one American. In June the same year, terrorists struck at Jeddah when they stormed the US Consulate, killing 5.[6]

From the account given above on the scale and nature of attacks by the jihadists, mainly the al Qaeda, it became evident that this new kind of terrorism was not going to be a local or even a regional affair. Rather it owed its origin, life, and duration in contemporary geo-political and geo-strategic realities of international politics, and it was here to stay.

US counter terrorism policies

First, I shall discuss the measures that the United States has taken, so far, to counter the threat posed by terrorism.

America's response to the Iranian hostage crisis in 1979 is believed to be the trend setter for the subsequent US counter terrorism policies. Some experts are of the opinion that America should have been more proactive and should have opposed the Iranian militant group, even with arms. They believe that the American conciliatory approach during that hostage issue hampered framing of tougher counter terrorism policies in the subsequent years. As a result, the emboldened Islamist terrorists, like the Hezbollah, frequently targeted American interests in Lebanon and elsewhere in the Middle East during the whole of 1980s. These terror groups became convinced that the US could be deterred and even pushed back by simply inflicting as many casualties on American targets as possible. The jihadists forced the US to withdraw from Lebanon in the aftermath of repeated attacks on its army barracks in the mid 1980s, and again, from Somalia in the early 1990s, following the killing of 18 American personnel. All these merely highlight the contradictions and hollowness of the longstanding US claim of not making concessions to terrorists. It must be remembered that most of the US counter terrorism policies that we have come to know today were framed during the last three decades of the last century, later strengthened and supplemented with amendments.

The US counter terrorism policies, like its other foreign policies, rely on a range of options from diplomacy, international cooperation, and constructive engagement to sanctions, covert and secret operations, protective security measures, and the use of military force. These are no different from its policies in other conflict situations around the globe. Thus the defining feature of the US counter terrorism policies has always been a greater reliance on its true and tried foreign policy options. In short, it won't be an exaggeration to say that the US counterterrorism policies, and even the War on Terror, happen to be the cause and consequence of American foreign policies. Until 9/11, there was no specific set of policies to deal with unusual and unanticipated threats by non-state actors on the American heartland. Prior to 1990, the US policy makers used to view international conflicts largely through the lens of superpower political exigencies. Thus the US anti-terrorism policies from the late 1970s to mid-1990s were aimed mostly at deterring and punishing states that were supposed to sponsor these terrorist groups. After 9/11, President Bush announced that 'things won't be the same again.'

Anti-terrorism and Death Penalty Act (AEDPA)

One of the basic assumptions of American counter terrorism policies till date has been that terrorists can't endure without help from sponsoring states. Hence, if their tap roots (state support) are cut, terrorism would lose its bite. Since the late 1970s, the US Congress was in favour of maintaining and publishing lists of sponsoring states. Such lists finally came into being, with the passage of Anti-Terrorism and Effective Death Penalty Act, 1996 (AEDPA). The principal objective of the AEDPA is to 'deter terrorism, provide justice for victims, provide for an effective death penalty, and for other purpose.'[7]

AEDPA marked a watershed in the US counter terrorism policies because it also contained provisions to combat the fund raising operations of terrorists making use of front companies and local sympathisers. Such fund raising issues came to light in connection with two terror attacks in Israel, first at the instance of Kahane Chai, and then the Hamas in 1994.[8] Besides categorising various banned terrorist organisations in a common list of 'Foreign Terrorist Organization' (FTO) under section 1189 of the Act, two other important provisions of the Act include (1) section 2332d that made it illegal on the part of a United States person (may be any person residing in the US, or a US citizen or national or a permanent resident alien or a juridical person), under penalty of fine or imprisonment, to enter into financial transaction with the government of any country (designated under section 6(j) of the Export Administration Act) and known to support terrorism;[9] and (2) section 2339B that metes out the same punishment to anyone in the US or in its jurisdiction providing material support and assistance to any designated FTO. This section also requires any US financial institution (unless authorised by the secretary) dealing in funds with terrorist links or having knowledge of such transactions, to possess or control the same, and to report to the Secretary in accordance with regulations issued by the Secretary. Material support to any FTO, as per the US law, includes currency or financial securities, financial services, training, lodging, food, shelter, false documenting and identification, expert advice, training weapons, communications equipment facilities or any other physical assets, among others.[10]

Another related area was the listing of designated state sponsors of terrorism and penalising them for their support of terror groups with funding, granting of visas, and other material support to such organisations. One of the pillars of AEDPA is the Export Administration Act (EAA) of 1979 that went through modifications over the years, including proscribing financial transactions of countries on the terrorist list and denial of tax credits for income earned in these countries.[11] Export of goods having dual use implications has always been an area of concern for the US policy makers. Libya and Iran used to take advantage of such exports both for defence purposes as well as for supporting terrorist groups. A third related area under AEDPA pertained to drug trafficking and money laundering, discussed in an earlier chapter.

Noteworthy, in this connection are the findings of the Congress that give an idea of the US perception of international terrorism. The Congress believed that international terrorism happened to be a 'serious and deadly' problem, detrimental to vital interests of the United States and needed appropriate laws, as guaranteed in the US Constitution, to penalise material support for the FTOs and to extradite members belonging to FTOs, in keeping with the provisions of the immigration and naturalisation law. The Congress further clarified that 'vital interests' related to the areas of trade, commerce, travel, and markets that were targeted frequently by the terrorists and emphasised the need for international cooperation. It admitted that many home-grown sleeper cells raised funds on behalf of terrorist organisations. It sought to block such activities by implicating FTOs as criminals. Thus, anyone helping them with funds would automatically fall in the same category as the terrorists. Currently, 42 groups are designated as FTOs by the Secretary of State.

USA Patriot Act, 2001

After 9/11, the US Justice Department drafted a bill, the Anti-Terrorism Act, 2001 and it was introduced as The Uniting and Strengthening America by Providing Appropriate Tools Required to Intercept and Obstruct Terrorism Act of 2001 (USA PATRIOT Act) in the House and passed by the House on October 12 as the Uniting and Strengthening of America (USA) Act (H.R. 2975) and then placed into the Senate as the USA Act of 2002

(S.1510). The Act, virtually a merger of two identical bills, H.R. 2975 and S. 1510 was passed by an overwhelming majority in both the Houses and signed by the then US president on 26 October 2001.

This Act, like the AEDPA, marked another watershed in the conduct of American counter terrorism policies. Some of the existing US Acts, like the Foreign Intelligence Surveillance Act of 1978 (FISA), the Bank Secrecy Act (BSA), the Electronic Communications Privacy Act of 1986 (ECPA), and the Money Laundering Control Act of 1986, had to be amended in the process. The USA Patriot Act has ten titles dealing with enhanced domestic security against Terrorism, enhanced surveillance procedures, tackling of international money laundering and anti-terrorist financing, protection of American borders, facilitating investigation on terrorism by removing some legal barriers, addressing the damage caused to the victims of terrorism, strengthening of criminal laws against terrorism, and emphasis on intelligence and information sharing.

Yet, the Act invoked widespread grievance and controversy, and several amendments were called for in the area of protection of individual rights, freedom, and security. Since most of the provisions were to expire after four years from its inception, the US administration enhanced the duration of such provisions, subsequently. Intense debates raged across the country over the provisions of the original Act that allowed intelligence and law enforcing agencies maximum freedom, like 'sneek and peek' searches to 'raid' any individual's house without search warrant, unlimited power to the FBI in obtaining business records and access to sensitive information from medical, library and book stores, expanding the scope of terrorism to cover even minor offenders, government watch on computer 'trespassers' without prior notice or court order, total secrecy in the conduct of domestic intelligence under the Foreign Surveillance Act (FISA), and no disclosure of subsequent information after investigations, monitoring of email and authorisation of 'roving wiretapping' by the FBI without the subject's knowledge, etc.

However, some of these problems were taken care of in the 2005 reauthorisation and compromise clauses, for example, efforts towards strengthening of civil liberty protections and permitting judicial review of the National Security letters (the centre of much debate), and doing away with the notorious Section 215 in securing medical, financial, and other personal information, and the legal rights of individuals to seek counsel and hire attorneys.[12] Michael Kraft believed that the Act contained several provisions, which if implemented fully, would not only enhance the surveillance of the US intelligence agencies but also extend their reach to other areas like cyber terrorism and even nuclear and biological terrorism. He commented, "I would classify the roving and warrantless wiretap provision as an effort to bring the counter terrorism effort into the modern computer age."[13]

Besides empowering the ability of law enforcement agencies to search telephone, email communications, medical, financial and other records, The USA Patriot Act sought to ease restrictions on "foreign intelligence gathering within the United States, the Secretary of Treasury's authority to regulate financial transactions, particularly those involving foreign individuals and entities", and to enhance the discretionary power of law enforcement and immigration authorities in detaining and deporting immigrants suspected of terrorism related acts. FBI was authorised to probe terrorist crimes perpetrated against Americans abroad. We have seen this happen when a FBI team interrogated the lone surviving terrorist (Azmal Qasab), held in Indian custody in connection with the Mumbai terror incident, in which six Americans were killed. An FBI team even went to Qasab's home in Faridkote, Pakistan. The Act also empowers the United States to try foreign nationals, accused of harming American citizens and American targets, in American courts. The US counter terrorism policy, as it stands now, permits families of terror victims to file civil suits against the states that sponsored terrorist groups in perpetrating these acts. Some of the victims of the 9/11 tragedy have already filed suits and demanded large sums from the Saudi government as compensation. It must be remembered that Saudi Arab has been the principal provider of finance and other important facilities for the propagation of Wahaabism on a global scale in the recent decades. Incidentally, at least, 15 Saudi nationals actively took part in the 9/11 terror strike on American targets.

Is the US safe after 9/11?

It is often argued that the US counter terrorism policies, particularly those after 9/11, have made that country safe from further terror attacks in its own territory. But can the United States rest content on the basis of such sweeping generalisations? It is important to note that prevention and thwarting of terrorist plots is as important as crushing actual attacks. Dr. James J. Carafano listed at least sixteen instances since 9/11 till March 2007 when intended terrorist attacks were actually thwarted or forestalled. For example, it is still fresh in the memory of common Americans that as far back as December 2001, Richard Reid, a British citizen and a self professed follower of Osama bin Laden, tried to use a match to ignite powerful explosives hidden inside his shoes, aboard a Miami bound flight from Paris. He was caught and found guilty of terrorist activities by a US federal court, sentencing him to life imprisonment. In all or most of the other attempted attacks, from the blowing of the Brooklyn Bridge to targeting the New York Stock Exchange, the needle of suspicion was on al Qaeda. Terrorist targets also included financial institutions in several American states, the subway station in Madison Square Garden, Los Angeles National Guard facilities, Synagogues, gas refineries, the Transcontinental Pipeline from the Gulf Coast to New York and New Jersey, Sears Tower in Chicago, the New York City train tunnels, the US army base in New Jersey, and a jet fuel supply line running beneath residential neighbourhoods leading to the JFK International Airport transnational pipelines. In some cases, terrorists used Pakistan as a transit point to establish contact with other terrorist groups.[14] Carafano concluded that forestalling of terrorist plots and consequent reduction or even absence of such attacks did not prove that the terrorist organisations had relinquished their activities. Eternal vigilance is indeed the price of liberty.

The US has always been threatened by three types of terrorist activities— loosely affiliated extremists, formal terrorist organisations, and state sponsors of terrorism. Loosely affiliated extremists, motivated by political or religious beliefs, may pose the most immediate threat to the United States. Al Qaeda relies on loosely organised groups and individuals, who work independently but are sympathetic to it. These 'sleeper cells' comprise individuals from varying nationalities, ethnic groups, tribes, races, and terrorist groups who work together, chiefly in support of extremist Sunni goals. One of the primary Sunni objectives is the removal of the US military forces from the Persian Gulf area. The only common element within these diverse individuals is their commitment to the radical international jihad movement, which includes a radicalised ideology and agenda for promoting violence against the "enemies of Islam" and to overthrow those 'apostate' Islamic states. A primary tactical objective of the jihadists is to plan and carry out large-scale, high-profile, high-casualty terror attacks against American interests and citizens and those of its allies, worldwide.

Interestingly, many of the local or regional political-secular terrorist groups that seemed to have run out of steam after the fall of communism, now draw blood through interactions with religious terrorist groups, especially the al Qaeda. Secondly, the US War on Terror has benefited the al Qaeda in another important way. As its members were flushed out from Afghanistan, they migrated to other parts of the world, particularly the conflict zones of Chechnya, Central Asia, Africa, the Balkans, Iraq, and Pakistan.

Any student of history knows that nothing matters more for human civilisation than migration. Human migration has played a vital role in the development of civilisation. In the post Westphalia arrangements, although nation-states enjoy defined territorial limits, two transnational phenomena, globalisation and cross border infiltrations, has resulted in the influx of huge 'illegal' immigrants. One of fallouts of a permissive immigration law in the US is the 'diasporic' effect. Myron Weiner believes that migration helps its own kind in the country of destination, thanks to the assistance, financial, advisory, and job seeking, offered by those already residing in these countries.[15]

To the extent that a diaspora secures influence in the land of destination, it develops a culture of its own and that culture is carried over from the country of origin. The presence of a few influential diaspora may even shape the policies of the federal authority of a country, for example, the Israeli lobby in Capitol Hill. Another inevitable offshoot of this trend is the rise in home grown and sleeper cells within the United States. The existence of 400 such cells in the United States has already led the US State Department to view jihad as a form of 'global insurgency. European countries have also suffered from their lenient immigration policies towards politically displaced persons. Thousands of extremists and jihadists, like the Mujahideen, have had little problem in entering these countries after the end of the Soviet

Afghan war, thanks to policies regarding 'guest-worker', 'family reunion' and 'political asylum'.[16]

Since major terrorist groups need an uninterrupted flow of arms, finance, information and intelligence sharing with other groups, they gained tremendously from contemporary developments such as globalisation, openness, democracy, human rights, and the proliferation of non-governmental organisations, non-banking organisations, cross border movements, legal or illegal immigration. They have even set up religious and educational institutions in foreign countries. By the same logic, counter terrorism has to have a global dimension, and that means that the United States must also listen to the viewpoints of other countries on how best to perceive the nature of terrorism on a global scale.

Domestic terror groups in the United States

As for the United States, it has suffered both from domestic as well as international terrorism. Holly Fletcher, in an article 'Militant Extremists in the United States' had observed, "Extremists across the political spectrum -- including white supremacists, Puerto Rican separatists, abortion opponents, and environmentalists -- have used a variety of terrorist tactics to pursue their goals." [17] Despite the massive casualties of the 9/11 terror attack perpetrated by foreign terrorists, domestic terrorism still poses serious challenge for the United States. According to the FBI, there were twenty-four terrorist incidents that occurred between 2002 and 2005, carried out by domestic extremists.[18] Domestic terrorist and militant organisations in the United States (discussed elsewhere in this book) comprise both right and left wing groups. In addition, there is another kind of extremist movement that embraces non-human factors like the animal rights movement, environmental and anti-nuclear movements, which is now known as special interest terrorism. The Earth Liberation Front and the Animal Liberation Front work for the protection of environment and animals. According to the same CFR article, 'Militant Extremists in the United States', extremists demanding better treatment of the earth and animals were responsible for twenty-three of the twenty-four terrorist attacks during 2002 and 2005.

The US domestic terrorism has almost the same definition as that provided by the various US government agencies, like the FBI, the State and the Defence Departments or the USA Patriot Act. It is sufficient to say that acts, like destruction, kidnapping, assassination, and others that violate criminal laws of the USA and pose threats to human life and property or are aimed at intimidating and coercing the civilian population or the government in order to shape the latter's policies for attaining political or social objectives, fall under the category of domestic terrorism too. The FBI has defined it as "the unlawful use, or threatened use, of force or violence by a group or individual based and operating entirely within the United States or Puerto Rico without foreign direction committed against persons or property to intimidate or coerce a government, the civilian population, or any segment thereof, in furtherance of political or social objectives." According to the USA Patriot Act, passed in the wake of the September 11 attacks, domestic terrorism could be construed as criminal acts that are "dangerous to human life" and seem to be meant to scare civilians or affect policy.

The roots of the left wing terrorism were planted on American soil in the closing decades of the nineteenth century by immigrants from East Europe, well versed with the doctrines of the international socialist and anarchist movements then sweeping throughout the length and breadth of Europe. Many of these Left wing groups had their heyday during the Second World War and the Cold War era because of the increased Soviet and Chinese communist influences across the globe. In the early 1970s, some ultra or radical groups like the Weatherman and the Symbionese Liberation Army (SLA) were active in the United States. No wonder, with the demise of communism, the influences and activities of the left wing groups subsided considerably, both in the United States and on a global scale. The only other time that they could make their presence felt was during the 1999 World Trade Organisation meeting in Seattle.

Right-wing domestic terrorist groups, on the other hand, focus their attention on issues relating to individual freedom and reduced government controls. Right wing militants groups may also have racial issues (the Ku Klux Klan) or issues related to social problems like abortion (the Army of God), or even immigration as their agendas. According to the FBI, right-wing terrorists often take the form of "racist and racial supremacy" and "embrace antigovernment, antiregulatory" platforms. Then there are far-right movements that make use of political rhetoric with racial undertones. Interestingly, the Black Liberation Army (BLA), a splinter group of the Black Panther Party, which used the platforms of both racism and Marxism to overthrow the US government, were responsible for carrying out at least 60 incidents of violence in 1970s till 1981.[19]

Members of a right wing militant group, Timothy McVeigh and Terry Nicols, were implicated in the 1995 Oklahoma City bombing. Timothy McVeigh claimed to have belonged to the Libertarian Party. Both these men were reportedly concerned about the increased UN involvement in American domestic policies. They opposed stricter gun-control laws, and were enraged by "several confrontations between members of right-wing groups and law enforcement officers at Waco, Texas, and Ruby Ridge, Idaho."[20] I have also referred to several other rightist groups that are active in carrying out domestic terrorism in the United States in the second chapter of this book. According to the FBI, it is the right wing organisations that are most likely to inflict greater damages as they have the potential and violent propensity to do so. Moreover, they are believed to be capable of amassing weapons and explosives on a large scale.

The counter terrorism drives taken by the UN

The United States has its own way of looking at terrorism. Consequently, there exists a lot of gap in the perception of the United States and other countries in this regard. The United States, being a super power, has to view international, political, and cultural issues through the prism of its present geo-political standing. What the successive US counter terrorism policies strive is to constantly narrow this gap of 'perception' with other countries. Accordingly, the US urges international bodies like the IMF, the World Bank, and the United Nations to play major roles in galvanising the support of the community of nations. The United Nations, in its turn, has always kept abreast in tracking the terrorist curve and has passed 13 universal legal instruments with 3 amendments in order to counter specific terrorist threats. Taken together, these thirteen UN Conventions have helped tremendously in a gradual but definite narrowing of the space for the terrorist activities on a global scale.

Earlier, civil aviation happened to be the favourite hunting ground of terrorists, since the hostage issue served several purposes: it could be used as bargaining chips for the release of terrorists held in the custody of the concerned states, for tremendous media coverage and wide publicity, and last but not the least, for securing a huge ransom for terror funding. It all started in the 1960s, with the formation of the PLO, and gained momentum during the 1970s and the 1980s. As a parallel trend, the maritime sector came under the radar of terrorist activities since the 1970s, culminating in the damage to the USS Cole in 2000. The terrorist links to the recent rise in piracy in the Arab-African waters must come under scrutiny because waterways may be used to carry nuclear bombs. Together these two sectors, aviation and maritime, account for at least 6 out of the proposed 13 UN Conventions. These are: (1) the 1963 Convention on Offences and Certain Other Acts Committed On Board Aircraft (Aircraft Convention); (2) the 1970 Convention for the Suppression of Unlawful Seizure of Aircraft (Unlawful Seizure Convention) (3) the 1971 Convention for the Suppression of Unlawful Acts against the Safety of Civil Aviation (Civil Aviation Convention); (4) the 1988 Protocol for the Suppression of Unlawful Acts of Violence at Airports Serving International Civil Aviation, supplementary to the Convention for the Suppression of Unlawful Acts against the Safety of Civil Aviation (extends and supplements the Montreal Convention on Air Safety) (Airport Protocol); (5) the 1988 Convention for the Suppression of Unlawful Acts against the Safety of Maritime Navigation (Maritime Convention); and the 2005 Protocol to the Convention for the Suppression of Unlawful Acts against the Safety of Maritime Navigation; (6) the 1988 Protocol to the Suppression of Unlawful Acts Against the Safety of Fixed Platforms Located on the Continental Shelf (Fixed Platform Protocol); and the 2005 Protocol to the Protocol for the Suppression of Unlawful Acts against the Safety of Fixed Platforms Located on the Continental Shelf.[21]

The other Conventions relate to crimes committed against individuals and persons, terrorist funding and explosives, bombs and nuclear issues. These are (7) the 1973 Convention on the Prevention and Punishment of Crimes Against Internationally Protected Persons (Diplomatic agents Convention); (8) the 1979 International Convention against the Taking of Hostages (Hostages Convention); (9) the 1980 Convention on the Physical

Protection of Nuclear Material (Nuclear Materials Convention) with Amendments; (10) the 2005 International Convention for the Suppression of Acts of Nuclear Terrorism (Nuclear Terrorism Convention); (11) the 1997 International Convention for the Suppression of Terrorist Bombings (Terrorist Bombing Conventions); (12) the 1991 Convention on the Marking of Plastic Explosives for the Purpose of Detection (Plastic Explosives Convention); and (13) the 1999 International Convention for the Suppression of the Financing of Terrorism.[22]

Besides, the UN Security Council was quick to respond to the 9/11 attack by resorting to Chapter VII of the UN Charter in adopting resolution 1373 (2001), condemning terrorist acts and incriminating all parties who supported or participated in financing, planning, and preparation of these acts. It further required member states to submit a report on their anti-terrorism measures to the Counter Terrorism Committee (CTC). Incidentally, the CTC, set up in 1999, now monitors compliance with resolution 1373, besides twelve other terrorism-related conventions and protocols mentioned just above.[23] Although over 500 reports had been submitted by 2004, the CTC experts feel that unless implemented in practice, such reports have little value. The Counter Terrorism Committee also oversees the progress made by member states in matching the provisions of refugee status in their immigration policies.

The UN Resolution 1267 adopted on 15 October 1999, required the Taliban not to let any portion of territory under its control to be used for the purpose of terrorist strike or training and it asked the Taliban to hand over of bin Laden to appropriate authorities. The other objectives of the Resolution relate to freezing of financial resources by other countries that may otherwise benefit Taliban and to cancel their air flights to Taliban dominated areas. The Resolution further asked other countries to submit reports within 30 days on the progress made in this regard. The UN Resolution 1373 adopted on 28 September 2001, seeks to restrict the movement and fundraising activities of terrorist groups and their capacity to organise terrorist camps, training, etc. It required other countries to modify their domestic laws to bring them more in line with anti-terrorist UN Resolutions and in criminalising terrorist acts. Intelligence and information sharing between member countries happens to be one of chief objectives of the Resolution. The UN Resolution 1390 requires member states to abide by various anti terrorist resolutions of the UN. There are indeed a dozen other such Resolutions, but those discussed above form the cornerstone of the UN counter terrorism measures.

The United Nations has a three pronged approach to its counter terrorism policies: the Security Council Resolutions, Conventions, and a counter terrorism strategy aimed at addressing conditions conducive to the spread of terrorism, whether economic or political, or otherwise, and helping member states build their capacities without violating human rights. This concern is reflected in the Global Counter-Terrorism Strategy adopted by the General Assembly on 8 September 2006, and in the corresponding Plan of Action, that attributed human rights violations, discrimination, political exclusion, and socio-economic marginalisation, as conditions conducive to the spread of terrorism.

According to Sheikh Haya Rasheed Al Khalifa, President of the 61st session of the General Assembly, launching the UN Global Counter-Terrorism Strategy on 19 September 2006, "The passing of the resolution on the United Nations Global Counter-Terrorism Strategy with its annexed Plan of Action by 192 Member States represents a common testament that we, the United Nations, will face terrorism head on and that terrorism in all its forms and manifestations, committed by whomever, wherever and for whatever purposes, must be condemned and shall not be tolerated." The General Assembly, in a Resolution, called upon its member countries to unequivocally and consistently condemn terrorism in all its forms and manifestations, participate without delay in the existing international conventions and protocols against terrorism, and finally, to implement all the Security Council Resolutions on terrorism.[24]

As for other global bodies, the G8 proved to be the main forum for the negotiation of many of the UN treaties, especially in the aftermath of 9/11. G8 leaders called upon the international community to enhance cooperation in regard to counter terrorism measures, like the expanded use of financial measures to stop the flow of terrorist funding, aviation security, control of arms exports, the identification and removal of terror threats, etc. In a report to the G8 Summit leaders by G8 Experts on International Terrorism and Transnational Organised Crime, the G8 members stressed the importance of the UN Global Counter-Terrorism Strategy, adopted by the General

Assembly in 2006. The G8 members also resolved to continue efforts to implement this strategy, and support the work of the Counter-Terrorism Implementation Task Force (CTITF). They expressed concern about bulk smuggling by the terrorists and asked other nations to ensure that no laxity remained in this respect. G8 laid further emphasis on blocking terrorist access to chemical, radiological, biological, and nuclear weapons. [25]

Conclusion

We see from the above discussion that most of the American counter terrorism policies and laws were already in place to combat violent and terrorist activities that had occurred in the earlier decades. 9/11 simply made the United States wake up to the reality that these had to be strengthened and made more comprehensive in order to cope with the ever changing tactics employed by the terrorists.

After 9/11, the United States sought to plug some loopholes in its earlier counter terrorism policies by ensuring better coordination and intelligence sharing between its various intelligence and investigative agencies and constantly tracking the new techniques adopted by terrorist groups. It follows up each incremental gain made by its anti terrorism policies in narrowing the room of manoeuvre for the terrorists. Eliot Schmidt of the Pennsylvania University rightly interpreted the above continuity in the US counter terrorism policies by saying that since terrorism has existed for long, it was not terrorism but the US policies that had undergone changes, depending on the response of successive Presidents, from Reagan to Bush and Clinton. [26]

Some authorities explain this continuity in the US counter terrorism policies in terms of two ring formations— defensive and offensive. The defensive ring ensures physical protection of the American Embassies and other key installations, army and civilian, American citizens and properties abroad. On a domestic level, it means protecting the lives of American citizens and safeguarding interests and targets at home. The offensive ring is supposed to secure the support, moral as well as active, of the allies and the international community, in waging a concerted battle against the terrorists in any part of the world commensurate with the US policies of 'no compromise' in respect to terrorism, destroying their roots, punishing their patrons, state or non-state entities. On a more proactive level, the United States is already on the job of upgrading the capabilities of many countries through training and security programs, workshops, meetings, conventions, intelligence sharing, joint exercises in the military sphere, diplomatic meetings, joint probing of appropriate legal options, and a host of other related measures.

The United States got the UN and NATO to take up the job of countering terrorism on a global scale. The United Nations passed several resolutions in this regard (1267, 1373, 1390, and 1467). Though the UN Resolution 1467 is prima facie concerned with small arms and light weapons, with specific reference to West Africa, its implication in respect to terrorism cannot be overlooked. The entire UN charter VII is devoted to Threats to Peace. The NATO, for the first time, invoked Article V of self defence clause in which an attack on a member state was to be construed as an attack on all.

Nevertheless, the implication of the Patriot Act in impacting fundamental American values needed to be addressed. In the same reauthorisation speech, Mr. Obama, commented, "This law didn't just provide law enforcement the powers it needed to keep us safe, but powers it didn't need to invade our privacy without cause or suspicion."[27] But he was quick enough to observe that the row over the Act had 'degenerated into an "either-or" type debate' between America's cherished principles and ensuring protection of the homeland from terror attacks. The president of Rutherford Institute, John Whitehead remarked, that the Patriot Act was the most invasive violation of constitutional liberties in his 28 years practicing law. Baldwin quipped in the same article, "Will someone please explain what good it does to dispose of a tyrant 7,000 miles away only to create one in your own backyard."[28]

But as I have mentioned earlier in this book, even extraordinary times may last long and may require extraordinary steps, particularly in matters of national security. For example, how can one be sure that the next man by your side doesn't have designs to disturb the security of a nation, be it through cyber crimes, aiding terror groups, or through actual terror attacks? It is now an accepted truth that a 'denial mode' may again precipitate a 9/11 attack, particularly in view of the presence of home grown cells that are to be found in abundance in the United States. An apparently innocuous person may be sympathetic, say, to the al Qaeda, and may independently carry on an attack or the same person may be tapped by terror groups for his 'proficiency' in manufacturing explosives or cyber hacking. Nobody knows. Since weak administration invites unwarranted and unseemly terror attacks, it is always better to have a stricter administrative apparatus to combat such threats till a decisive victory is achieved or a workable and honourable compromise is reached with the terrorist groups. Nevertheless, the entire issue highlights one important point mentioned in the opening chapter of this book—terrorists can succeed in their mission if the United States acts with indiscretion or even remain careless in guarding its borders.

Since the 1980s, the United States has based its counterterrorism policies on four principles: (1) make no concessions to terrorists and strike no deals; (2) bring terrorists to justice for their crimes; (3) isolate and apply pressure on states that sponsor terrorism to force them to change their behaviour; and, (4) bolster the counterterrorism capabilities of countries that work with the United States and require assistance.

The US government has a long drawn plan to counter terrorists. It knows that it has to exercise utmost patience in convincing other nations through indefatigable persuasion, in order to avoid divisions within the international community. In short, the United States hopes to combat terrorists through a combination of international diplomacy, law enforcement, covert actions, and military force, simultaneously.

Law enforcement is designed to put individuals behind bars, but is not a particularly useful tool in combating state sponsors. With the passage of the USA Patriot Act, the effectiveness of law enforcement measures has been upgraded to make up the inadequacies at both the domestic as well as international levels. Thus, efforts to bring terrorists increasingly into the legal net and ensuring international cooperation have become the two main pillars of the US counter terrorist policies after 9/11. In this respect, the role of the international community led by the United Nations is crucial.

The United States strives, adroitly, to use multilateral world bodies to perform those tasks that could otherwise pose constitutional and other socio-political problems for it. This is indeed an ingenious way of countering global terrorism. But a snag still remains—would the 'enraged' jihadists relent or would they summon and sustain that inner fire of revenge that possessed the enemy of Rome, the great Hannibal, till the US pulls out of the Middle East?

References

[1] Frontline: "Target America" handout, www.pbs.org/wgbh/pages/frontline/teach/terror/classroom/target.pdf

[2] ibid,

[3] " Terrorist Attacks on America Before Osama Bin Laden was born'. Nigerian Times, July 13, 2005, nigeriantimes.blogspot.com/2005/07/terrorist-attacks-on-america-before

[4] November 2001, revised in February 2002.

[5] 'List of Terrorist attacks against America', Daniel Pipes, www.FactsOfIsrael.com.

[6] ibid, Nigerian Times.

[7] Anti-terrorism and Death Penalty Act 1996, Wikipedia: the free encyclopaedia.

[8] 'Terrorist Organisations: Equal Opportunity Reaffirmation', Micahel Kraft ,Counterterrorism Blog, October 18. 2006

[9] Anti-terrorism and Death Penalty Act, US Code, Title 8- 'Aliens and Nationality',Ch.12- Immigration and Nationality. Available at http://www.treas.gov/

[10] Anti-terrorism and Death Penalty Act, US Code, Title 18- 'Crimes and Criminal Procedure', Part1- Chapter113. Available at http://www.treas.gov/

[11] "The Evolution of U.S. Counter terrorism', Michael Kraft, Counter terrorism Blog.

[12] Homeland, Security, 16 February 2006, Floor Statement of Senator Barack Obama, S-2271- USA PATRIOT Act Reauthorization

[13] Counterterrorism blog Event Transcript: The Evolution of U.S. Counterterrorism Policy, February 18, 2008, Michael Kraft, p.6

[14] U.S. Thwarts 19 Terrorist Attacks Against America Since 9/11, James Jay Carafano, Backgrounder, No 2085, 13 November 2007, www.heritage.org

[15] Myron Weiner, The Global Migration Crisis: Challenge to States and to Human Rights, New York, Harper and Collins, 1995.

[16] Robert S. Leiken, 'Europe's Mujahideen: Where Mass Immigration Meets Global Terrorism', April 2005, Center for Immigration Studies. Available at http://www.cis.org/articles/2005/back405.html

[17] Holy Fletcher, 'Militant Extremists in the United States', Council on Foreign Relations, 21 April 2008.

[18] ibid, Fletcher

[19] Domestic Terrorism in the United States, Wikipedia: the free encyclopaedia.

[20i] ibid, Fletcher

[21] UN website untreaty.un.org/English/Terrorism.asp

[22] ibid, UN website

[23] UN Chronicle, 'Combating Terrorism while Protecting Human Rights'.

[24] United Nations, General Assembly, A/Res/60/288.

[25] Report to G8 Summit Leaders from the G8 Experts on International terrorism, 2008.

[26] The Evolution of US policies Against Terrorism, Eliot E. Schmidt Statement of Senator Barack Obama

[27] Floor Statement of Senator Barack Obama, S2271-Patriot Act Reauthorization, February 16, 2006

[28]Chuck Baldwin, 'All Americans Should Want To Know The Details About The USA Patriot Act, But They Don't', The Covenant News, 8 April 2003. Available at http://www.chuckbaldwinlive.com

CHAPTER VI

STATE SPONSORED TERRORISM

There is a difference between state sponsored terrorism and state terrorism. The state, in its capacity as the law enforcement authority of a country, can make use of all the elements of state power— the police, the judiciary, and even the army, to quell disorders and rebellions in any part of the state. There is no definite way to determine if such acts by a state could be termed as state terrorism because of the relative nature of the issue. For example, rebels may feel that they are being harassed and tortured by the state despite their justified demands while the state may feel otherwise. Both dictatorial and democratic states use the law and order 'problem' as a pretext to suppress genuine grievances of the masses. The concerned state authority may feel that a particular insurgency movement may result in the overthrow of the incumbent government. However, the spread of democracy and awareness about human rights, the press and the electronic media, these days, serve as checks to state terrorism.

State sponsored terrorism, on the other hand, means state patronage that includes, among other things, financial, logistical, and training facilities for a terrorist organisation, situated either within its own territory or in the territory of other states, far and near, in order to secure political mileage that may benefit both the sponsoring state and the concerned terrorist group. Pakistan's support for several Islamist terrorist groups operating against India offers a good example of state sponsored terrorism. There are numerous instances when the United States, the bastion of democracy, used to resort to such activities to punish the 'unfriendly' states in its backyard. India's alleged support for the LTTE a couple of decades ago was dubbed by many as an example of state sponsored terrorism. Iran, Saudi, Arabia, and Jordan have the dubious record of sponsoring terrorism. One important advantage of state sponsored terrorism is that it serves the purpose of war without the risk of retaliation (unless the adversary happens to be the United States or Israel), at lesser costs. It can be said that state sponsored terrorism has changed the face of modern warfare, albeit to a certain extent, by turning it into low intensity warfare that can be continued indefinitely. Needless to mention, stakes and casualties here happen to be less and the gains substantial.

During the Cold War days, both the super powers indulged freely in state sponsored terrorism, for instance, the American support for Israel and Soviet support for Palestine and other Arab countries. As the Cold War intensified, state sponsored terrorism assumed a global dimension spanning Europe, Africa, Asia, and Latin America. Only Oceania remained free from such threats.

According to the Country Reports on Terrorism released by the Office of the Coordinator for Terrorism on 28 April 2006, "State sponsors of terrorism provide critical support to non-state terrorist groups. Without state sponsors, terrorist groups would have much more difficulty obtaining the funds, weapons, materials, and secure areas they require to plan and conduct operations." The Report expressed concern that since such 'rogue' states have the capability to manufacture Weapons of Mass Destruction (WMD), these can fall into the hands of the terrorists. The countries listed in the Country Reports stand to face strict sanctions, like ban on arms related exports and sales, prohibitions of economic assistance, certain controls over exports of dual use items that could significantly enhance the military capability of these countries or their ability to support terrorism, imposition of other kinds of restrictions, like the US opposition to loans that could otherwise be obtained from international financial institutions, and withdrawal of diplomatic immunity that would enable the terror victims to file suit against these countries. Yet, there are many other states that are believed to sponsor disruptive and subversive activities, overtly and covertly, besides those listed above. Paradoxically, the mother of them all, the United States, is currently engaged in fighting the very Frankenstein that it had created more than three decades ago during the Soviet-Afghan war. Let me deal with some of these cases. India is often accused by its neighbours of supporting 'separatist' and insurgent groups. Nevertheless, these are more in the nature of accusations than evidences.

India

As mentioned above, India has long been accused by its immediate neighbours, especially Sri Lanka, China, Pakistan, and even Bangladesh, of fomenting disruptive activities in their respective territories through its external intelligence agency, the Research & Analysis Wing (RAW). Pakistan and China saw an Indian design to dismember a theocratic state in its own geo-political interests through the creation of Bangladesh. RAW was blamed for imparting training, finances, arms, to the Mukti Bahini that used to carry out the fight against West Pakistani troops, based in the then East Pakistan. However, extraordinary circumstances (huge influx of Bangladeshi refugees pouring endlessly into the Indian border) and support for a genuine freedom struggle cannot be categorised as sponsoring terrorism. Later on, RAW was also blamed for assisting the Tamil Tigers in Sri Lanka, demanding a separate and independent state for ethnic Tamils. India, however, had long ceased to help the separatists. In the late 1980s it had sent its own forces on a peace keeping mission to fight the LTTE. Moreover, it signed the Indo-Sri Lanka Peace Accord in 1987. As per this arrangement, the Lankan government agreed to a devolution of power to the provinces and withdrawing its army, on the condition that the LTTE should lay down its arms. India has also been charged with inciting ethnic violence in Balochistan, Peshawar, and Sind. However, there is little truth in such accusations. Otherwise, Pakistan, still a fragile state, would have long ceased to exist as a federal entity.

Cuba

For over the last four decades, Cuba has always been critical of American policies and actions. According to the above mentioned Country Report on Terrorism, Cuba virtually refused to agree with the US requests to support the latter in its War on Terrorism. Cuba, according to the report, has not, so far, made any attempt towards tracking, blocking, or seizing terrorist assets despite legal provisions to do so. Cuba had never spoken against either the al

Qaeda or any other group designated in the FTO list, the report claims. Nor did Cuba embark on any counter terrorist drives or join any international or regional forum on counter terrorism issues. The report points out that the Cuban Government has still friendly ties with Iran and North Korea. Regular visits take place at the governmental level between Cuban, North Korean, and Iranian officials for signing of treaties and protocols. The Cuban Government had not obliged the US by sending American fugitives back, despite repeated requests. Strangely, the same report says that the United States has no proof of Cuba harbouring and abetting terrorism!

The contradiction in the report is evident. While it states, "The Government of Cuba maintains close relationships with other state sponsors of terrorism such as Iran and North Korea, and has provided safe haven to members of ETA, FARC, and the ELN", it also admits that there is no information regarding terrorist activities of these or other organisations in Cuban territory and that the United States is not aware of any specific terrorist enclaves in that country! Yet, Cuba happens to be in the list of state terrorists prepared by the State Department.

Since the United States has no definite proof of Cuba's involvement in sponsoring terrorism, the above charges against Cuba's non compliance with American counter terrorism policies fall flat. After all, no country can force another to do its bidding. Cuba has not harmed American interests in any way, except causing some embarrassment and being defiant, which the US finds difficult to digest. Neither has Cuba indulged in any terrorist activities against the United States so far. Does the US work on paranoia and complex in branding its enemies. Has the War on Terror been waged on the basis of any such complex and hubris?

Iran

The CRT Report brands Iran as the most active state sponsor of terrorism, as its two wings, the Islamic Revolutionary Guard Corps (IRGC) and the Ministry of Intelligence and Security (MOIS), were found "directly involved in the planning and support of terrorist acts and continued to exhort a variety of groups, especially, Palestinian groups with leadership cadres in Syria and Lebanese Hezbollah, to use terrorism in pursuit of their goals."

The report charges IRGC with supplying assistance to Iraqi militant groups to destabilise Iraq.

It is believed to be shielding al Qaeda militants. Iran has never responded to repeated calls by concerned states to send back the perpetrators of terrorist crimes, either to these states or to any third country, for prosecution. The United States and Israel have always accused Iran of harbouring an anti-Israeli stand and with abetting anti-Israeli terrorist activities through training, funding, and supplying arms to the Hezbollah, the Hamas, and other Palestinian terrorist groups like the Palestinian Islamic jihad, the al-Aqsa Martyrs Brigades, and the Popular Front for the Liberation of Palestine-General Command (PFLP-GC). Some of these groups, the US suspects, may have strong al Qaeda connections. Iran is also accused of providing funding, safe passage, and arms to insurgent elements in post Saddam Iraq.

To add to the American concern, Iran pursues WMD and even nuclear programs and is capable of manufacturing chemical and biological weapons. The United States fears that such weapons, in the possession of a state actively engaged in sponsoring terrorism, could be dangerous as they may fall into the hands of the terrorists who could hold Israel and other contiguous Arab states to ransom. Iran was designated as a state sponsoring terrorism by the State Department, on 19 January 1984. Interestingly, this move by America did not deter it or Israel from striking a deal with Iran for the release of hostages in the 1980s. Iran, on its part, dismisses all the above allegations as bogus. Iran has recently snubbed President Obama's offer of 'reconciliation' as insincere because it feels that such words never match actions.

Syria

The Syrian Government, as per the CRT report, continues to provide material assistance to both the Hezbollah and other Palestinian terrorist groups, like the Hamas, the Palestinian Islamic Jihad (PIJ), the Popular Front for the Liberation of Palestine (PLFP), and the Popular Front for the Liberation of Palestine-General Command (PFLP-GC), to carry out anti-Israel terror attacks. Hezbollah, incidentally, accounted for the bulk of terrorist attacks on American targets in Lebanon and took the maximum toll of American lives prior to 9/11. The CRT report is of the view, "Syria continued to permit Iran to use Damascus as a transhipment point to resupply Hezbollah in Lebanon."

The Syrian officials, however, considered the Palestinian and Hezbollah terror attacks as "legitimate armed resistance" in occupied territories. The CRT report, however, noted that no acts of terrorism against American citizens have taken place in Syria in the last few years. The American administration charged Syria of being lenient in letting the 'military age' Arab citizens to move to Iraq to fight the American and Iraqi forces. Syria, however, claims to have stepped up physical security in its borders. Syria has reportedly sent back more than 1200 foreign extremists and arrested over 4000 Syrians willing to go to Iraq for the same purpose. However, the United States remains open to changes in the Syrian attitude in sponsoring terrorism. Syria continues to be in the US State Department's list of countries sponsoring terrorism since 1979. Yet, Syria discourages terror groups based on its soil from attacking westerners. Syria ended a twenty five year long diplomatic stalemate with Iraq, at the end of 2006, to combat terrorism and to fortify its borders. Yet, both the 2006 Country Report and the UN investigation on the killing of the Lebanese Prime Minister, Rafiq Hariri, cast serious doubts on the involvement of top Syrian officials in that incident. Syria even shared intelligence about the al Qaeda and bin Laden with the US. Thus, Syria has been termed by experts as a 'passive' supporter of terrorism.

Libya

Though Libya once happened to be the most active state sponsor of terrorism, it now, by and large, relinquished its terror activities of the 1980s that had held the world community at ransom. Rather, it now cooperates with the United States and the international community in their fight against terrorism. Libya has cooperated with Britain in curtailing the 'terrorism-related acts' of the Libyan Islamic Fighting Group (LIFG) and in extraditing a member of the terror cell charged with bombing (in which three tourists were killed in a Cairo bazaar), to Egypt. Earlier, it had shown its good intentions by expelling the Abu Nidal Organisation, closing terrorist camps on its soil, and cutting ties with the Palestinian militants.[1] Consequently, Libya and the United Kingdom signed an agreement that allowed Britain to send back suspected Libyan nationals. Another reason for this change of attitude was that the economic sanctions had hurt the Libyan economy badly. The then US Secretary of State, Rice, had praised Libya's change of attitude towards terrorists as historic. She justified the US decision to strike out Libya's name from the list of state sponsors of terrorism because of "Libya's continued commitment to its renunciation of terrorism." The United States now feels that Libya is a reliable partner in the War on Terrorism.

Nevertheless, Libya was implicated in the assassination of the Saudi Crown Prince Abdullah in 2003 and was subjected to sanctions again. According to the CRT report, a terrorist named Abulrahman Alamoudi pled guilty of his Libyan connection and admitted his involvement in the plot to 'assassinate the Crown Prince at the behest of Libya officials'. Alamoudi was subsequently sentenced by a US federal judge to serve a 23 year imprisonment.

Besides cooperating in the Lockerbie Pan Am 103 bombing investigation, Libya had assured the United States in 2003 that it would 'renounce terrorism in all its forms' and not support international terrorism or any other acts of violence that target civilians. Libya has since refused to provide safe havens to international terrorists.

Sudan

Like Libya, Sudan has also turned a corner. Bin Laden was based in Sudan in the mid 1990s when the al Qaeda carried out some of its deadliest terrorist attacks on the life and property of American citizens. However, there is no visible presence of the al Qaeda in Sudan now. It has driven out Laden from its territory after pocketing the $300 million aid that Laden allegedly gave to that country (for developmental purposes), much to the latter's annoyance.[2] Sudan is firmly committed to denying any foreign or domestic terror outfit to use its soil. It has a porous border and there are disturbances in Darfur and other border areas, particularly along the Red Sea coast. Nevertheless, Sudan has seen to it that the flow of weapons to its eastern and northern neighbours ceases or slows down considerably. The Report has found that "Sudan produced desired results against international terrorist elements and the facilitators that support them." Yet, the US has doubts about Sudan's commitment in countering terrorism. As a result, Sudan continues to stay in the list of state sponsors of terrorism, despite the fact that the United

States and the international community have lauded Sudan's recent counter terrorism initiatives. Sudan has condemned terrorism in various regional or global fora and it takes part in many international conventions dealing with counter terrorism issues. But it is yet to stamp out the Lord's Resistance Army (LRA), a terrorist organisation led by a Ugandan, from its soil. Sudan has offered to mediate between LRA and neighbouring countries like the Democratic Republic of Congo.

Another area of concern has been the movement of 'jihadi' fighters who use Sudan as a transit route for escaping into Iraq. The CRT report says, "The Sudanese have taken steps, through self-initiation and encouragement by the United States and other international actors, to disrupt jihadists both travelling to and returning from Iraq, however, significant gaps in knowledge and capability to identify and capture such individuals remain."

North Korea

North Korea, once dubbed as 'the Axis of Evil', by the former US President George Bush, had its name removed from the terrorism blacklist on 12 October 2008, due to its willingness to allow inspection of all its nuclear programs. Earlier, the standoff over the nuclear issue between the United States and North Korea had nearly reached a flashpoint and the EU and Russia had to negotiate with North Korea to avoid a war on the Korean peninsula. Later on, in October 2007, a six party talk that included China, Russia, USA, South Korea, and Japan, prevailed on North Korea to renounce its nuclear programs. After some intransigence and deliberation, it finally agreed to open its nuclear facilities for inspection and verification purposes. However, in an extremely disturbing development, North Korea test fired a series of missiles, since May 2009, much to the annoyance of Japan and the United States.

Nevertheless, North Korea is not known for abetting and harbouring terrorist activities outside its field of activity, that is, the Korean peninsula and Japan and that too infrequently. In November 1987, North Korea was believed to have been involved in the bombing of Korean Air 858. It had also given refuge to a few members of the dreaded Japanese Red Army for their alleged involvement in a 1970 jet (flight 351) hijacking. North Korea is believed also to have supplied nuclear and ballistic missiles to Yemen and

Pakistan. Just a couple of years ago, a North Korean ship containing WMD material was held by India.

Soviet Union

Prior to 1945, the Soviet Union used to employ repressive and terror tactics— 'red terror'— in the name of safeguarding the fatherland from the 'reactionary' and 'subversive' elements of society, that is, the intelligentsia, the kulaks, the business class, religious organisations, and the media. Obviously, such activities definitely qualify as acts of state terrorism. Besides, the Soviets had helped rebel and insurgent groups fighting national liberation wars against the European colonial powers since the early 1920s, in various parts of the world. Such assistance ranged from invitation of communist delegates from different parts of the world to the Soviet Annual Congresses to financial and arms aid that continued till the end of the Cold War. But the Soviet support of rebels and insurgents took a different direction after 1945 to suit its geo-political interests. Obviously, it looked for soft spots, like spreading of communist ideals and guerrilla wars in Latin and Central America and securing strong footholds in Africa and Asia, in a bid to marginalise the United States in world politics. How far they succeeded in their mission is another matter, but that was the rationale behind Soviet sponsorship of terrorist activities.

Ion Pacepa, former acting chief of Communist Romania's espionage service said, "In the early 1970s, the Kremlin established a 'socialist division of labor' for persuading the governments of Iraq and Libya to join the terrorist war against the US."[3] According to him, it was the KGB that created the PLO, the National Liberation Army of Bolivia (created in 1964), the National Liberation Army of Colombia (created in 1965), the Democratic Front for the Liberation of Palestine in 1969, and the Secret Army for Liberation of Armenia in 1975.[4] Besides these, the Soviet role in Angola, Vietnam, Laos, and Cambodia need special mention.

Pakistan

Pakistan's complicity with terrorism is very well known. Pakistan happens to be the breeding ground of various jihadist groups and their proliferation. Pakistan's two neighbours, India and Afghanistan, have been the worst suffers of Pakistan sponsored terrorism in the recent decades. Quite a number of terrorist camps operate from within the Pakistan occupied Kashmir (PoK). Their leaders stay in the Pakistan mainland, for example, Karachi, Lahore, and Islamabad, besides staying in the border regions of the Federally Administered Tribal Areas (FATA). Recently, Salman Rushdie complained that the Pakistani President, Zardari, ordered an armoured vehicle to be used by the LeT chief. The United States —the 'intelligence' giant and the 'know-all' country— is well aware of Pakistan's involvement in sponsoring and abetting terrorist activities against India and Afghanistan. The Government of India has, from time to time, given numerous proofs, but America has continued to turn a deaf ear to all such allegations. Some members of terrorist organisations enjoying the blessings of the Pakistani army and its intelligence wing, ISI, had also told various media sources that they had training camps within Pakistan occupied Kashmir. Just a few years back, the Government of India had received highly classified inputs regarding the existence of 5,000 odd militants from J&K in various camps in Pakistan.[5]

The only terrorist captured in the recent Mumbai terror attack, Azmal Qasab, has given chilling accounts of not only the rigors of training that terrorists had to undergo in those camps, especially, in Pakistan occupied Kashmir (PoK), but also how the planning and timing of any particular terrorist attack was designed, including, the monitoring of 'live' attacks, by the masterminds sitting in the main cities of Pakistan. Pakistan has consistently denied these charges. What is more intriguing and perplexing is that Pakistan was on denial mode for a good period after 26/11 regarding the claim made by Qasab that he was a Pakistani national. It had refused to take back the body of nine other terrorists killed during the Mumbai attack, despite solid proofs given by India about their particulars, that is, their names, whereabouts, etc. Strangely, Pakistan has now lodged an FIR against Qasab and other terrorists directly involved in the Mumbai carnage!

Intelligence agencies from Britain and the United States have carried out investigations and interrogated Qasab. Acting on the Indian lead, one FBI team even went to Faridkote, Qasab's hometown in Pakistan. Strangely not much is known about their findings although the FBI believes that Pakistan had a hand in the 26/11 attack on Mumbai. The United States finds it hard to defend Pakistan's misdeeds in the light of solid proofs given by India. But, as I have mentioned earlier, it was only concerned about its six nationals who were killed during the attack, while the Indian casualties hardly mattered. China, the closest ally of Pakistan, believes that Pakistan's support for terrorist organisations has had spill-over effects in its Xin Xiang province. Yet, China had defended Pakistan in the Mumbai case. China maintained that the blast might have been the handiwork of Indian terrorist outfits. Incidentally, many such home grown terrorist cells receive active support from the ISI.

Pakistan and the ISI have been implicated by Indian authorities in almost every serial attack that has taken place in various Indian cities from Ahmedabad to Guwahati, Bangalore, Hyderabad, Varanasi, Delhi, and Mumbai, in the recent past. The Afghan head of the state, Hamid Karzai accused Pakistan of harbouring and training various terror groups. The United States was convinced that the recent bombing of the Indian embassy in Kabul was done at the behest of Pakistan. The United States had, in fact, carried out several attacks on terrorist camps operating from within the Pakistan borders and in the FATA region. The recent Drone attacks have drawn so much ire from people living in these tribal zones. Pakistan was kept in the watch list of states sponsoring terrorism for six months by the Clinton administration in 1993. As stated earlier, the then Secretary of State, Madeline Albright, recently commented that Pakistan happened to be a 'migraine' for the international community through its support for terrorism. The US Ambassador to India, David Mulford, has clearly said, on many occasions, that Pakistan was responsible for the Mumbai carnage.

The US President Barrack Obama has recently warned Pakistan of sponsoring terrorism. He feared that unless the sponsors of terrorist groups are completely stamped out, there would be unceasing 'copy cat attacks' of the Mumbai type, by various terrorist groups in other regions in the future. This is a clear admission that Pakistan is a state that sponsors terrorism. Obama was definitely not referring to any other neighbours of India when he talked about the Mumbai terror tragedy. The FBI has collected satellite images that clearly show the existence of terror camps in Pakistan. Indian external Intelligence Wing, RAW, has sufficient proof of the existence of quite a number of terrorist camps in Pakistan. Some non-partisan sources are also convinced that there are quite a number of terrorist sympathisers in Pakistan's military and Inter Services Intelligence. Pakistan, however maintains that it only provides political and moral support to secessionist groups. The ex-Pakistani President, Pervez Mussaraf, told the Indian politicians when he visited New Delhi way back in 2001, that what was going on in Kashmir was not terrorism but a freedom movement and that Pakistan would continue to assist these 'freedom fighters'.

What is more intriguing is that many of the terrorist organisations that are banned by the United Nations continue to operate under different names in Pakistan. For example, Lashkar-e-Toiba assumed the name of Jamat-Ud-Dawa. The United Nations had asked Pakistan to ban Jamat. The United Nations has, time and again, expressed its displeasure ver Pakistan's inability to restrict the activities of Taliban leaders, in the Pakistan-Afghan border. In fact, many countries suspect Pakistan of following a double standard: carrying out occasional raids on the terrorist hide outs and providing them with shelter, at the same time. The Pakistani army, in the recent past, carried out flushing operations in Lal Masjid in which so many dreaded terrorists had taken refuge. Pakistan has provided safe passage and safe haven to terrorists like Dawood Ibrahim, Masood Azhar, Zarrar Shah, and many others. Some believe that bin Laden might be hiding in Pakistan, though this does not sound convincing in view of Laden's suspicions about the country. Yet recent US intelligence report point to the possibility of Laden staying in Pakistan.

How can one account for the failure of the US campaign in Afghanistan, after its success in the initial three months? The needle of suspicion again points towards Pakistan. Many Taliban and al Qaeda members had little difficulty entering, first, the Afghan-Pakistan border regions, then the FATA, and, thereafter, the Swat valley in Quetta. Now the Pakistani army has declared war on Taliban to flush them out of the region. The US, much to its consternation, woke up to the reality that despite the War on Terror that has been going on for nearly eight years, al Qaeda and Taliban have regrouped in large numbers not only in many parts of Afghanistan but also in Pakistan.

An Indian national TV news channel recently aired a short video description of the presence of Taliban leaders in Pakistan. Taliban had taken control of the Swat valley in the North West Frontier Province of Pakistan, just about 160 kilometres from the Pakistani capital. It is only recently that Swat has been freed by the Pakistani army from the Taliban fold. It is well known that the Islamic cleric Maulana Fazlullah made use of 30 illegal FM radio broadcasts to spread the message of jihad against the Pakistani forces, in retaliation for the Lal Masjid operations. These broadcasts also prohibit women's education and the running of schools and music shops in many parts of Swat. Other Taliban commanders in the Swat valley are, Maulana Durrani who had fought the US forces in the 2001 Afghan war, Ghaznavi a very competent army commander, Muslim Khan and Shirazuddin, who work tirelessly to revamp new recruits, not to speak of the Haqqanies. One Pakistani official even pled helplessness in blocking these illegal FM radio stations! Ted Galen Carpenter commented that the US intelligence agencies had evidence that ISI operatives were again aiding the al Qaeda and the Taliban. He lamented, "With "friends" like Pakistan and Saudi Arabia, America doesn't need any enemies".[6]

Noted Pakistani journalist, Ahmed Rashid has accused the ISI of providing help to the Taliban. Ted Galen Carpenter, Vice President for Defence and Foreign Policy Studies in the Cato Institute had written that the US intelligence agencies had uncovered evidence that ISI operatives were helping the Taliban and al Qaeda again and that Washington should ask Pakistani authorities to 'clean out terrorist sympathizers from the military and the ISI'.[7] Stephen Schwartz observed that Pakistan had provided considerable financial and human assets to the al Qaeda and had effectively handed over much of its North West frontier to the Taliban.[8] Daniel Byman is extremely critical of Pakistan's role in using terrorist groups to fight a proxy war against India.[9] Recently, in an article in the Brookings Institution website, Byman, senior fellow of the Saban Center for Middle East Policy, states that much of the problem of state sponsorship today involved countries that are not on the American list of state sponsors of terrorism at all and that Pakistan had long aided a range of terrorist groups fighting against India in Kashmir and is a major sponsor of the Taliban forces fighting the US-backed government in Afghanistan.[10] He further observes, "The nightmare of a terrorist group acquiring nuclear weapons is far more likely to involve Pakistan than it is Iran or North Korea."[11]

It would be a folly to defend Pakistan on the grounds that it itself happens to be a victim of terrorism and that it is rather powerless to control these terror groups and that it is ill equipped to combat them. This argument does not hold because terrorist groups don't operate in a vacuum and there are many weak states, in terms of political and economic development, like Sudan, that have had little problem in ousting bin Laden and his al Qaeda network from their soil. Unless a government supports the terrorist outfits, there is no way that these groups can carry out attacks on targets in another country. It is a truism that if one plays with fire one may run the risk of getting gutted. The result is that it is now Pakistan that is bleeding more from Taliban attacks than any other country.

The folly on the part of the United States is its misplaced trust on Pakistan. It is one thing to have an Islamic state as an ally fighting against Soviet communism but the same tactics won't work against fellow 'Islamic brethren'. It is beyond imagination why the US has failed to comprehend this simple truth. As far back as December 2000, Jessica Stern had written an article in the *Foreign Affairs*, virtually challenging Pakistan for its tacit support to radical Islamic group and the latter's strong presence in the Pakistani military. Can the US rely on such a State to wage war on its 'brethren'? The Pakistani case has also been dealt with elsewhere in this book.

The United States

If any country that has made rampant use of terror activities, bestriding all the three categories of terrorism discussed above, that is, non-state terrorism, state terrorism, and state sponsored terrorism, then that distinction must go to the United States. This is neither a moral evaluation of the United States nor finding fault with making use of all the above three categories of terrorism since it has to discharge a host of conflicting duties as a super power. I have admiration for the great nation, as I have explained in my earlier book *Tracing the Eagle's Orbit*. But time has come to make a sober estimate and probing into the why, how, and when of terrorism. This book makes a critical evaluation of the real causes leading to the present form of terrorism and the United States cannot escape its responsibility in bringing modern terrorism to its current religious manifestations.

The United States, more than any other great power in history, has resorted to all the above mentioned categories of terrorism. It has done so as a non-state entity in its war of independence. Reputed British historians also hinted that during that War, American revolutionaries used coercive tactics to maintain and augment the level of its war recruits, needed in a protracted war of that kind. The US war against the Indians would definitely qualify as a stark example of state terrorism although the purpose was 'noble'. The atrocities committed on the national liberation forces in Philippines certainly come under the category of state terrorism. The American overtures in Mexico, prior to the First World War, were definitely examples of state bullying and terrorism.

However, even after the Second World War, the United States has made rampant use of state and state sponsored terrorist tactics. The entire Cold War period is replete with examples in which both the super powers made unbridled use of both these forms of terrorism. In that respect the Cold War conflict contributed in large measure towards lifting modern terrorism to its new heights. However, the United States in the post war period had a plausible excuse, rightly or wrongly—the bogey of Communism. Thus, it was easy to internationalise America's tirade against a political ideological opponent, having global networks and influence. It can be debated whether the United States would have done so had the post-Second World War international order been a multi-polar one. The United States, during the period of European colonialism, in various parts of the world, had adopted an isolationist approach and acted only when it saw its chances of breaking that shackle, of course, at European costs.

The United States took a little time after 1945 till the Truman Doctrine gave a blank cheque to carry out its anti-communist and anti-Soviet tirade. America preferred to proceed along the lines of least resistance. It started with disciplining its own backyard with a cleaning up operation of the Soviet infiltration in some Central and Latin American countries that had developed a fancy for the red flag. It all started in Guatemala with the overthrow of the democratically elected government of Jacob Arbenz when he was replaced by the coup manager, Castilo Aramas. A noted historian, Patrice McSherry had remarked in her book, that with Aramas at the head of government, "the United States began to militarize Guatemala almost immediately, financing and reorganizing the police and military."[12] The same author has revealed that the extent of such atrocities and covert plots, hatched by the US can put other state sponsors of terrorism to shame. In her book she has vividly described how Operation Condor, a covert Latin American military network, was created during the Cold War, to facilitate the seizure and murder of political opponents across state borders. Human rights expert, Michael McClintock remarked that the national security apparatus in the post Arbenz regime was virtually oriented toward countering subversion and that the key component of that apparatus was an intelligence system set up by the United States. It maintained a 'blacklist', that is, a detailed record of potential subversive actors, the names of communist party members, pro-Arbenz organizations, teacher associations, and peasant unions. This list was handled and monitored by the CIA officers.[13]

What was conceived, in the beginning of the 1950s, as mere counter insurgency measures, became a regular US prescription on a global scale, to combat Soviet communist influences. The American ploy of effecting regime changes was but another form of state sponsored terrorism to destabilise established regimes, dictatorial or democratic, by opposition or dissident groups. Cuba had to be the next target as that country, under the able leadership of Fidel Castro, set up a new government, 'unfriendly' to the United States by ousting the dictatorial and corrupt Fulgentio Batista. The CIA lost no time in trying to initiate a regime change by organising and training expatriate Cuban rebels. The failure of Operation Mongoose, the name of that coup, carried out at America's behest, made the United States more desperate.

Cuba had filed a $181.1 billion lawsuit on behalf of the Cuban people in Havana's Popular Provincial Tribunal against the United States, alleging that for over forty years, the United States had used terrorism as an 'instrument of American foreign policy against Cuba'. Richard Helms, former CIA Director, while testifying before the US Senate in 1978, admitted that the United States had task forces that were regularly targeting power plants and sugar mills. "We were attempting to do all kinds of things in this period. This was a matter of American government policy."[14]

Leaving aside the happenings in the Dominican Republic, the next target was Chile where the United States left no stone unturned to destabilise and even overthrow the democratically elected socialist government of Salvador Allende. Prof. Stohl writes, "In addition to non-terroristic strategies… the United States embarked on a program to create economic and political chaos in Chile".[15] The Allende government was overthrown in a violent military coup and many experts strongly believe that the coup was engineered by the CIA that had financed the opposition groups and the right wing paramilitary group, Patria y Libertad in Chile. This is further reinforced by the Professor Gareau's observation that the CIA had close relations with the Contreras, during 'the height of terror' in Chile. He has further written that, "Washington's service as the overall coordinator of state terrorism in Latin America demonstrates the enthusiasm with which Washington played its role as an accomplice to state terrorism in the region."[16]

However, the US role in encouraging terrorism couldn't have been more brazen anywhere than in Nicaragua where it armed, trained and financed the 'Contras' to destabilise the Sandinista government, pursuing progressive social and economic programs. Nicaragua went to the International Court of Justice, accusing the United States of indulging in unlawful and subversive acts. The Court found the US guilty of breaching the sovereignty of another country through "direct acts of US personnel and by supporting Contra guerrillas in their war against the Nicaraguan government and by mining Nicaragua's harbors." Noam Chomsky wrote that the very fact that the World Court had accepted the case and gave a long and detailed judgment and asked the US to pay large sums as compensations for resorting to unlawful use of force proved that the United States resorted to "international terrorism."[17] The Court further ruled that the US "by producing in 1983 a manual entitled Operaciones sicologicas en Guerra de guerillas, and disseminating it to the contra forces, has encouraged the commission by them of acts contrary to general principles of humanitarian law."[18] Since then, the United States has preferred to defy and ignore the World Court rulings in international disputes involving the United States by saying that its judgments were infringements on America's sovereignty. Paradoxically, the United States gleefully highlights those international arbitrations, including those of the World Court, when the judgments go in its favour!

Twenty six years ago, President Reagan made a reference to the word 'terrorism' while justifying his decision to invade Grenada. Professor Wendell

Bell, in a brilliant article,[19] had conclusively shown how tenuous were the three reasons given by the then Reagan administration to justify invasion of Grenada. Since that decision was taken prior to any student being targeted (one of the chief reasons given by the Reagan administration to invade Grenada was to ensure the safety of American medical students there) by the 'disruptive' forces in Grenada, Dr. Bell rightly discerned, in these superficial reasoning, a vain attempt on the part of the US administration to 'transform hindsight' (the 1979 Iranian hostage issue) into 'foresight'. He rightly observed, "Rather, I am referring to the ways in which the range of consciousness shrinks, systematic efforts are made to extinguish thought, and the idea begins to grow that the external world exists largely—if not entirely—in the mind.".[20]

The Regan administration offered another reason to justify the US invasion of Grenada. This had to do with the US concern that militarisation of Grenada was aimed at exporting 'terrorism' or 'revolution' to neighbouring Latin American countries. The United States always displayed a sort of paranoia for progressive socialist movements in its backyard during the entire Cold War period. The third reason given in justification of the US campaign in Grenada was borrowed from the memories of the Cuban missile episode. It has, indeed become a defining feature of the US foreign policies to predicate actions on past 'apprehensions' that almost never recurred. Professor Bell was again right in interpreting this in an ingenious way, "Whether believed or not, assertions about the future cannot be proven absolutely to be true or false at the time they are made. They concern the future, and by its very nature the future remains uncertain until it becomes the present. There are no memories of the future and no future facts, only future possibilities and probabilities".[21] History repeated when the 43rd US President decided to invade Iraq on extremely superficial and flimsy charges. Dr. Bell rightly calls this the 'systematic assault on truth that prepared the way for the attack on Iraq of March 19, 2003.'[22] I have already dealt with the Iraqi case, in detail, in my earlier book.

While these acts of 'state terrorism', barring the Iraqi case, could be blamed on the Cold War rivalry, how can one justify more brazen acts of state terrorism perpetrated by a super power under the guise of unilateralism in the post Cold War era? Since every action evokes reaction, American bullying in the Middle East came under challenge, albeit from non-conventional forces. American soft powers, viewed by many in this part of the globe as mere instruments of cultural intrusion, increasingly came under the scanner. Such reactions eventually manifested in radical and extremely violent ways, culminating in the September 11 attack in the American heartland. Modern terrorism, especially Islamist terrorism, is the sum total of America's past policies (chiefly the US support for Israel that has served as a red rag to a 'green' bull). America's licentious use of unilateralism, again, in the Middle East, came to be viewed by these fundamentalist elements as American ploys to defend Israel. President Bush rightly emphasised that a reasonable and agreeable solution to the Israeli-Palestine issues held the key to peace not only in the Middle East, but also on a global scale. The reference was clearly to Islamist terrorism.

After the first Gulf War, most other low to medium intensity conflicts were fought on ethnic and religious issues, from the Balkans to the Caucasus, and in the far flung regions in Africa. Although, terrorists with religious bias did take part in most of these conflict situations, the United States kept a low profile as all these wars took place far away from its mainland. It is only when American cities were attacked that the United States lost no time in declaring War on Terrorism.

The US act of aggression on Iraq in 2003 was based on false charges. Both President Bush and his deputy admitted this truth a few days before the end of their tenure, but they passed the blame on to poor intelligence reports. However, it is worth remembering that both of them had prior knowledge of the findings of the United Nations Special Commission (UNSCOM) that there was no evidence of Iraq either possessing or even preparing any WMD. The US overtures in Iran in the recent past also remind others of the same American excuses to invade that country. The same provocative ploys of the Cold War days were brought to bear in the Iranian case— fomenting ethnic unrest, supporting opposition groups, aiding selected terrorists to collect intelligence information in Iran's border, like the Sunni militant organisation, Jundallah, (identified by both Pakistan and Iran as terrorist organisation), trying to assess Iran's defence capability by flying reconnaissance planes in its borders, etc. The US reportedly encouraged Jundallah and the People's Mujahideen of Iran (PMOI) or the Mujahideen –e-Khalq (MEK) to attack

Iranian targets in order to destabilise the current Iranian regime. The United States has reportedly persuaded Pakistan to allow the MEK to reach the Iranian border in lieu of an offer to drop a long standing US demand to hand over A.Q. Kahn (who had a vast network of intelligence for disseminating nuclear materials/information to non state actors) to the United States for interrogation. Also, the United States is reported to have framed Azerbaijan to allow US bases to operate on its soil so that it can launch a ground assault on Iran at a lower cost and in lesser time.

This is what the United States means by the War on Terrorism— re-enactment of its Cold War model, by replacing the bogey of communism with the bogey of terrorism. In this regard, the United States seems to have made a serious miscalculation. For example, the victory against Communism was made (I would request my readers to have a look at the various statements made in various platforms by successive US presidents, from Truman to Reagan) on stamina and inner conviction, in addition to military and economic prowess, and the allied unity. However, as things stand now, the United States is at the receiving end in all these four areas in its War on Terror. It is now clear that the United States is tired of using force, evident from observations made by reputed counter terrorism experts and those of its military personnel. To be honest, the United States is on a flight as it wants to retreat both from Iraq and Afghanistan. Just the other day, President Obama clearly stated that America was not winning the war in Afghanistan and proposed a 'divide and rule' policy to isolate the hard liners from the moderates in the Taliban ranks.

In the economic front, the United States has run out of steam. The ever expanding defence budget might blow up any day and the crisis may worsen further in the climate of deep and prolonged recession gripping the United States. Incidentally, the entire cost of carrying out the War on Terror is being met, largely, through foreign borrowing that entails substantial interests. As for stamina and inner conviction, I am afraid, the United States this time is definitely on a wrong foot. No measure of 'material' injection by the US can replace the level of stamina and inner conviction of the jihadists. It is now a common knowledge that the NATO bombings in the border regions of Pakistan and Afghanistan produced more jihadists than it killed. Can one deny that War on Terrorism has already snowballed into a miniature form of the Great Crusade as Muslim youths incessantly migrate to the scene of conflict from various parts of the world? Yes, I repeat, they (the jihadists) too can win provided the US goes on committing foreign policy blunders.

But no book on terrorism is complete without a reference to the US role in Afghanistan from 1970s till now. Available sources clearly point out that the United States started to fish in the troubled waters of Afghanistan a few months before the Soviet invasion took place in December 1979. Prior to 1979, it was the Soviet Union that used to exert influence on a land traditionally inhabited by fierce and unruly tribes engaged in incessant infightings. Afghanistan plunged into chaos in the years following the overthrow of Zaheer Shah's corrupt regime by Daoud Khan in the 1970s. But corruption continued to engulf the Daoud regime and made him more repressive, till he was murdered by army officers sympathetic to the pro-Soviet People's Democratic Party of Afghanistan (PDPA). But the broad coalition government led by Khalq, one of the two PDPA factions, soon unravelled as the reform led by the Tarakki government seemed either too fast or too cumbersome. Government officials preferred to use extreme and repressive measures in the name of reform. As the government tried to quell the rebellion that had spread to many parts of Afghanistan, the Mujahideen, reputed for their ruthlessness in annihilating opponents, emerged as the principal force of resistance in Afghanistan.

In September 1979, Prime Minister Hafizullah Amin had Tarakki murdered and took over as the President. But his anti-Soviet stance angered the USSR who had been nurturing the 'exiled' Afghan leader Barbrak Karmal (belonging to a rival Parcham faction. He was in the coalition government led by Khalq) to become the future president of Afghanistan. Soon, the Soviet army entered Kabul with 5,000 troops. Amin was killed along with 2000 loyal members of his armed forces. As the number of the Soviet troops increased exponentially in the coming days, the United States became worried. According to the then US President Jimmy Carter, the Soviet occupation of Afghanistan had harmed America's vital interests and posed a threat to the Gulf countries. However, the truth is that the US was already helping the Mujahideen to carry on their jihad against the Soviet forces, a few months before the Soviet invasion. Zbigniew Brzezzinski, in an interview given in 1998, clearly said that America was helping the rebels prior to the Soviet invasion.[23] According to him, that secret operation was an excellent idea. It had the effect of drawing the Russians into the Afghan trap, as hoped for. "The day that the Soviets officially crossed the border, I wrote to President Carter: We now have the opportunity of giving to the USSR its Vietnam War."[24]

Many American diplomats had also keenly hoped at that time that Afghanistan could become the Soviet Union's Vietnam. For this, they were prepared to go to any length, uncaring of the consequences, even if it meant the establishment of a regime based on fundamentalist ideology. The United States hoped to realise its long cherished dream to control the oil and the energy rich region of Central Asia and Caucasus, in addition to those of the Middle East and, more importantly, to deny the same to the Soviet Union. So the United States went all out to ally with regional forces, friends or foes, Iran, Pakistan, China, Egypt, and Saudi Arabia, in forming an inexhaustible storehouse of finance, weapons, training, and reserve recruits to drive the Soviets out of that region.

While each of these new found allies had their own political interests, it was the Mujahideen and associate groups that made the most of these finances and weapons, later to be used against the United States itself. Following the Soviet withdrawal, Afghanistan once again plunged into chaos and anarchy, but the United States got busy in Europe as the Cold War drew to a close. The United States had to leave something for its new tribal allies who had done so much to pull down the Soviet empire. It simply allowed some grace period for such free riding by Pakistan and various other factions in Afghanistan. Eventually, a more radical and fundamentalist group, Taliban, emerged out of this chaos. With the help of the Pakistani army, Taliban consolidated its total grip on many parts of Afghanistan. This is how the phoenix of radical Islamist movement arose out of the ashes of the Soviet-Afghan war, at America's behest. The United States thought that residing with several fanatic Islamic fellows was a better option than sharing a bed with the Soviet Union. After all, these roaming tribal fellows were not supposed to pose hindrances to its trade and empire. But the United States had forgotten, perhaps momentarily, that Afghanistan has been the graveyard of so many empires and that having crossed the Rubicon (the Soviet hurdle), America would meet it fate in the shallow waters of Afghanistan.

References

[1] Eben Kaplan, How Libya Got Off the List, Updated October 16, 2007, Council on Foreign Relations, www.cfr.org/publication/10855
[2] Abdel Bari Atwan, 'The Secret History of Al-QA'IDA', Abacus, 2007
[3] 'From Russia with Terror', Interview with Ion Mihai Pacepa, 1 March 2004. Available at FrontPageMag.com
[4] ibid.
[5] '5000 Kashmiri Militants, in various Pak Camps' J&K News, December 2002, the Daily Excelsior. Available at http://www.jammu-kashmir.com/archives/2002/kashmir20021230c.html
[6] The latest news is that Pakistan has declared war on Taliban to drive it out of Buner, Swat, and Dir.
[7] Ted Galen Carpenter, 'With Friends Like These', 4 August 2008. Available at http://www.tedgalencarpenter.com/blog/?p=6Journalist.
[8] Stephen Schwartz, 29 December 2007, 'Terror's New Theater', the New York Post.
[9] Daniel Byman, 2005, Deadly Connections: States that Sponsor Terrorism, Cambridge University Press.
[10] 'Changing Nature of State Sponsorship of Terrorism', June 30, 2009, Saban Center Analysis Paper, Brookings Institution. Available at www.brookings.edu.
[11] ibid, Byman
[12] Predatory States: Operation Condor and Covert War in Latin America, 2005, Rowman & Littlefield Publishers Inc.
[13] Michael McClintock, American Connection: State Terror and Popular Resistance in Guatemala, 1985, Zed Books.
[14] House Select Committee on Assassinations Report, September, 1978 Volume IV, pp.125.
[15] Michael Stohl and Professor George A. Lopez, 1984, The State as Terrorist: The Dynamics of Governmental Violence and Repression, Greenwood Press, pp.51.
[16] F.H.Gareau, March 2004, State Terrorism and the United States: from Counterinsurgency to War on Terrorism, Clarity Press, pp.78-9.
[17] Noam Chomsky, 'Interview on Pakistan television by Pervez Hoodbhoy'. Available at www.chomsky.info (retrieved on 30 August 2006).
[18] Official Name: Military and Paramilitary Activities in and against Nicaragua (Nicar V. U.S.) Jurisdiction and Admissibility, 1984 ICJ REP. 392, 27 June 1986.
[19] 'The American Invasion of Grenada: A note on false prophecy, Foresight: the Journal of futures studies, strategic thinking, and policies, Vol. 10, no.3, pp. 27-42.
[20] ibid.,
[21] Bell, 2003a.
[22] ibid.
[23] 'The CIA's Intervention in Afghanistan: Interview with Zbigniew Brzezzinski', NSA to the Carter Administration, Le Nouvel Observateur, Paris, 15-21 January 1998. Posted at www.globalresearch.ca on 15 October 2001)
[24] Ibid.

CONCLUSION

Terrorism chiefly has two forms— religious and secular political. However, the agenda behind both these is definitely political, at least in the short term. Islamist terrorism has re-emerged with gusto and filled up the hiatus created by the withdrawal of left wing terror groups following the demise of communism. This means that the enemy happens to be the same— neo colonial and the imperial United States. Although many parts of the world have experienced terrorist attacks, these are more pronounced in the Middle East, India, Pakistan, and the United States. Most of the US counterterrorist efforts, prior to 9/11, were devoted to countering drug trafficking in its neighbourhood, that is, Columbia and Mexico. According to the Country Report on Terrorism, released until the recent past, the Revolutionary Armed Forces of Columbia (FARC) and the Colombian drug peddlers used to account for bulk of terrorist activities against American US targets. On the opposite side of the globe, it is India that has been the target of most of the terror strikes sponsored by Pakistan as part of its support to various separatist groups, particularly, in the border states of the North East and Kashmir. After the 1992 Babri Masjid demolition, fundamentalist groups based in Pakistan, sometimes, independently, and, sometimes, through connivance with home grown cells in India, increased the scale and lethality of terror attacks even in the main cities of India. The Indian case has been discussed in a separate chapter in this book.

During and after the Cold War period, till prior to 9/11, most of the terror strikes in the western hemisphere, especially the United States, were carried out by domestic terror groups— both left wing and right wing groups. The United States used to provide its neighbours, affected by drug trafficking and communist guerrilla activities, with all sorts of help. On the other hand, it had little concern for other terrorism affected countries like India, Sri Lanka, and even the Middle East, as long as its own interests remained somewhat unharmed. For example, the United States used to turn a blind eye to all the evidence provided by India regarding Pakistan's complicity with various terror groups. Thus, the United States has little excuse and credibility when it declares a War on Terrorism on a global scale.

Prior to 9/11, radical Islamic forces used to focus their activities largely in the Middle East, albeit on American targets. The Hezbolla and Abu Nidal's terror groups used to target American, Israeli, and European interests and citizens outside the Arab heartlands. This fact alone proves that these Islamic radical groups had an agenda directed against American foreign policies. For example, the al Qaeda, immediately after its formation in 1989, took advantage of the post Soviet international political situation and mobilized its resources on the job of training and funding jihadists in Chechnya, Georgia, Azerbaijan, Yemen, Algeria, Egypt, and Kashmir.[1] Most of these (Muslim dominated) regions were undergoing political turmoil following the breakup of the Soviet empire and Soviet communism. Al Qaeda's agenda was political— to use religion as a means to garner support of the Muslim community. The United States itself has never desisted from driving a wedge between various religious and ethnic factions to achieve its political objectives, for example, the surge movement in Iraq. Meanwhile, the presence and activities of the al Qaeda and other Islamic terror groups in the Middle East increased in proportion to the US meddling in the region, especially, Iraq. The al Qaeda, the Hezbollah, and the Hamas continued to target American facilities and installations in Saudi Arabia, Kuwait, and Iraq during this period.

9/11 was, in some senses, a culmination of the successive fatwas by the al Qaeda leadership resulting from the frequent American interventions in the Middle East and the Gulf after the end of the Cold War. Earlier, the al Qaeda limited their activities in areas far off from the American homeland. But as the net of the US counter terrorism policies spread to bin Laden's operational areas such as Saudi Arabia and Sudan, Laden grew more restive and aggressive. Once the US heartland was attacked, the United States went all out to combat terrorism, especially the al Qaeda after 9/11.

Under these circumstances, Laden increasingly resorted to religious rhetoric as the al Qaeda prepared for a showdown with the American military colossus. Despite his apparently unrealisable goal and idea, Laden's persistence seemed to have turned the tide, to some extent, in his favour, as the War on Terror dragged on indefinitely. By now, Laden has created such a base (al Qaeda indeed means a 'base') for jihadists that even if he gets caught , dead or alive, it would simply catapult him to the status of a legend or a hero, like the great Saladin during the Great Crusade. It is now that the American policy makers have come to realise that the al Qaeda movement would not lose momentum after Laden's death or disappearance. After all, Al Zarqawi's killing failed to stop the flow of new recruits into al Qaeda. In a statement released on the Internet on 30 June 2006, Laden had said that the death of one lion (al Zarqawi) would bring forth other lions into the arena and that the fight against the US and its allies would go on.

The United States made a wrong assessment of the post Cold War international political realities. It seems to have ignored the lessons of its Vietnam debacle—that even a mighty power like the United States can't prevail over an opposition motivated by an ideological doctrine and fighting in its own land. It failed miserably in that war but managed to find an exit route. It is committing the same blunder by relying only on its military prowess instead of diplomatic policies in the Gulf and adjacent areas. Will it be able to escape from the ongoing war on terrorism midway?

Both George Bush and Donald Rumsfeld admitted that America can't retreat from this war for the fear that the al Qaeda would chase them back all the way to America. Liz Cheney, the former Principal Deputy Assistant Secretary of State for New Eastern affairs, once recalled one member of the Lebanese Parliament telling her how the Sunnis, Shias, and even Christians were lining up with Iran and Syria to fight their counterparts in Iraq, fighting alongside America and its allies. Of late, American foreign policy experts have started talking in more a conciliatory tone as they realise that application of force alone would lead America nowhere. It is only the other day that President Obama admitted (the same day he signed to approve deployment of additional troops to Afghanistan) that military means were not the solution and that diplomacy must be given its chance. This is in the backdrop of long standing US policy of not to make any concession to terrorists! President Obama further acknowledged that the United States was not winning the war in Afghanistan.

When I say that the jihadists can do it, I am not talking of al Qaeda's victory over the United States. What I mean is that the al Qaeda would gain some of its major objectives, like the retreat of the United States from the Middle East and a transformation of the United States from 'arrogant' to conciliatory and compromising. Even then, the al Qaeda would have every reason to celebrate what they would deem as their greatest achievement.

Another chief cause of the US failure in its War on Terror may be attributed to its misplaced hope on Pakistan. During the Soviet invasion of Afghanistan, America feared that Pakistan could be the next Soviet target. That apprehension never came true. After 9/11, the United States feared that Pakistan might fall into Taliban's hands. So, a war had to be waged to destroy Talibani forces. That policy seems to have backfired. Taliban has, in fact, regrouped and consolidated its base in Pakistan because of the war.

The fact is that Pakistan has been playing a dirty game since the beginning of the War on Terror in Afghanistan. The then Pakistani President, Pervez Musharaff, was alarmed not only by the disappearance of the Pakistan friendly Taliban government in Kabul but also by the installation of the India friendly Northern Alliance government in Afghanistan. Pakistan seemed to weave its fiendish plots to make way to reinstall the Taliban regime in Afghanistan as soon as possible. Many American authors and politicians have said, in various fora, that Pakistan was double dealing with America in its War on Terror.

There was another dimension to the above Pakistani design— to permanently tie the United States in this region to act as a guardian, safeguarding itself from hostile overtures by India and Russia. Sadly enough, the United States played into Pakistan's hands. The US knew of Pakistan's central role in the War on Terror. It hoped to secure Pakistan by 'rewarding' it with the 'Kashmir' package, should the latter fight alongside America in the ongoing War on Terror till it was won. Things turned otherwise. The United States is not winning the war and Pakistan has rather added to American problems. Pakistan never deviated from two of its primary objectives— Kashmir and Taliban. It was quick to realise that the Afghan war might geld its anti-Indian stand (an unacceptable proposition) by diverting its focus from the Kashmir issue for an indefinite period consequent upon its prolonged engagement in the Western front. So, it began to double deal with the United States, upgrading its defence capabilities with American funds meant for use in the War on Terror, while enhancing the American dependence on itself.

Before launching the War on Terror, the then US president declared that even the state sponsors of terrorism would be treated in the same way as the terrorists. Instead, we have seen a phenomenal rise in Pakistan sponsored terrorism, especially, in Kashmir. Pakistan simply can't cohabit peacefully with India. Its federal integrity depends on its anti-Indian stance. This is where the American policy makers erred. The inevitable outcome is that Pakistan has all but lost interest in a war that it feels might blunt its anti-Indian 'teeth' for good. Conversely, it is equally true that should the United States resolve the Kashmir issue in Pakistan's favour, we'll see a new surge in the Pakistani army in favour of the War on Terror. What an irony!

One of the major causes of the US failure in War on Terror is Pakistan's half-hearted approach in this war. It is not that the United States was unaware of this but, like a helpless 'guardian,' it preferred to turn a blind eye to Pakistan's 'misdeeds'. Pakistan government's concession towards the fundamentalists in the Swat valley in allowing Taliban to re-impose the Sharia was a clear message to India not to bother it with repeated charges of sponsoring terrorism. Otherwise, it would hardly mind letting the Taliban forces loose on Indian border areas. This, incidentally, served also as a veiled warning to America against supporting India, lest the war and, for that matter, the Taliban and the al Qaeda forces would spread deep into the subcontinent. The message to America is clear— Pakistan military would be 'fight' only when bestowed with sufficient arms and funds and with an anti-India focus. Pakistan knows that the fate of the WOT and that the post WOT scenario largely depends on it.

According to a Pew Global Attitudes Project, released in June 2007, the American credibility on a global scale had suffered since 2002 and this position is especially worse in the Muslim countries of the Middle East and some other parts of Asia, as many of America's oldest allies get weary of the War on Terror. President George Bush in a speech at the National Endowment for Democracy in Washington in 2005, while making a case for continuing the Iraqi war, said, "The militants believe that controlling one country will rally the Muslim masses, enabling them to overthrow all moderate governments in the region and establish a radical Islamic empire that spans from Spain to Indonesia."[2] The al Qaeda and Taliban have since used Iraq as the launching pad to spread anti-American jihad to other parts of the world, by providing training and forming deep rooted bonds between the 'jihadists'. Even Mullah Dadullah, a key commander of Taliban, in an interview in Al Jazeera in 2006, admitted how the Iraqi Mujahideen had sharpened the Taliban's fighting capacity. Dadullah noted that "we have 'give and take' with the mujahideen in Iraq."[3] It is the policy blunders of the previous Bush administration that has contributed to phenomenal success of the al Qaeda.

The United States has now resorted to the policy of creating division and hatred amongst various factions of Muslims in Afghanistan and Iraq. This is nothing new. American policies during the entire Cold War period, especially in the Middle East, are littered with CIA efforts of setting one group against the other. After so many wasteful years spent on the War on Terror in Iraq and Afghanistan, the United States now feels that it is be better to separate moderate elements from the hardliners within the Taliban ranks, that is, the 'good' and 'bad' Taliban, and to negotiate with the former in order to marginalise the latter. However, this ploy may not work as Taliban is already cautious about America's divisive policies. Moreover, India has conveyed its doubts over the effectiveness of such American policies.

Conversely, Muslims, in general, don't subscribe to the view of the jihadists that it would ever be possible to recreate the Caliphate on a global scale. A reference to the Arab empire of the seventh and eighth centuries serving as a model for the twenty first century won't help. First, as Fukuyama rightly said, the weight and influence of modern western civilisation, with its train-load of enlightened economic and political ideas, stretching over half a millennium, is too imposing to think of any other alternative. Such a condition was absent when the West, as a viable civilisation, was yet to emerge out of its barbaric fold in the Middle Ages. Secondly, the Middle Ages lacked the modern means of communication and information networks. Today's military conflicts won't take place on horse backs with swords but would mostly resemble high tech computer simulated wars. That is why bin Laden lamented that unlike the Soviets, the Americans didn't engage in open battles. Thirdly, the advantage that the Arabs enjoyed at that time over their adversaries, in respect of their new techniques and weaponry, now lies with the West and that could be decisive in the end. Fourthly, the international order is being led by a military-economic colossus and no decisive outcome to any conflict situation would emerge without American initiative or arbitration. Fifthly, demographic factor may not work to the advantage of the Islamic world as it may cut both ways, for example, it may swell the ranks of moderate Muslims too. So, the American retreat could be extremely temporary and localised because there is no other major power round the corner. Such a retreat would result in a temporary curtailment of the American power potential in world politics with the injection of some limited dose of multi-polarity.

Yet, there are lessons for the United States to learn from this failed war. The United States would learn the hard way that any respectable solution to a war on an adversary bent on making it a religious issue (despite the American claim that it is a fight against the radicals and that radicals don't speak for the Muslim majority) cannot be arrived at by merely creating divisions within various groups of the same community or religion. Dr. Fareed Zakaria had written a couple of years back, about how America ought to exploit such divisions when he said, "Rather than speaking of a single worldwide movement—which absurdly lumps together Chechen separatists in Russia, Pakistani-backed militants in India, Shiite warlords in Lebanon and Sunni jihadists in Egypt—we should be emphasizing that all these groups are distinct, with differing agendas, enemies and friends. That robs them of their claim to represent Islam. It describes them as they often are—small local gangs of misfits, hoping to attract attention through nihilism and barbarism".[4] Yet the fact is that the course and outcome of both the ongoing sanguine Shia-Sunni conflicts (and between their supportive terror groups) in Iraq and of the American backed Sunni tribal groups' decision to fight against the Iraqi al-Qaeda sorely depend on the continued presence of American troops there Does America have an exit route this time? Incidentally, in the same speech mentioned above, President Bush described the jihadists as immune from bribes or any game of persuasion.

The United States has already learnt to its mortification that unless it can arrest or block the regular flow of new young jihadists, the War on Terror would remain un-winnable in Iraq and Afghanistan and may even spread to other regions. How can one awake a sleeping giant (almost everybody in this part of the world knows how peaceful the Afghans are and how they like to live within their cabals) and not expect it to carry on a reign of terror? According to National Intelligence Estimate of July 2007, the Iraqi jihad has shaped a "new generation of terrorist leaders and operatives, and that the Iraq conflict had become the cause celebre for the jihadists "breeding a deep resentment of US involvement in the Muslim World and cultivating supporters for the global jihadist movement."[5]

The US policy makers were perhaps in a denial mode and never imagined that a few stateless actors could wreak so much havoc in Iraq and Afghanistan. Just a few years back, Barry Posen, professor of political science at MIT, admitted this when he remarked that the US and its Iraqi allies were rather fighting a tough counter insurgency 'against determined, deadly, well funded, and well equipped foes', comprising the remnant Baathist elements of the earlier Iraqi regime, in league with the fundamentalist Iraqi militants and foreign radical Islamic terrorist, like the al Qaeda.[6] He recommends a well planned disengagement through reduction of military, economic, and political costs.

Nir Rosen, an experienced journalist in Afghan-Iraq campaigns, rightly observed that the Iraqi insurgency is concerned with the liberation of their country from foreign control. "They are not interested in Salafi Islam, Crusaders, Jews, the Caliphate, or any international jihad."[7] He too feels that Iraq is threatened by a widespread civil war between various warlords, religious factions, and political parties that might destroy it. Thus the US indiscretion in attacking Iraq might recoil heavily on the American pride. The million dollar question remains, even if America pulls out of Iraq and Afghanistan, will it be allowed a safe exit route?

In this connection it would not be wrong to construe that Iraqi militants and their sympathisers believe that they are engaged in a second national liberation movement against the United States. Since national liberation movements also tend to draw on religious passions, like the great Indian Sepoy Mutiny, only a political solution can provide an answer to such a rebellion. The great Indian historian Nandalal Chatterjee underlined this aspect of politico-religious passion when he wrote that during the great Indian Sepoy Mutiny in 1857, many dreaded dacoits voluntarily left their 'professions' to join the uprising against the British. People can only be aroused when they see a concrete political goal before them in which religion acts as a means and not an end. So, the claims of those scholars who try to vilify Islam as a violent and aggressive religion are unfounded. Even the al Qaeda knows this and that is why they are fighting for a political agenda, albeit in the guise of religion.

Unfortunately, one of the shortcomings of the United States is that it simply lacked the experience of the erstwhile European colonial powers that had good knowledge of the culture and motivations of the people in this region. Fareed Zakaria feels that neither Britain nor the United States, nor any other country has so far successfully addressed the root causes of jihad. He feels that this has something to do with the alienation of the Muslim community and their inferiority complex and fear of being left out of the mainstream forces of society.[8]

What has the United States gained after wasting billions of dollars in Afghanistan and Iraq, in the name of war on terror? Nothing creditable. The United States and the West for that matter, failed to get the much coveted free access on Iraqi oil resources— one of the chief motives behind the 2003 Iraqi invasion. Mr. Maliki's government has no intention of going back to the days of the 1960s when the Western powers, under the Power Sharing Agreements (PSA), reaped huge profits from sale of oil that they extracted from Iraqi oil fields. Rather, the current official Iraqi position is that foreign companies may, at best, enter into a service contract with major oil companies, like the Iraqi National Oil Company (INOC), instead of being allowed participation in the production process.[9] This perception stems from the new government's decision to adhere to the Constitution that considers oil and gas as the property of the Iraqi people.

Further, the course of the war rather portends either an American retreat, for several years, from the Middle East or an extremely prolonged infighting within various factions in Iraq, not unlike Lebanon in the mid 1980s, but on a much magnified scale. Recently, the United States, in a bid to prolong the US troop presence in Iraq, prepared a draft arrangement under the Status of Forces Agreement (SOFA), which met with widespread opposition in Iraq. Atul Aneja, the West Asia Chief of Bureau of the Hindu, considers all these developments as assertion of Iraqi sovereignty and the

Iraqi government's defiance of the United States. What is more ominous for the United States is that Iran may run away with all the attendant benefits at the expense of America. Israel's stability could also be in jeopardy, with Iran becoming so active in the region with its two surrogates— Hezbollah based in Lebanon and the Hamas based in the Gaza strip. But there is one silver lining— the age old mutual suspicion of the two neighbours in the backdrop of contemporary developments like political stability in Iraq and Iran's burgeoning geo-political interests in the region may eventually work in America's favour.

Finally, as discussed above, the War on Terror has so far not achieved American objectives— reducing and exterminating terrorism, especially, Islamist terrorism of the al Qaeda type and consolidating its grip over the strategically important Middle East, and above all, securing American leadership in world affairs. After well over half a decade into the Afghan and the Iraqi war, the United States now finds that it has opened a Pandora's Box with all the attendant 'evils' following it.

The US strategy at the beginning of the War on Terror both in Afghanistan and Iraq was to overpower and overawe its adversaries to such an extent as to make them shudder at the sight of the nightmare of death and destruction, in order to bring them down to their knees and submit unconditionally to the American might. However, that was not to be. American atrocities have simply furthered the resolve of the jihadists, to carry on their fight till finish. To make matters worse, the US War on Terror has in fact aided in rapidly fanning out the passion for 'global jihad'. So many jihadists had crossed over to Iraq from various parts of the Muslim and Arab world and have developed and sharpened their fighting skills. In all probability, these jihadists are certain to carry those skills either to other conflict zones or to their respective countries of origin once America decides to retreat from Iraq by the end of 2011. One such example is North Africa, where nationalist-Islamic movements are being co-opted by the al Qaeda. A recent report prepared by a panel of experts from Jamestown's 2008 Conference entitled, 'The Expanding Geography of Militant jihad' concludes in its premium report, that "the nationalism that once fuelled the Mujahedeen in North Africa is giving way to a new emphasis on global jihad, reinforced by ties to al-Qaeda."[10]

One of the most intriguing features of the US terrorist hunt in Afghanistan is that its campaign lacked long-term planning and imagination, relying instead on sheer force component. The result is that, the al Qaeda and the Taliban, who were marginalised by the US and the Northern Alliance forces into pockets surrounding Kandahar, subsequently migrated to the Afghan-Pakistan border and now into Pakistan. The US and the UN forces did little to capture the retreating Talibanis, allowing them 'free zones' in the Pakistan-Afghan border areas instead. Perhaps, the US policy makers knew subconsciously that the War on Terror was after all not a 'war.'

Things came to a head when the United States invaded Iraq in 2003. These same al Qaeda fighters found a safe haven in the troubled regions of Iraq. By 2004, the al Qaeda was a force to reckon with in Iraq. In a 2005 publication, *Terrorism Monitor*, while exploring the Salafi-jihadist base that helped al Zarqawi to draw new recruits, Murad Batal Al-shishani (based on a list of mujahideen posted on the al-Saha web forum, http://alsaha.fares. net) found that a major portion of such recruits encompassed the entire Arab world, with Saudis being the majority (200 fighters—53 per cent), 13 per cent from Syria, 8 per cent from Iraq, 5.8 per cent from Jordan, 4 per cent from Kuwait, 3.8 per cent from Libya.[11] Iraq proved to be a great bonanza and happy hunting ground for the al Qaeda because of its geography as it can be easily reached from other parts of the Arab world. This was what led al-Zawahiri to say, "Here is America among us. So, come take revenge on it and extinguish your thirst with its blood".

Now, the United States has woken up to the reality that a speedy and viable solution to the Iraqi issue must be found at the earliest to cut the tap roots of al Qaeda, which are firmly entrenched there and are threatening to spread jihad to other Muslim states with Iraq as its model. But there are several considerations. First, how are the returnees from Iraq to be blocked from waging another jihad in their lands of origin or in other Muslim states? The United States has hit upon an idea to tackle this menace: allowing these jihadists to return to the mainstream socio-economic process by giving them jobs and other avenues of earning money needed for a respectable life style. Already, the United States officials have prevailed upon the incumbent Shiite-dominated government in Iraq to put Shiite insurgents (whom the American military had paid $300 per month for guarding American checkpoints and installations) on government payroll.[12] This is part of a great American design to forge and guide the recent Awakening movement (in 2006 in the Anbar province the Sunni tribal leaders had decided to fight alongside the US forces against the al Qaeda) in the direction of a grand coalition leading prior to Iraqi Parliamentary elections at the end of 2009. This coalition is supposed to consist of the US-backed Sunni movement along with other influential Sunnie leaders, the influential Shiite militant cleric Moktada al-Sadr, Maliki's Shiite group, and secular groups of Alawi and Mutlak.[13]

In this connection, it could be said that one of the principal features of American foreign policy has always been to soften the adversary through application of hard power and then through injection of carrots to heal wounds and do its bidding. This has so far been employed in every theatre of conflict in various parts of the world. Would this ploy succeed in countering an ideologically equipped group bent on driving America out of the Middle East? At best, this may offer an exit route for America (not a respectable one) from Iraq and the Middle East and, at worst a renewed surge of conflict in the region.

The second problem is Iran. The only country to gain from the American misadventures in Afghanistan and Iraq is their neighbour, Iran. A strong Iran does not bode well either for Israel or any other surrounding Arab states. The United States is already on the job of organising these 'unfriendly' Arab countries against Iran. On the other end of the extreme, American policy makers offer the option of negotiations with Iran. The most notable of this gesture has been the recent goodwill message to Iranian people and their leader on the occasion of the Persian New Year Nawruz by the American President, Barack Obama. He even went to the extent of calling Iran by the name of 'Islamic Republic' while lauding the contributions of the great ancient Persian civilisation towards the world community in various fields. Obama called on Iran to understand the future that America seeks. He went on, "It is a future with renewed exchanges among our people, and greater opportunities for partnership and commerce. It is a future where the old divisions are overcome-where you, and all your neighbours and the wider world can live in greater security and greater peace."[14] Predictably, this has drawn both praise and criticism from foreign policy experts. The Iranian Supreme leader, Ayatollah Ali Khamenei dismissed such overtures as mere words. He said, in a speech before tens of thousands of people in the northeastern city of Mashhad, that, "They chant the slogan of change but no change is seen in practice."[15] Khamenie said that the US velvet looking glove must have a cast iron mould inside. Whatever be the real situation, it is the United States that is now learning the hard way to negotiate properly with the rest of the world.

In respect of Afghanistan, President Obama's recent package appears to be too late, coming at a wrong time and place. The United States has so far failed miserably in 'disrupting, defeating and dismantling' the al Qaeda and Taliban. These two groups have not only enhanced their influence in Afghanistan and Pakistan, but are now threatening to engulf the entire subcontinent. Recently, the Indian Intelligence Bureau has reported that scores of Taliban fighters are attempting to infiltrate into India through the Line of Control (LOC). This means that whereas prior to 9/11 Taliban remain closeted within Afghanistan with occasional forays elsewhere, it has assumed unmanageable proportions by 2009. Would the US ploys of forming a regional contact group including Iran, Pakistan, Afghanistan, and possibly India, pay at a time when the US is retreating from both the major theatres of the War on Terror? The omen is that all these four countries would be transformed into tinderbox regions, thanks to America's 'purification' policies of first destroying indigenous ways and cultures and then remaking them in the Western mould.

Nevertheless, the Obama administration has begun to read the writing on the wall. While Obama's new plan has been termed by many as a 'strategy for success', in effect, his recent policies on Afghanistan emphasise stability on both sides of the Pakistan-Afghan border that would make it easy for American troops to be pulled back. This is the long and short of the American war on terror— internationalising a conflict situation that had little in it to develop into a global insurgency but for the US indiscretion. In the face of all this, doesn't Obama's new plan of creating a new military command in southern Afghanistan point toward a geo-strategic consolidation in this region and can't we say that this has been one of the hidden agendas of the Bush administration in the name of a War on Terror?

Or would the US divine another ploy and raise the bogey of nuclear weapons falling into terrorist hands as a pretext to prolong the War on Terror? Readers may note that I have somewhat underplayed the 'nuclearisation' of terrorism. There are reasons for it. First, such an outcry or alarm would in fact hasten the realisation of the very premonition that the Untied State least wants. Secondly, even if the terrorists get hold of those weapons they would lack the necessary infrastructure to conduct nuclear attacks on a big scale. Is it not pragmatic to have an open approach and to make preparations to counter conditions that may arise consequent on the jihadists' possession of WMD materials? Are we not living with another 'weapon of mass destruction'— the IEDs? Thirdly, if the United States could successfully combat the nuclear leviathan, the Soviet Union, will it be any problem for the 'high-tech' US to neutralise the 'invaluable' advantage that may accrue to the terrorists?

Not every conflict, unlike Vietnam, would offer an honourable exit route for the United States. A small retreat from its present unilateralism and a small dose of multi-polarity can save the present international political order from being defined along cultural lines and from frequent wars that remind us of the pre-Westphalian days. I am sure that the United States, as a responsible and mature power, would read the demands of time and make necessary adjustments in its foreign policies in order to avert further calamities. But the question remains— was all this necessary to resurrect a slumbering ideology at such a big American cost, particularly, that too at a time when the United States was going great guns with its liberal democratic polices on a global scale? Wouldn't economic sanctions and other counter terrorism measures, including efforts to cut off the supply lines of terrorist funds and arms, have been sufficient to avert the War on Terror? And more importantly, even if the United States manages to get out of this war successfully, would it have the same credibility of the pre 9/11 days?

References

[1]Rohan Gunaratna, 2002, Inside al-Qaeda: Global Network of Terror, New York: Columbia University Press.
[2] Bush: Iraq crucial in war on terror, Politics, October 7, 2005, www.cnn.com
[3] 'Taliban Commander: We have a "give and take" relationship with allies in Iraq', Mother Jones, March/April 2007, National Security Network, Report 14 August, 2008, www.nsnetwork.org/node/938
[4]'Losing the War Against Radical Islam', James Joyner, 25 June, 2007, Outside the Beltway, www.outsidethebeltway.com/archives/tag/fareed_zakaria

[5] 'IRAQ HAS UNDERMINED THE U.S. STRATEGY FOR COMBATING VIOLENT EXTREMISM', NIE 07/07, www.nsnetwork.org/node/974

[6] Barry R. Posen, Jan/Feb. 2006, 'Exit Strategy, How to disengage from Iraq in 18 months', Boston Review. Avalable at http://bostonreview.net/BR31.1/posen.html

[7] Nir Rose, 'Once the Americans leave, Sunnies will have no common cause with foreign Mujahideen' Boston Review, January/February 2006, Available at http://bostonreview.net/BR31.1/rosen.html

[8] ibid. Losing the War on Terrorism.

[9] Atul Aneja, 17 September 2008, 'Is America losing out on Iraqi Oil?', the Hindu, Available at http://www.thehindu.com/2008/09/17/stories/2008091756161100.htm.

[10] The Jamestown Foundation, 'The Changing Face of Militancy in North Africa', 17 March 2009. Available at http://www.jamestown.org/programs/books/.

[11] The Salafi-jihadist Movement in Iraq: Recruitment Methods and Arab Volunteers, Publication: Terrorism Monitor Volume: 3 Issue: 23, December 2, 2005, jamestown.org/programs/gta/single/?tx_ttnews[tt_news]=621&tx_ttnews...

[12] New York Times, September 22, 2008, Awakening Movement in Iraq, http://topics.nytimes.com/top/news/international/countriesandterritories/iraq/awakening_movement/index.html

[13] The Washington Post, New Alliances in Iraq cross Sectarian Lines, Anthony Shadid, March 20, 2009, A01, http://washingtonpost.com

[14] Obama Calls for 'New Beginning' in Message to Iran, Paula Wolfson, 20/3/09

[15] Iran's Supreme leader dismisses Obama overtures, Ali Akbar Dareini, The Associated Press writer,Teheran, Iran, 21 March, 2009

SELECT READINGS

Muhammad, Asad, *The Principles of State and Government in Islam*, Islamic Book Trust, Kualampur, 1999

Abdel Bari Atwan, *The Secret History of AL-QA'IDA*, Abacus, 2006.

Maloy Krishna Dhar, *Fulcrum of Evil, ISI-CIA-Al Qaeda Nexus*, Manas Publications, N. Delhi, 2006.

Burke, Jason, *Al Quaeda, The True Story of Radical Islam*, Penguin Books, London, 2004.

Gunaratna, Rohan, *Inside al Qaeda, Global Network of Terror,* New York, Columbia University Press, 2002

Lewis, Bernard, *The Crisis of Islam, Holy War and Unholy Terror,* Phoenix, London, 2003

Al-Zawahiri, Ayman, *Knights Under the Prophet's Banner,* A-Shaeq al-Aswar, Cairo, 2001.

Pape, Robert A., *Dying to Win; The Strategic Logic of Suicide Terrorism,* Random House, New York, 2005.

Randal, Jonathan, *Osama: The Making of a Terrorist,* Alfred A. Knopf, New York, 2004.

Rachel, Ehrenfeld, *Funding Evil, Updated: How Terrorism is Financed and How to Stop It,* Paperback ed., Bonus Books, California, Expanded Edition, 2005

Michael Scheuer, *Imperial Hubris: Why the West is Losing the War on Terror,* Potomac Books. Inc., London, 1st ed., 2004

Hassan Abbas, *Pakistan's Drift into Extremism: Allah, then Army, and America's War Terror,* M.E.Sharp, London, 1st ed., 2004

Jessica, Stern, *Terror in the Name of God: Why religious Militants Kill,* Harper Perennial, London, 2004.

Steve, Cole,	Ghost Wars: *The Secret History of the CIA, Afghanistan, and Bin Laden, from the Soviet Invasion to September 10, 2001,* Penguin Press HC, 2004
Reuvan Firestone,	*jihad: The Origin of Holy War in Islam, Oxford University Press, USA, 1999.*
Bruce Hoffman,	*Inside Terrorism,* Columbia University Press, USA, 1999.
Noah Feldman,	*The Fall and Rise of the Islamic State* (Council of Foreign Relations), Princeton University Press, March 2008
Raymond Ibrahim	*The Al Qaeda,* Broadway, August, 2007
Angel Rabasa,	*Beyond al-Qaeda: Part I: The Global Jihadist Movement (Pt.1),* Rand Corporation, 2006
Walid Phares,	*Future Jihad: Terorist Strategies Against America,* Palgrave Macmillan, 2005
Mohammad Ayoob:	*The Many Faces of Political Islam: Religion and Politics in the Muslim World,* University of Michigan Press, 2007 John Esposito &
John O. Voll.	*Islam and Democracy,* Oxford Univesity Press, 1996
H.A.R. Gibb,	*Mohammedanism: An Historical Survey,* London, OxfordUnivesity Press, 1950
Arnold Toynbee	*A Study of History, Vol XII,* Oxford University Press, 1961.

INDEX

(USA) Act (H.R. 2975) 150

arms iii, vi, 8, 18, 19, 22, 26, 27, 32,
33, 36, 56, 59, 62, 78, 79, 85,
90, 105, 107, 108, 109, 110,
111, 112, 113, 114, 115, 128,
133, 139, 144, 147, 155, 160,
162, 167, 168, 170, 174, 193,
202

arms bazaars 107
arms dealers 108
arms export 111
arms market 110
arms production 106
arms supplies 105
arms trafficking 107, 114
arms transfer 111, 113
army 26, 28, 32, 41, 70, 79, 92, 93,
99, 113, 119, 126, 134, 135,
137, 138, 148, 153, 161, 166,
168, 175, 177, 178, 186, 187,
193

Army of God 156
arsenals 106
Arshad, Hafiz 120
artillery 107, 108
artillery shells 107
Asad, Muhammad 22
Asia 11, 88, 167, 174, 193, 197
Asian Tribune 95, 116
Assam 135
assassinations 95
Athens 145
Attila 66
Atwan 31, 52, 53, 83, 115, 188
Atwan, Abdel Bari 9, 141, 204
Aukar 145
Australia 15, 119, 133
Austria 55, 140
Avienius 66
Ayodhya 135
Azerbaijan 110, 185, 190

Azhar, Masood 135, 177
Azhar, Maulana Masood 135
Azhar, Mohammed Masood 89
Aziz, Abdullah Bin Abdul 71
Aziz, Tariq 2
Azzam 9, 78
Azzam, Abdullah 9

B

Baadar Meinhoff Gang 59
Baathist elements 196
Babri Masjid 124, 135, 189
Badawi Refugee camp 59
Baghdad 12, 38, 82, 107
Bakr, Abu 74
Bali car bombing 87
Balkan crisis 80
Balkans 93, 100, 154, 184
ballistic missiles 173
Balochistan 168
Bandipore 133
Bangalore 124, 176
Bangladeshi refugees 168
Bangladeshi terrorist group 124
Bangladesh Rifles 40
Bank Secrecy Act. See BSA; See
BSA
Banna, Hasan al 70
barbarism 195
Barcelona 140
barometric bomb 106
Barua, Paresh 107. See
base security 37
Batista, Fulgentio 181
battery of army 129
BBC probe 121, 130
BBC television 121
beaches 137
Begin, Menachem 32
Beirut International Airport 145

216

Marx, Karl 1
Masada 24
masjids 71
Matunga 124
May, 2005 134
Mazagaon dock 119
McClintock, Michael 181, 188
McDonald's 110
McSherry, Patrice 180
McVeigh, Timothy 146, 157
mechanical failures 144
media 16, 29, 39, 48, 89, 126, 127,
    158, 166, 174, 175
media terror cell 16
Mediterranean Sea 145
mega power 47
Mehsud, Baitullah 114
metals 91, 103
Metro Cinema 119
Mexico 180, 189
microfinancing 96
Microfinancing Terrorism 96
micro-nationalism 44
Middle East v, 2, 3, 4, 6, 9, 11, 13,
    15, 20, 25, 34, 42, 46, 49, 50,
    52, 55, 60, 61, 69, 76, 77, 79,
    80, 81, 83, 85, 87, 88, 99, 100,
    103, 108, 115, 116, 143, 147,
    148, 164, 178, 184, 187, 189,
    190, 192, 193, 194, 197, 198,
    200
Middle Eastern Studies 55
Militant Extremists 155, 164
militant Islamic organisation 144
militant organisation 88, 184
militarisation of Grenada 183
military age 171
military capability 167
military force 163
military interests 90

military operations 37
military prowess 191
Military rebellion 30
Military spare parts 109
militia 24, 80, 125
Million Mom March 114
Mindanao 59
minority 4, 119
missile 113
misuse by authorized users of weap-
    ons 111
Mizo 139
Mizo National Front. See MNF
mobile phones 17, 89, 122, 130, 140
modern civilisation 114
modern communication 140
modern communications 32, 114
Mogadishu 48
Mohammad, Din 107
molotov cocktail 106
money 12, 18, 37, 44, 56, 60, 78, 79,
    90, 94, 97, 98, 99, 100, 101,
    102, 103, 105, 108, 141, 150,
    151, 199
money launderers 101
money laundering 86, 91, 102, 105
Money Laundering Control Act 102
Money Laundering Control Act of
    1986 151
Mongols 74, 76
Moon, Patrick 92
moral 69, 77, 78, 99, 161, 177, 179
Morocco 55, 138
mortars 112
Moscow 42, 92
mother of battles 5
Muhammad Asad 83
Mujahideen iii, v, 8, 9, 16, 43, 56,
    70, 78, 79, 125, 135, 139, 154,
    164, 186, 187, 194, 203